D0915961

# THE GOLDEN DREAM

# THE GOLDEN DREAM

## A History of the
## St. Lawrence Seaway

Ronald Stagg

DUNDURN PRESS
TORONTO

Editor: Allison Hirst
Design: Courtney Horner
Printer: Transcontinental

**Library and Archives Canada Cataloguing in Publication**

Stagg, Ronald John, 1942-
        The golden dream : a history of the St. Lawrence Seaway / by Ronald Stagg.

Includes index.
ISBN 978-1-55002-887-4

                1. Saint Lawrence Seaway--History. I. Title.

FC2763.2.S715 2010            386'.509714        C2009-900304-X

1   2   3   4   5        14   13   12   11   10

We acknowledge the support of the **Canada Council for the Arts** and the **Ontario Arts Council** for our publishing program. We also acknowledge the financial support of the **Government of Canada** through the **Book Publishing Industry Development Program** and **The Association for the Export of Canadian Books**, and the **Government of Ontario** through the **Ontario Book Publishers Tax Credit program**, and the **Ontario Media Development Corporation**.

Care has been taken to trace the ownership of copyright material used in this book. The author and the publisher welcome any information enabling them to rectify any references or credits in subsequent editions.

*J. Kirk Howard, President*

Published by The Dundurn Group
Printed and bound in Canada.

www.dundurn.com

Dundurn Press
3 Church Street, Suite 500
Toronto, Ontario, Canada
M5E 1M2

Gazelle Book Services Limited
White Cross Mills
High Town, Lancaster, England
LA1 4XS

Dundurn Press
2250 Military Road
Tonawanda, NY
U.S.A. 14150

*To my parents,*
*who introduced*
*me to the Seaway.*

# CONTENTS

# PREFACE

I was quite intrigued when I was asked by the publisher Dundurn Press to write a book on the history of the various St. Lawrence River canals and their competitors to mark the 50th anniversary of the opening of the St. Lawrence Seaway. I have had a long and diverse association with the subject.

My first exposure to the St. Lawrence Seaway was as a young teenager in 1956 when my parents took me on a road trip to the Maritime provinces. This was before the days of superhighways, expressways, and thruways, and accommodation was usually in cabins, hotels (sometimes railway hotels), or privately built motels. Our first day was spent driving on Highway 2 from Toronto to Kingston, a trip which now takes less than three hours but at that time took most of the day as we meandered through towns and villages and large swaths of rolling farmland. On our second day we drove much of the way along the St. Lawrence, travelling through more towns and villages. My father explained that this area was going to be flooded and that many of the buildings would be moved or demolished. We passed the old cut-stone canal at Cardinal and ate lunch beside the canal at Iroquois. It seemed as if you could reach out and touch one of the "14-footers," those unique ships specially built to haul freight from Prescott, through the narrow canals, to Montreal. We saw a building being moved, a rather rare sight at the time as house-moving was in its infancy. We undoubtedly passed the Long Sault Rapids also, famous to generations of travellers on the river, but I have no memory of them.

I have returned to the area many times since, either to visit Upper Canada Village, a collection of salvaged buildings judged to be of architectural and historical merit and arranged in the form of a village to portray life in the early nineteenth century, to explore the Lost Villages Museum, a collection of minor buildings from several villages that no longer exist, or to camp on the Long Sault Parkway. The latter is built on the tops of hills that rise above the flooded farms, connected by a series of causeways. Here one can see the beginning of walkways that no longer exist that once led to houses that no longer stand; a rather surreal experience is seeing the old Highway 2 rise out of the water, cross the high ground, and disappear into the water on the other side. An outdoor presentation centre marks the site where divers can descend to the lock of the original canal that used to be located near the Long Sault Rapids. This now lies some 50 to 60 feet below the surface of the water. Some nights, camping on the parkway, the throb of ships' engines and propellers approaching the canal on the American side about a mile away is enough to wake campers from a sound sleep. At Cornwall, while crossing the high-level bridge to the United States, one can look down on the remains of the old Cornwall Canal which lead to a dead end near the massive dam and powerhouse — major features of the St. Lawrence Seaway.

In the 1990s I helped friends bring a sailboat from Albany up through the Erie and Oswego canals, early competitors for the St. Lawrence route, to Lake Ontario. I had long been curious about the first of these, an early North American canal. It turned out not to be the waterway of my imagination. Officially renamed the New York Barge Canal years earlier, it no longer ran along its original route for its whole length, serving towns and cities along the way, and it was wider and deeper than the original. It was a wonderful trip, nevertheless, as much of the canal runs through rural New York State. We passed and sometimes stopped at waterside inns, travelled long distances in which trees hanging over the water obscured most of what lay beyond, making it seem like we were in another century, and saw the remains of factories once served by the canal. Partway up, in one bucolic setting, a sign on the shore pointed to the remains of locks from the original canal. Shallow and narrow, these were suitable only for small barges pulled by horses. On the way home from Oswego to Toronto by bus, a street name in Syracuse indicated the path of the original canal before it was rerouted in the late nineteenth century.

My association with the Ottawa–Rideau route from Montreal to Lake Ontario has been somewhat episodic, crossing it by car or on foot rather than travelling it by boat. Skating on the canal during winter in Ottawa is the closest thing to being on the water that I have experienced. From the step locks beside the Parliament Buildings, where the Rideau begins (a site seemingly more appropriate to a European city than to the capital of a North American country), to the industrial remains beside the locks at historic Merrickville (once an important spot along the Rideau Canal, but now more an attractive bedroom community for those working in Ottawa), to viewing the canal at Smiths Falls or at rural spots beside the highway, one has a sense of what it is like to travel the canal. The scenery alongside the canal is generally so attractive that it conveys no sense of the horrendous conditions encountered by the labourers who constructed it in the early nineteenth century.

Curiously, until I began to work on this book, I was least familiar with the canal closest to my home in Toronto which is officially part of the St. Lawrence Seaway. I knew that there had been several Welland canals, but had never visited them. Every few weeks I drive along the Queen Elizabeth Way and over the Garden City Skyway, which looks down over the twinned triple-step locks, the major feature of the current Welland Canal, yet I had never taken the time to visit them as many tourists do each year. I had driven under the canal at one point where this is possible, and had driven beside a short section in the course of my travels, but the modern Welland and the remnants of its predecessors remained for me largely unexplored.

None of these experiences made me an expert on the subject of the St. Lawrence Seaway and its rivals, but each made me aware of a portion of the story and piqued my curiosity. In researching the remainder, I must acknowledge the work of several of my predecessors. They all contributed to make the task a much easier one. In particular, I owe a debt to Robert Legget, who dealt with many of the engineering aspects of the canals. Also, to Carleton Mabee, who covered in great detail the complex regional rivalries in the United States over which transportation system or systems would win out in the struggle to control the trade of the American Midwest, and who provided a firsthand account of the building of the Seaway that dealt not just with machines, cement, and steel, but also with how the workers and the inhabitants coped with the mammoth undertaking. He also donated a large collection of interviews and clippings to St. Lawrence University. This collection has been of considerable help in understanding the political and social climate surrounding the building of the Seaway. In addition, Mabee provided a good deal of information derived from the records of the Great Lakes–St. Lawrence Tidewater Association and from other Midwestern sources, some of which are now unavailable, and some of which the publishing deadline did not allow me to locate and consult. William Willoughby dealt with some aspects of mid- to late-nineteenth-century American canal building, especially with the political background, as well as information on the political manoeuvring of the twentieth century. This saved me considerable time and effort locating material. John Heisler provided some details on early Canadian canals, particularly on the financing aspect and on government policy, which filled gaps in my knowledge. Lionel Chevrier contributed a delightful self-deprecating account of his role in getting the Seaway approved in Canada, of negotiating with the United States, and of being in charge of building the Canadian portion of the Seaway. Other works which were useful are mentioned in the bibliography, but these are the ones that I feel have provided the most background information on issues involved in the Seaway story as I was pursuing my own research. Much new published information has become available concerning the multitude of threads that are woven together in the story of the Seaway, and concerning the many players that have participated in the struggle to control the trade of the Great Lakes. Since the last accounts were written some 30 years ago, access to this new information has made my task much easier, as researching the many interwoven stories, in addition to the main story of the Seaway itself, would have taken many years.

As a researcher used to the traditional method of spending countless hours in archives and libraries, I have been pleasantly surprised to find out how much material is available on the Internet. Apart from the usual numerous sites of dubious authenticity, there are many sites maintained by universities, museums, government agencies, and public bodies that provide helpful information on many of the topics covered in this work. There are also entire books, reports, government documents, and papers of important individuals. Some of these I have located through diligent searching; others have been discovered quite by chance. All have made my task much easier, saving me months of searching and travel, and in some instances providing information that I would not have discovered otherwise.

In writing my own book, I have tried to accomplish several things. Dealing with every engineering and construction feature of the various canals, or with every twist and turn in the half-century struggle to build the Seaway would be too much detail for all but the ardent student of technology or of politics. I have tried to provide an account that balances the need for a significant amount of detail with the desire to provide a history that will be appropriate for both the general reader and the serious student of the subject. Each of the existing histories of the struggle to control trade with the centre of the continent has emphasized certain aspects which the particular author has felt important. In so doing, the context in which certain actions took place is not always adequately explained. In the case of the Canadian context, authors have not always fully understood why certain steps were taken. I have attempted to provide a broader explanation of the context in which decisions in both countries were made, while at the same time re-examining the reasons behind decisions made in Canada. The roles of the provinces of Ontario and Quebec in the debate over the Seaway perhaps have not been as fully acknowledged as they should be in the histories, and I have also scrutinized these in more detail. The story that I tell covers ground that has been covered before, up to the 1970s, but I have re-examined many of the conclusions of earlier authors, have broadened the scope of the account, and have viewed the history from my particular perspective, as all historians do. Since the story is a complex one, I have chosen to place some of the information in the endnotes so as to limit the digressions in the main thread of the history. Those readers who wish to know more should consult these notes in conjunction with the text. Lastly, since the previous generation of histories dates from the 1950s to the late 1970s, I have brought the story up to date. When these accounts were written, the "Golden Dream" was still widely accepted. Every port of any size along the Great Lakes believed that increased prosperity was within easy reach in the 1950s, and even 20 years later there were still high hopes because of dramatically increased traffic. The last 30 years have brought several challenges for which solutions have not yet been found.

I have discovered the issue of providing measurements a difficult one, as this book is designed for two audiences who use different systems. After giving the matter considerable thought, I have used the original measurements, which were in feet, inches, and miles. Such an arrangement is in keeping with the original plans of the builders and is in most cases slightly more accurate than the metric equivalent. When discussing tonnage figures on the Seaway, I have included the metric conversion (tonnes) because that is the way that both the Canadian and American entities responsible for the Seaway list the amount of cargo carried on the system.

Where terms are used that might not be familiar to the reader, I have included a brief explanation. In dealing with indigenous people, I have attempted to use terms which will be recognizable to the majority of readers. This decision means, for one thing, that I have not employed words in the languages of the indigenous peoples. The term *First Nations*, which is much used in Canada, is not a descriptor in widespread use in the United States. I have settled on the use of the words *native people(s)* or *natives* as an accurate representation of the people who were here before Europeans arrived. Of course, if a particular linguistic group or tribe is mentioned, I have used the commonly used term to describe that group.

While researching this book, I have tried to visit as many of the current and abandoned canals as I could. I have now driven under two more canals, at the Eisenhower Lock and the Beauharnois Lock, with the tunnel at the latter being so far below the lock that there is not the same sense of being able to drive under a ship. I found that the Lachine Canal (1825–1970; enlarged in the 1840s) and the Soulanges Canal (1899–1959) are the most intact of the earlier canals, and that the latter's predecessor, the original Beauharnois Canal (1845–1905), and the Cascades Canal (1805–about 1890) are the least, as all but a few hundred yards of the Beauharnois and all of the Cascades have been filled in. Seeing all of these canals, including some from the eighteenth century, has helped me to understand the issues involved in building them and, I hope, has allowed me to better portray these issues and the appearance of the canals than I would have been able to do otherwise.

I would like to thank the staff of the Archives of Ontario, who were unfailingly patient as I searched through hundreds of photographs that were not always adequately catalogued, requiring the recall of various boxes of the collections, and who also helped locate material in one collection that had only been catalogued on a preliminary basis. My thanks, also, to the staff of the Owen D. Young Library, Special Collections and Vance University Archives of St. Lawrence University, who helped me to navigate through the extensive St. Lawrence Seaway collection that the library maintains. Archivist Mark McMurray offered helpful suggestions, and Mrs. Darlene Leonard was ever ready to bring out boxes of documents or photographs, photocopy documents, suggest other sources, and even volunteer information on places nearby to get a good meal. Curator Patricia Maus of the Northeast Minnesota Historical Center, located at the University of Minnesota–Duluth, provided not only a better copy of a photograph that I had located, but also suggested other photographs, and looked through the archives' holdings for documents related to my work. She even searched collections in other repositories for materials that might be of help to me. The staff of Library and Archives Canada assisted me in searching the various collections of photographs which relate to the Seaway. As in my previous experiences with the Archives, the staff was universally helpful. I would particularly like to thank Dr. Jill Delaney and the staff of the Preservation Centre of the Archives who went to great effort to locate an album of early photographs. Unfortunately, the collections and the pre-ordering system at the Library and Archives seem to be in a state of partial disarray and I was only able to see a portion of the material that I wished to view during my two visits. This situation did not create a major problem, however, as a great deal of other art and cartographic and photographic material on the Great Lakes exists in various repositories. A considerable amount can be ordered from the Archives over the Internet, though without being able to view it beforehand in most cases. The staff who handle online orders were helpful in my several dealings with them. All orders arrived ahead of the schedule posted on the Archives website, except for one that went astray until a frantic phone call about publishing deadlines brought a quick response. I would also like to thank Eric Nixon, a canal enthusiast who was generous with his time and advice during my quest to visit remnants of the previous Welland canals.

I would like to express my appreciation to my colleagues Ross Fair and David MacKenzie for reading portions of the manuscript and offering helpful suggestions, and to my colleague Carl Benn for discussing with me how best to identify native North Americans in terms that readers in both Canada and the United States would understand. My editor at Dundurn, Allison Hirst, went beyond merely editing the text by bringing possible factual errors to my attention. For this I am very grateful. Nadine Dennis kindly acted as my sample general reader to ensure that the book would appeal to more than an academic audience. The Ontario Arts Council, through the Writers' Reserve Fund and the History Department of Ryerson University have both provided funding that assisted in the research for and the preparation of the manuscript. This assistance was much appreciated.

In asking me to write this history, Dundurn Press has done me a great service. My research has allowed me to return to a subject that I first experienced and was fascinated by more than 50 years ago. As I learned more about the diverse group of characters whose enthusiasm and persistence created the different canals over the centuries, and as I saw the results of their work, much of which survives today, my own enthusiasm only grew. I hope that I have been able to do them justice.

# INTRODUCTION

It began as a matter of necessity, developed into an international and interregional rivalry, and ended in international co-operation.

The St. Lawrence River first attracted Europeans as a possible means to reach the wealth of China — a golden dream. After this conclusion was quickly proven to be an illusion, French settlement began in the St. Lawrence Valley. To the south, British and Dutch settlers moved into the Hudson and Mohawk River valleys to the extent that their native allies, the Iroquois who lived in the area, would allow them. The rivers were their means of transportation; roads were few. To the north, the Ottawa River–Lake Nipissing–French River–Georgian Bay route took fur traders into the interior. To the east, the Richelieu River–Lake Champlain–Hudson River corridor was used until the end of the American Revolutionary War as an invasion route, one that worked both ways. After Britain took over New France in 1763, then lost the American colonies in 1783, the population of the British colonies to the north and of the United States of America to the south began to expand, though at different rates. Expansion of settlement required transportation, and transportation for the next several decades depended heavily on waterways.

The problem with rivers is that they do not provide unimpeded travel. Each of these river routes involved portaging around rapids and, in the case of the Richelieu–Lake Champlain route, and in particular the Hudson–Mohawk route, a substantial body of land lay between the end of one body of water and the beginning of the next. A look at a map of North America will suggest that the St. Lawrence–Great Lakes route was the most efficient way for European settlers to reach the interior of the continent, but from the beginning, international considerations impeded its use. Initially it divided British from French territory. After the Revolutionary War and the implementation of Jay's Treaty in 1796, in which Britain surrendered claims to the area below the western Great Lakes, much of the route became the division between the two rival nations, with the entrance, the St. Lawrence River, being in British hands for nearly its entire length. Each nation looked for alternative routes which would be entirely in its own territory, and a strong rivalry developed among supporters of the various possibilities, including new ones which emerged.

Officially, the St. Lawrence Seaway includes the St. Lawrence canals, the river from Montreal to the western end of the International Rapids section of the St. Lawrence, east of the Thousand Islands, and the Welland Canal, which bypasses Niagara Falls, and which was largely completed nearly 30 years before the remainder of the Seaway. It is doubtful that anyone living at the western end of Lake Superior would see the system in this light, however. The whole point of the Seaway is to allow ships of a substantial size to travel as far as they need to up and down the Great Lakes and the St. Lawrence. From the Atlantic Ocean to the western end of Lake Superior is approximately 2,350 miles. Over that distance, the height of the water rises in numerous steps until it is just over 602 feet above sea level. These steps consist of falls and rapids and constitute another reason, aside from international rivalries, that the St. Lawrence–Great Lakes system did not early on become the method of choice for reaching the interior.

Like the Ottawa River, the Lake Champlain system, and the Hudson–Mohawk route, the St. Lawrence–Great Lakes are products of the effects of the last ice age. While the glaciers stripped the Canadian Shield of its soil and threw up the Adirondack and Appalachian mountains, they left channels through which water could flow, but that were of different depths and were partially choked by debris in places. The most extreme effect of this glacial grinding is to be found at Niagara Falls, where the level of Lake Erie is twice as far above sea level as that of Lake Ontario. In order to overcome these barriers, humans would have to intervene on a grand scale to make easy transportation of bulky goods possible.

To do this would also require that jealousies between regions within the two countries, and fears of the motives of each county on the part of the other, be put aside.

Another reason that the St. Lawrence system would logically have prevailed as the way into the interior much earlier, had international issues not intervened, can be seen by looking at a map. If Canadians in the interior regions of the Great Lakes had been trading with Americans on the eastern seaboard, the St. Lawrence, with its mouth well to the north, would have been at a considerable disadvantage, but trade for those regions was, from the beginning, overwhelmingly with Europe. It is a considerably shorter and more direct route from Britain or mainland Europe to Quebec or Montreal than to their chief rival on the Atlantic coast, New York. The harbour in New York does not freeze in winter, but the Hudson–Mohawk water route, which became the Erie Canal, does freeze, giving the St. Lawrence the advantage in terms of distance travelled during navigation season. Only the advent of the railways, with their year-round travel, gave New York the advantage over its rivals to the north. In addition, other proposed competing canal systems emerged over time on both sides of the border. As a result of the international situation, and competition from the railways and other water systems, the St. Lawrence system did not prevail, and for a century and a half it was not clear if it would ever become the system of choice to transport goods by water in and out of the Great Lakes.

Certain factors influenced decisions concerning the building of canals in the Great Lakes region, and some of them represent recurring themes in the struggle to dominate trade. The issue of power generation, either water in the early years, or hydroelectric in later years, was a major factor in the building of a number of the canals. The St. Lawrence region has a distinct advantage over contiguous areas in the United States in terms of providing the conditions to generate hydroelectric power. With numerous rivers flowing long distances down the Canadian Shield to the Great Lakes, a consistent flow of water from the lakes into the St. Lawrence and numerous drops in level along the route, conditions were ideal for power generation in Canada. Other great North American rivers, such as the Columbia, have an extremely variable rate of flow and are much more difficult to harness. Nowhere in the United States close to the Great Lakes, except at Niagara, where the flow of water passes through both countries, do the right conditions exist to generate large quantities of power. The mountains of New York State and New England are too close to the St. Lawrence to provide a sufficient head of water, and farther west, not far south of the Great Lakes, the rivers drain slowly south into the Mississippi.

Defence issues form another recurring theme. A number of the early canals were the product of tensions between Britain and the United States. In the twentieth century, defence was used as a reason to build the Seaway by its proponents and as a reason not to build a joint seaway by some of its opponents. It was only after the two nations put aside suspicions of the other's motives and recognized that common interests, including defence, outweighed national jealousies and regional rivalries that the Seaway acquired sufficient backing to be built.

Another recurring theme involves rapidly changing technology. Canal systems were often built slowly because of the great costs involved and fluctuations in political will. As a consequence, shipbuilding technology often made the canals obsolete within a few years of opening. This, in turn, created a demand for a new canal, with larger locks and deeper channels. Such technology evolved much more quickly in the mid-twentieth century, creating an even greater challenge for canal builders.

The Seaway story, then, is one with many threads, spanning some 400 years. Geography, politics, technology, economics, and national pride all played a part both in holding back and in moving forward the seaway concept. All of these threads interacted in a complex arrangement, involving far-sighted personalities and greedy individuals, political intrigue, engineering brilliance, self-serving corporations, and selfless, civic-minded proponents. States and regions, provinces and countries struggled, formed alliances, and dissolved alliances, creating an ever-changing pattern of support for the Seaway and its competitors. When at last the seaway concept triumphed, there were high hopes that the Golden Dream, first conceived by Jacques Cartier in 1555 as he gazed over the mighty St. Lawrence, would finally become a reality.

# The Age of the Innovators:
# The Early Canals, to 1848

The story of the Seaway really begins before Europeans first arrived in North America. Native peoples in what is now Quebec used the St. Lawrence, the Great Lakes, and the Ottawa River to trade and to fight with other nations farther west. Thus, when Europeans arrived, the inhabitants of the St. Lawrence River valley were able to give them some idea, albeit rather vague and general because of the limited distances that they travelled, of what lay beyond the valley.

The first known European to visit the St. Lawrence was Jacques Cartier, a pilot from Saint-Malo, France. Cartier had been introduced to the king, Francis I, as someone who had voyaged to Brazil and the "New Land." With the king's blessing and support, Cartier set out in 1534 to discover a western passage to China and India, a dream of European rulers at the time. It was believed that such a passage would bring untold wealth to Europe. His voyage that year led him to the mouth of the St. Lawrence, but at the time he did not know what he had found.[1] The following year, again supported by the king, Cartier sailed up the St. Lawrence, hoping, like other explorers of the American hemisphere before him, that he had found a through route to the Orient. He visited the native settlements at Stadacona (now Quebec City) and Hochelaga (now Montreal), having been told by his two native guides that he had taken back to France on his first trip that the river turned to fresh water and went "so far that no man has been to the end." At Hochelaga, he stood on Mount Royal and saw a raging torrent farther up the river, later named the Lachine Rapids. Using sign language, the inhabitants explained that three more rapids needed to be circumvented and that the river then ran on for a very great distance. A large tributary ran off to the north beyond these rapids (the Ottawa), from which gold and silver came, but which was inhabited by enemies of the Iroquoian peoples who inhabited Hochelaga.[2]

Cartier was to make a third voyage, confident that gold and furs would make up for the lack of a route to Asia. He made that voyage in 1541, this time as the deputy of Jean-Francois de La Roque, known as Roberval, and although he found a path which led around the rapids, it is not clear if he went farther. The gold and diamonds that Cartier took back to France turned out to be iron pyrites and quartz, and the settlement founded by Roberval in 1542 was abandoned after just one winter.[3]

France made one other feeble attempt in 1600–01 to colonize "Canada," as Cartier had dubbed a portion of the territory he had travelled, but no permanent settlement was made until 1608. In 1603, an expedition found the Iroquoian peoples gone from the St. Lawrence Valley, perhaps displaced by their enemies, the Algonquin, who travelled through but did not settle in the valley. These people, who came from the north and the west, were able to provide a fairly accurate description of the Great Lakes and the St. Lawrence, including Niagara Falls, to the French. Their description of what is now Lake Huron as having "bad" water led Samuel de Champlain to conclude that this must be the eastern sea that would lead to China.[4] It was to be some years before the dream of reaching the wealth of Asia through North America was finally put to rest by French explorers. The Ottawa River then became the main route used by these early explorers and fur traders to reach the interior, as it was a much faster route; the Great Lakes were little used.

In the meantime, French settlement progressed slowly, gradually filling the banks of the St. Lawrence as far as Lachine. It was there in 1689 that the first attempt to build a canal on the St. Lawrence took place. New France was divided into seigneuries, areas of land held by seigneurs from the king of France as long as they fulfilled certain ongoing requirements. In turn, these lands were divided into small farms and given to habitants who had their own set of obligations to the king and the seigneur. A sizeable number of the seigneuries were held by various orders of the Catholic Church. The island of Montreal was held by the Suplican Order, whose Superior, Dollier de Casson, was concerned about the limited supply of water to power mills that ground wheat for bread. He proposed to build a canal from Lake St. Louis, a widening of the St. Lawrence west of Montreal, to a lake near the centre of the island. From the lake, the St. Pierre River flowed parallel to the St. Lawrence and emptied into it near the middle of the island. Not only would this increase the flow of water to mills on the St. Pierre, but it would also allow canoes to circumvent its rapids.

To build the canal, de Casson initially proposed paying to have the work done, but when his superior in Paris refused the expense, he proposed using the labour of habitants who had not paid their yearly seigneurial dues, usually paid in the form of labour on the seigneur's lands. In June of 1689, work began, but it was brought to an abrupt and bloody halt on August 5. Near the rapids, derisively named after La Chine (China), the goal of early explorers, was a settlement, Lachine, which took its name from the raging torrent of water nearby.[5] In the struggle to dominate the Great Lakes region, the French had allied themselves with native peoples who inhabited the region north of the lakes and the St. Lawrence, while the British had allied themselves with the Iroquois, or Five Nations, who lived south of the St. Lawrence and Lake Ontario. The French had carried out numerous raids on the Iroquois, and their opponents had responded in kind, but nothing had been seen of the Iroquois for some time, and the last French campaign had resulted in a preliminary peace treaty. As a result, the people of Lachine had let down their guard. The Iroquois, hearing that Britain and France were at war, slipped across the St. Lawrence under cover of a storm on the night of August 4, and attacked at dawn the next day. More than two-thirds of the homes in the settlement were burned, some 24 inhabitants were killed, and between 70 and 90 were carried off, either to be slowly tortured to death, adopted into native families, or to escape and find their way back. All work on the canal was abandoned.[6]

Dollier de Casson did not give up the idea of a canal. In 1700 he contracted with a self-taught engineer, Gedeon de Catalogne, to have the work done, as well as to have a second small river diverted into the St. Pierre. Unfortunately, de Catalogne had not taught himself very well, for, after expending considerably more money than the contract allowed for and completing only part of the work, he succeeded only in flooding some adjacent fields. The Suplican superiors in France were outraged at the waste of so much of their limited funds, and North America's first attempt to build a canal was at an end.[7]

Defence, not the need for power, was behind the next canal building project. New France passed into British hands at the end of the Seven Years War, in 1763, and not long afterward the British government was at odds with a substantial portion of the population in the Thirteen Colonies to the south, resulting in the American Revolution and the Revolutionary War. The British forces in Quebec, as the new colony was known, were at a disadvantage in the latter conflict, as only a small contingent was stationed in Quebec for much of the war, and all supplies had to be brought from Britain. The two most difficult tasks were supplying the small British population which lived near Lake Ontario and supplying the military posts which protected the Great Lakes. This problem became more acute after 1783 when some seven to eight thousand United Empire Loyalists, who had left the Thirteen Colonies in order to remain under British rule, were settled along the north shore of the St. Lawrence, from west of the Ottawa River to the Bay of Quinte area on Lake Ontario. In the early years, they did not even produce enough food to feed themselves.

While some rudimentary works may have been undertaken on a shoreline canal, the primary means of transporting goods across the Island of Montreal was by a well-established portage road. Beyond Lachine, goods had to cross the widening of the St. Lawrence known as Lake St. Louis, into which the Ottawa River flows. From this point, the St. Lawrence becomes quite narrow, and is interrupted by a series of rapids: the Cascades at the beginning of this section; the Split Rock, or Rocher-Fendu; the Cedars; and the Coteau. All of these are found within a distance of about 13 miles. Whenever possible, goods were transported across the ice and frozen land in fall and winter, as far as Coteau-du-Lac, to be shipped from there, but this method could not handle the large volume of goods. Beginning in 1779, Loyalist troops — American colonists who fought on the British side — and Cornish miners, directed by an officer of the Royal Engineers, hacked a narrow, shallow canal (six or seven feet wide and about two and a half feet deep, hardly much deeper than what a modern bathtub can hold) out of the rock at Coteau-du-Lac, for a distance of over 330 feet. Three locks raised boats about six feet.

This was the first canal with locks built in North America. Completed in 1781, it only partially solved the problem of getting goods around the various rapids.[8] Additional canals had to be built to bypass the Cascades and Split Rock rapids. These were quite primitive facilities. At Cascades Point, one canal, La Faucille, was largely excavated from the marshy shoreline only yards from the river.

Goods in this period were transported in bateaux, conveyances built like long, narrow rowboats that were 35 to 40 feet long and slightly narrower than the canals. At the entrance to the canal, about three-quarters of the cargo and any passengers would be unloaded and portaged by wagon across the Cascades Point and up to the head of the Cedars Rapids, about four miles ahead. The bateau would then be pulled through the canal and around the point through the edge of the rapids. Not far beyond the point, the boat would have to go through the Trou-du-Moulin Canal, which cut through a small projection of land in the rapids. Here an earlier channel, dug during the French regime, was replaced by a larger cut containing a lock. Not far beyond that, the Split Rock (or Rocher-Fendu) Canal was constructed. The Cedars Rapids, farther along the waterway, could be ascended by pulling the bateau, with most of the cargo and the passengers still removed, up through the edge of the rapids.

These three canals were finished by 1783. All of this would raise the bateau only about 15 feet. Finally, the bateau would reach the Coteau Canal, and from there would be able to access Lake St. Francis, another widening of the St. Lawrence.[9] This body of water, on which it might be possible to put up the sail, brought only temporary relief from the drudgery of portaging and dragging, as between Lake St. Francis and Lake Ontario lay the mighty Long Sault Rapids, along with the Lachine Rapids the most challenging on the St. Lawrence, and a series of smaller rapids beyond that.[10] It is no wonder that the trip from Montreal took around two weeks to complete, or that the men who undertook this work shared a unique way of life. Mostly French Canadian, they worked very hard by day, were famous for dancing, singing, and drinking well into the night, and usually retired at an early age, worn out from constant exertion and often suffering from aches and pains brought on by many nights sleeping on damp, cold ground. Any passengers, who were often immigrants, would be able to sit and watch the bateaux go by, perhaps enjoying a "picnic" lunch among the pleasures of a Canadian spring or summer, blackflies, flies, and mosquitoes in the thousands. If there was no kind farmer to put them up at night, or no inn was available where the bateau stopped, they, too, would sleep on the ground.[11] Because of the time and effort involved, transportation of goods from Montreal to Lake Ontario was very costly, and more than one well-to-do immigrant found out the hard way that the cost of bringing furniture and other bulky items from Great Britain exceeded the value of the goods transported.[12]

Going back downstream from the mouth of Lake Ontario took only about four days, and slightly more cargo could be carried, as the boats shot the rapids rather than using the canals.[13] No one knows who first dared try to navigate the channels that would safely take boats through the churning waters, but going through was the normal course of events. Sometimes the breaking of an oar used for steering, or some other momentary mishap would lead to disaster, as the bateau turned sideways and overturned.

The average bateau carried about three and a half tons and fit easily into the canals. But an increasing population on the St. Lawrence and Lake Ontario and the beginnings of export from the lower lakes created a demand for bigger boats on the St. Lawrence, and this created a need for larger canals. By the early nineteenth century, Durham boats had been introduced from the United States, where they had been George Washington's boat of choice to ferry his forces across the Delaware River in his famous crossing. These were more ungainly than bateaux, but carried far more cargo. They could be over 60 feet long and the average width was about eight feet. Flat bottomed, with a small keel, they typically could hold up to 20 tons, yet required only 28 inches of water when fully loaded. More like a wooden barge with pointed ends than a rowboat, they could be rowed, sailed, or poled. Wooden walkways on each side allowed the crew members to walk the boat up through the rapids with iron-tipped poles, and a long "sweep" rudder could be used on either end. Fully loaded, the top edge of the boat was only 12 to 14 inches from the water.[14] The crews, usually composed of five men, were not bothered by this, but riding so close to the water must have given some passengers the odd fright. One traveller, going downriver in 1818, told of a somewhat harrowing trip in a slightly wider and longer Durham boat which was heavily loaded with "26 tons," resulting in the top of the sides being only "a few inches" from the water. These areas above the water had been reinforced with heavy planks nailed on, so that when the craft hit a rock in the rapids the heavy weight of the boat would not result in the side being crushed.[15]

The increased use of Durham boats, and the fact that the La Faucille and Trou-du-Moulin canals were close to the river and subject to ice damage in winter, resulted in the Royal Engineers widening the Split Rock and Coteau canals. The other two canals were abandoned after a new Cascades Canal was cut diagonally across Cascades Point for 1,500 feet, with three locks and a maximum width of 20 feet (19 feet in the lock gates), effectively bypassing the Cascades Rapids, and bringing boats into the St. Lawrence closer to the Split Rock Canal than before. This work was completed in 1805, and by 1817 the two remaining original canals, the Split Rock and the Coteau, had been doubled in size and deepened to 3 feet, 6 inches.[16] This allowed for much greater upstream traffic on the river and, by the turn of the nineteenth century, it was theoretically possible to travel all the way to the head of Lake Superior by boat.

The biggest obstacle on the route was at Niagara Falls, where a drop of 327 feet between the lakes had to be overcome. There was a portage road on what is now the American side by the mid-eighteenth century, but it had to be abandoned after the Revolutionary War and Jay's Treaty dictated that the land south of the Great Lakes was to be American. A new portage was completed in the 1790s, and was used to transship cargo on wagons, the contents of which would then be loaded onto ships on Lake Erie, an expensive and time-consuming process.[17] From there it was an easy trip to the narrows at the head of Lake Michigan, where a portage road overcame the 20-foot difference in height at the site of the St. Marys Rapids. In 1798 the North West Company, a fur-trading company operating out of Montreal and a supply depot called Fort William at the head of Lake Superior, built a crude canal around the rapids, similar to the early canals at Cascades Point. This canal was the first built specifically to exploit the resources of the central interior of North America, a desire that would find its ultimate expression in the Seaway. Few, with the exception of fur traders and the military, went beyond the settlements at Detroit and at Amherstburg on the Canadian side. Most, including the North West Company, used the long-established Ottawa River–Lake Nipissing–French River–Georgian Bay route to the Upper Lakes. This was a faster, easier route for the large freight canoes used by the North West Company. The canal that bypassed the St. Marys Rapids was later destroyed during the War of 1812 and was never rebuilt. In 1821, the North West Company amalgamated with its long-time rival the Hudson's Bay Company, and soon all trade was being done through Hudson Bay, which provided a shorter and much less expensive route into the Far West.[18]

By the early 1800s, a two-way trade had developed on the St. Lawrence–Lake Ontario–Lake Erie corridor. On the way back down the St. Lawrence, bateaux and Durham boats transported potash, the product of burning trees cut from developing farmland, a product that was used in the British cloth-making industry. They later carried wheat and flour, as farms developed, to feed the British masses. Along with these came timber rafts, bringing timber for use in the building of British ships. Trees were felled and the four sides squared up. They were tied together in "drams" averaging 33 by 100 feet, and about 10 drams were lashed together into a massive raft. A crew of men travelled on each dram, which was complete with housing, a fire pit on which to cook, steering poles and sails, and sometimes a cargo of wheat or flour. When rapids such as the Long Sault were reached, the larger rafts were broken down into small drams which could more easily shoot the rapids and be reassembled below. At Quebec City, the timbers were loaded into the same ships that brought immigrants to Canada from Britain, providing a lucrative return cargo.[19] The Great Lakes were beginning to show their economic potential.

In the first half of the nineteenth century the region experienced a boom in canal construction. For the first two-thirds of this period, roads were scarce, generally in poor condition, and unsuitable for long-distance bulk transport. Until the railway era in the 1850s, water transportation was the preferred means of travel for both people and goods going any distance, and canal improvements were a necessity.

The United States completed the first canal, the Erie Canal. This was an audacious project that involved the construction of a canal that was 363 miles long, cut through largely uninhabited, virgin forest, in an area where engineers had to contend with a rise of about 600 feet between one end, at Albany, and the other, on Lake Erie. Its purpose was twofold: to open up western New York to settlement and to make the port of New York the terminus of trade with the West. This was the first canal specifically designed to link the interior around the Great Lakes with the seacoast, and as such was to become one of the main rivals of the St. Lawrence.

The wealthy and well-connected Gouverneur Morris, bon vivant, senator, and former American minister in France, is often given credit for coming up with the idea of a canal that would stretch from the Hudson to Lake Erie. Morris was a man of boundless enthusiasm for life who did not let the lack of one leg slow him down either in politics, business, or pleasure. In fact, several others had proposed it before him, going back as far as a bill in the New York Legislature in 1787 and, in more general terms, to a proposal in 1724; however Morris's personality ensured that the concept was widely discussed among his peers.[20] During the Revolutionary War, Morris had speculated about a water connection from the Hudson to the "great western seas." It was after a trip in 1800 up the Hudson and Lake Champlain route to Montreal, and then on through the St. Lawrence and Lake Ontario to Niagara, where he saw nine ships anchored on the "western sea" of Lake Erie, that he began to talk and dream about a canal linking the Atlantic with Lake Erie.[21] Although Morris remained an active supporter of the canal idea, others did much of the work.

Elkanah Watson, later a famous agricultural reformer, wrote extensively in the 1780s about the benefits of connecting the Mohawk River through Oswego to Lake Ontario. General Philip Schuyler, the wealthy leader of the Federalist forces in the New York Legislature, who became a great believer in internal improvements in New York, helped to pass two bills in 1792 based on Watson's ideas. These bills created two private companies, one to develop a waterway from Albany to Oswego, and one to build a canal from the Hudson to Lake Champlain. Each company intended to divert the wealth of the eastern lakes through New York, with hopes of bringing prosperity to the state. Half of those who bought shares in the companies were either holders of large blocks of vacant land in western New York, or land speculators. Others were bankers and merchants in New York City, and all of them saw immediate personal benefits in such developments. Morris was a landholder, as was Schuyler, but they and some of the others were not involved just for personal gain. In the aftermath of the American Revolution, they saw themselves helping to build a new state and a new nation. Schuyler became president of both companies, and Watson a director.[22]

The two private companies were not very successful despite the State of New York investing a sizeable amount of money in them. Only a small amount of work was done on the Hudson–Lake Champlain route before the company went bankrupt. The second company survived for a decade and made some improvements on the Mohawk River and Wood Creek, but nothing was done to connect the works with Lake Ontario through the Oswego River. In addition, seasonal variations in water level and obstacles on the Mohawk that could not be overcome meant that much traffic still went by road. After 1803, the company became inactive, but many of those involved continued to support canal construction and became active in endorsing the Erie Canal.[23]

Several men in the first decade of the nineteenth century began discussing, both in print and in public, specific ideas for a canal from Albany to Lake Erie, translating Morris's vague idea into specific routes and projected costs. Most notable, perhaps, was Jesse Hawley, who had a freight-forwarding business in Geneva, New York, and knew the difficulties of shipping to New York City. Working only from maps and books, he came up with almost the exact route that was later followed, as well as a general explanation of how it could be done using the height of water in Lake Erie to supply the canal. He also detailed how freight from Canada would pay the cost of upkeep and immigrants would pay the operating costs. The cost of building the canal, which he calculated fairly accurately, he believed should be borne by the federal government as a nation-building expense.

Hawley's published ideas formed the basis for future action, although it became apparent when the route was actually examined that it would take more than water running downhill from Lake Erie to supply the needs of the canal. A survey was undertaken of the practicality of the scheme in 1808, and some advocates warned that, if the canal went to Lake Ontario instead, there was a danger that Canada would get control of all of the trade.[24] The hope of the backers was that the national government would back a project that would so benefit the country, but when approached about financing, President Thomas Jefferson called the plan "little short of madness."[25]

The scheme could go no farther until the Republicans in the state Legislature came onside. The existing, dormant canal company was heavily dominated by Federalists, and if the state was to pursue such a project, it would require the support of both groups. The leader of the dominant Republican faction in the state Senate in 1810 was De Witt Clinton. From a long-established and wealthy Dutch family that had a history of public service, Clinton had previously served in the New York Assembly and the New York Senate, had been in the United States Senate, and was mayor of New York from 1803 to 1807 and from 1808 to 1810. Like other backers of the canal plan, he was a land speculator, and held a single share in the dormant company. He had a great desire to see New York City rival other great cities of the United States, and believed the canal was the key. He agreed to back a Federalist bill to survey both the Lake Erie and the Lake Ontario routes to see which was the most practical. Gouverneur Morris was the president of the board of the canal commissioners, which was appointed to do the survey. Clinton was also a member. In 1811, the commissioners issued a report favouring the Erie route, and Clinton made the project his own from then on.[26]

Congress would not finance what the commissioners argued was a plan of national importance, and the War of 1812 made it difficult to advance the project, especially since the war was fought on the northern frontier. Clinton, too, suffered setbacks, losing a bid for the presidency as the peace candidate in 1812 and later losing the New York City mayoralty, which he had again held between 1811 and 1815. Clinton's response, with the support of other believers, was to engineer a grand petition at the end of 1815 to send to the state Legislature. Clinton's was one of 30 petitions submitted in 1816 favouring the canal, but it was the best-argued and most influential. He even accepted the idea of building a canal to Lake Ontario, which some of the opponents of the canal favoured, as long as it was built in conjunction with a canal to Lake Erie so as to prevent Montreal from gaining control of trade in northern New York.[27] In 1816 a move in the Legislature to start the canal was defeated, but in 1817 a bill to construct it by first building a test section succeeded with the support of Clinton's Republican rival in the state Senate, Martin Van Buren, who had become convinced of the benefits of the project. On the strength of his championing of the canal, Clinton was elected governor in 1817. Resistance from his political opponents and from sections of the state which felt they would not benefit from the canals (the short Champlain Canal was also authorized), particularly southern areas and working-class neighbourhoods of New York City, led to the canal being dubbed "Clinton's Ditch" and "Clinton's Folly."[28]

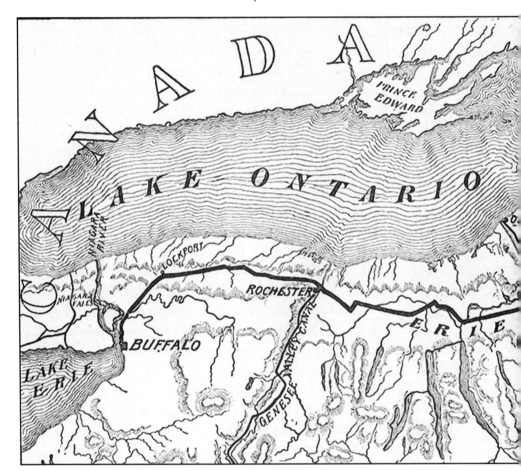

**Map 1.** The Erie Canal, its feeder canals, the Oswego Canal, and the Hudson–Lake Champlain canals, *circa* 1850. Adapted from Thomas Curtis Clarke, "A Map of the Country Traversed By the Erie Canal," *Scribners Magazine*, Vol. 19, No. 15, 1896, and

While there were no professional engineers in the United States who could handle such a project, amateurs, often surveyors or artisans, trained themselves as they went along, and several ingenious inventions sped up the process. Instead of laboriously shovelling earth into wheelbarrows and carrying it away, a form of scraper or plow that could be dragged by horses was invented, which significantly speeded up the work. Special winches were created which quickly ripped trees and stumps out of the ground. After much experimentation, a type of cement was invented which would harden underwater, thus solving one of the greatest problems in canal building.

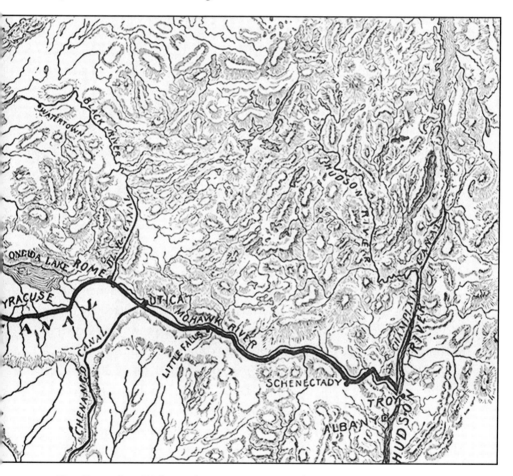

Van Rensselaer Richmond, state engineer and surveyor (supervising editor), *Map and Profile of New York State Canals*, Annual Report of the New York State Engineer and Surveyor, 1860.

The canal was built 4 feet deep and 40 feet wide at the top, with sloping sides. A tow path would run along the side so that horses could pull the barges and boats along the canal. Locks were 90 feet long by 15 feet wide, limiting the size of Durham boats or barges that could use the canal to a displacement of 3.5 feet and about 12 feet in width. Not too many years after it opened, though, many boats using the canal were upwards of 14 feet wide, leading to numerous scrapes against the lock walls and collisions in the channels.

At one point, 9,000 men and hundreds of horses and oxen laboured on the canal, which opened in sections as they were completed, the test section having proven that the canal could be built, and the Legislature having voted to continue with the project. The Montezuma Swamp on Lake Cayuga caused considerable illness and death among workers, and had to be excavated in winter to avoid swamp fever.[29] The two other great obstacles builders faced were the large rivers, such as the Genesee, that had to be crossed, and the steep rise at Niagara approaching Lake Erie. Several long aqueducts, some over 1,000 feet in length, were constructed along the route to carry the canal over rivers or to bring supplies of water to the canal. To cross the valley of the Irondequoit Creek, a 70-foot-high hill was built for a distance of a quarter-mile, nearly 250 feet wide at the base. At the approach to the Niagara River, a creek bed down the side of the escarpment was enlarged and a double series of five step locks installed, literally a series of connected locks that looked like elongated steps climbing up the escarpment. Above that, a deep channel was blasted through a high ridge using black powder, an extremely dangerous undertaking that resulted in numerous injuries being inflicted by the rocks which were scattered in all directions. So difficult were these two portions of the construction that the State, in a highly unusual move, had to take over the supervision of the project from the contractors. As the canal neared completion, a fierce rivalry developed between Buffalo and Black Rock, a short distance down the Niagara River, which had been vying for the position of terminus on Lake Erie since 1817. Neither possessed a good harbour and each tried to convince the canal commissioners and the Legislature that it could construct a suitable one. Buffalo had to contend with a persistent sandbar and Black Rock with the strong current in the Niagara River as well as strong winds that blew against departing vessels. Ultimately, Buffalo won, although Black Rock was left as a second harbour on the canal. Problems persisted, however, forcing the state to take over both harbours in 1828. The rivalry did not completely subside until Black Rock was absorbed by a rapidly expanding Buffalo in 1853.[30]

As the canal progressed, an increasing number of individuals wanted to invest in it, and money was therefore always available to push ahead with construction. The Hudson–Champlain canals were finished in 1824 and the Erie in 1825, eight years after it was started. De Witt Clinton, however, nearly did not receive the credit for the finished project. A vindictive politician who punished his enemies and felt no need to conciliate either the opposing faction within his own party or the Federalists by favouring their candidates for various posts, he had increasingly alienated those in the Legislature whose support he needed. Old enemies eventually came to embrace the canal concept, which was increasingly popular, but to oppose Clinton. At the end of 1822 his party did not nominate him for another term as governor due to his unpopularity among politicians, and in 1824 he was removed as a canal commissioner by a legislature filled with his opponents. Realignment of state politics with the creation of the People's Party, however, gave him a new political base. His popularity as the champion of the canal, combined with anger among the electorate at his seemingly undeserved removal as a canal commissioner, overcame his many failings, and he was swept back in as governor in time to celebrate the opening.[31]

In a symbolic and politically astute move to celebrate the opening of the entire canal, Clinton led a flotilla of canal boats from Buffalo in the *Seneca Chief*, specially outfitted for the occasion, and carrying produce not only from New York, but also from Ohio and Michigan. Filling a cask with water from Lake Erie, he poured it into the Atlantic off New York in an elaborate ceremony, and then repeated the process, carrying a cask of water from the Atlantic back to Lake Erie. All along the route there were celebrations of what was a remarkable achievement. Jesse Hawley, who had conceived the general plan for a canal to Lake Erie commented during the celebrations that New York had "made the longest Canal — in the least time — with the least experience — for the least money — and of the greatest utility of any other in the world."[32]

While there was a small measure of exaggeration in this, he was essentially correct. It was a great engineering achievement and a great financial success. It made money even before it was finished, as the portion that had opened before 1825 was already bringing in revenue. So much money came in from tolls in succeeding years that the commissioners tried to buy back the stock, but because it was worth so much they decided to loan the toll money to banks along the route instead, which in turn was loaned to farmers and business people whose success brought more traffic to the canal. Even though a great deal of money was loaned, by 1845 the principal on the original construction had been paid off as well. By 1847, goods coming through the canal from the West exceeded those being sent from western New York. Thousands of immigrants used the canal to fill up the lands of western New York, much of it once the hunting grounds of the Iroquois Confederacy, which had interrupted the building of the canal at Lachine in the seventeenth century. The Iroquois had been displaced from parts of the area south of Lake Ontario after a portion of the Confederacy, mainly Mohawk, had taken the British side in the Revolutionary War. Many other settlers went on to fill up the lands of the Midwest, and to send their agricultural goods down the canal in return for manufactured goods such as furniture.[33] Whereas the produce of Lake Erie settlers had almost entirely gone down the St. Lawrence until the Erie Canal was finished, that changed radically after 1825, and the St. Lawrence was at a decided disadvantage.[34] When the Oswego Canal opened in 1828, one of a number of feeder canals for the Erie, it brought even more Lake Erie business down through the canal, and some Canadian business, as well. The Canadian backers of the St. Lawrence route knew that they would have to compete more effectively or lose out on the ever-increasing business of the West.[35]

Three canals or canal systems were started in Canada in the decade after the Erie was begun: one for defence purposes, one for defence and commercial reasons, and one both to attract the trade of the West and to provide power for mills. During the War of 1812, the weaknesses of the St. Lawrence system had become even more apparent than they were in the Revolutionary War. The difficulties of transporting military supplies, including foodstuffs, from Great Britain to the troops in Upper Canada, the present Province of Ontario, were immense. William "Tiger" Dunlop, a Scottish writer and later an employee of a land company in Upper Canada, wrote of his experience as an assistant surgeon in the war:

> Troops acting on the Niagara frontier, 1,000 miles from the ocean were fed with flour the produce of England, and pork and beef from Cork, which, with the waste inseparable from a state of war, the expense and accidents to which a long voyage expose[d] them, and the enormous cost of internal conveyance, at least doubled the quantity required, and rendered the price of them at least 10 times their original cost. Not only provisions, but every kind of Military and Naval Store, every bolt of canvas, every rope yarn, as well as the heavier articles of guns, shot, cables, anchors, and all the numerous etceteras for furnishing a large squadron, arming forts, supplying arms for the militia [all adult males had to serve when called] and the line [regular soldiers], had to be brought from Montreal to Kingston, a distance of nearly 200 miles, by land in winter, and in summer by flat-bottomed boats, which had to tow up the rapids [partially unloaded] and sail up the still parts of the river …[36]

In the fall of 1814, even the entire wooden frame for a 55-gun frigate and all the fittings were sent from Britain to Lake Ontario in pieces by this route.[37]

An added problem which did not exist in the earlier war was the threat to the transportation system posed by the proximity of the United States. Although there was almost no American settlement along the shore, the river marked the boundary between British territory and American for much of the way from Montreal to Kingston. As Dunlop put it, the boats came up the river

> … (in many places not a mile in breadth, between the British and American shores,) exposed to the shot of the enemy without any protection; for with the small

body of troops we had in the country, it was utterly impossible that we could detach a force sufficient to protect the numerous *brigades* of boats that were daily proceeding up the river, and we must have been utterly undone, had not the ignorance and the inertness of the enemy saved us. Had they stationed four field guns, covered by a corps of riflemen, on the banks of the St. Lawrence, they could have cut off our supplies without risking one man.... They rarely or never troubled us. If they had done so with any kind of spirit, we must have abandoned Upper Canada ...[38]

In 1828, testifying before a House of Commons committee about the defence of Canada, the Duke of Wellington, a national hero in Britain after his defeat of Napoleon at the Battle of Waterloo, commented,

I have been astonished that the officers of the army and navy employed in that country were able to defend those provinces last war; and I can attribute their having been able to defend them as they did only to the inexperience of the officers of the United States in the operations of the war, and possibly likewise to the difficulty which they must have found in stationing their forces as they ought to have done upon the right bank of the St. Lawrence.[39]

Wellington, in fact, became a strong advocate for a canal system to bypass the narrow stretch of the St. Lawrence in the years after the war ended in 1815.

American forces demonstrated this danger to Upper Canada with an attack on Montreal in the fall of 1813 designed to cut the lifeline to Upper Canada. The war was generally poorly fought on both sides. The British were hampered by the fact that they were fighting Napoleon in Europe and could only send a small force to defend Canada and by the fact that about 60 percent of the population of Upper Canada, which experienced most of the fighting, consisted of recent immigrants from the United States, attracted by free land. The Americans, who had the benefit of being located close to the Canadas, were not successful in taking advantage of this for a variety of reasons. Among these was the fact that most of the senior commanders at the beginning of the war were junior officers in the Revolutionary War who had worked their way up in the ranks without ever commanding an army, and proved to be incompetent. In addition, many of the troops they led were recent recruits who were not well trained, and the state militias, not required to serve outside state boundaries, were reluctant to do so.[40]

The senior American commander in the area, Major General James Wilkinson, an officer who was not even respected by his fellow officers, led an army of 8,000 men, a considerably larger force than the entire body of British regulars in both the Canadas, by boat down the St. Lawrence, while his junior, Major General Wade Hampton, who later resigned in protest at serving under Wilkinson, brought his 4,000-man army up from Lake Champlain. The New York State militia refused to accompany Hampton, and his own men were poorly trained, but he had been working hard to prepare them, with liberal use of the lash and executions. As well, he faced a resistance of only a few hundred men, mainly French-Canadian militia and native allies. This latter force, partly sedentary militia (untrained) and partly embodied (trained and equipped) beat off Hampton's attack southwest of Montreal, and Hampton retreated with minimal casualties to wait for Wilkinson. Wilkinson's brigade of boats was badly mauled by October storms and harassed by a small force of British regulars, militia, and natives, supported by gunboats, about 800 or 900 men in all. Needing two days to get his boats through the Long Sault Rapids, Wilkinson landed a force to clear the road to Cornwall, and another, of about 2,000 men, to drive off the British and Canadians. In a battle on John Crysler's farm, the American forces fought well, but the British commander had chosen his position carefully. The Americans were not expecting to face British Regulars and their commander committed his forces piecemeal. In a hard-fought battle the Americans suffered heavy casualties before retreating. While the road to Cornwall was now open and he still had almost 8,000 men, Wilkinson took a message from Hampton refusing to meet him near Montreal as an excuse to call off his advance, since Hampton could be blamed. Though the campaign failed, it drove home the point that the narrow section of the St. Lawrence west of Montreal was a critical point in the security of Upper Canada, and it would not be the last time Crysler's farm figured in the history of the St. Lawrence waterway.[41]

Even before the war ended, the commander of the British forces in the Canadas was contemplating the possibility of bypassing this stretch of river by creating a canal system to take supplies up the Ottawa River and down to Kingston, the naval base on Lake Ontario, by way of the Rideau River. This would involve a long detour, but provide a route safe from American attack. The British government took up the issue of the Ottawa–Rideau system as well as that of a canal to bypass the Lachine Rapids, both equally necessary if war materials were to reach Upper Canada easily. Surveys were carried out by the military on both the Ottawa and on the Rideau to Kingston routes in the years immediately after the war, and Upper Canada paid for another survey of the Rideau route in 1822–23, concerned about the deleterious effects that the small St. Lawrence canals were having on trade. Neither, however, was prepared to pay, and the project languished. Meanwhile, the Americans built two military roads along the St. Lawrence to facilitate the movement of troops.[42]

Only a small start was made on a canal at Carillon on the Ottawa River, thanks to the intervention of the governor general of Lower Canada and commander-in-chief of British forces in the Canadas, Charles Lennox, Duke of Richmond. He took a personal interest in the Ottawa–Rideau route as a defensive measure, and approved the building of a small canal at Carillon on the Ottawa River only a few months after he arrived in Canada in 1818, as a preliminary step in construction of a whole system of canals. Unfortunately for the project, the Duke decided to explore the entire route himself, and while visiting Sorel on the St. Lawrence on the way to the Ottawa, he was bitten by a pet fox which happened to be rabid. While exploring the Rideau route, he took ill and died, leaving behind no specific instructions as to what was to be built, and there was no one in the colony to continue support for the project. In the absence of any specific instructions, the Royal Staff Corps of the British Army, a little-known and short-lived branch of the army which did essentially the same type of work as the Royal Engineers, decided to build a canal with the same dimensions as the proposed canal around the Lachine Rapids.[43]

Work progressed slowly, with both money and men in short supply, but the project was given a boost through the efforts of the Duke of Wellington, who had been appointed Master General of the Ordnance, a cabinet-level position responsible for fortifications, military supplies, artillery, and other physical needs of the military. Because of his keen interest in defence in British North America, he dispatched a commission of engineers in 1825 to study defence issues in all of the colonies. Commenting on the Ottawa–Rideau route, the commission recommended that, in order for the route to be used for military purposes, locks would have to be built around the other rapids on the Ottawa, and suggested that the surveyed Rideau route was quite practical. Wellington then urged the British cabinet to commence work on both rivers. In 1826, Colonel John By of the Royal Engineers was selected to build the Rideau Canal system.[44]

By was chosen because he was seen as a competent manager, but, like many of the people associated with building the early canals, he was also a rather remarkable individual. Like Jesse Hawley, who envisioned the Erie Canal in detail before it was built, and who also envisioned other canals in the eastern states which were later built, By looked to the future, not just to the present. Not long after he arrived in Canada, he urged his superior in London, the Inspector General of Fortifications, to authorize the building of locks on the Rideau and the Ottawa large enough to handle steamboats then in use on the Great Lakes, and timber cribs and spars for the British navy, instead of locks the size of those on the Lachine Canal, which had recently been completed. He urged work on the channel north of Montreal, which would allow steamboats to bypass the smaller locks of the Lachine Canal and be able to reach Lake Ontario by the Ottawa and Rideau route. He reasoned that this would prevent Americans from taking over the trade of the Great Lakes with their canals, and would allow armed steamboats, rather than just gunboats, to enter the Great Lakes and defend Canada. In addition, since the Americans claimed control of the navigable channel in the St. Lawrence near Cornwall, they could easily interrupt all commerce between the colonies. He also recommended enlarging locks on the Richelieu River so that Lower Canada could dominate the trade from that area of the colony and the trade from the United States around Lake Champlain. By even suggested opening the waterways all the way to Lake Superior. He also pointed out that an earlier estimate of the cost of building the canal was far too low.[45]

Since the British government was very reluctant to spend money on the colonies unless absolutely necessary, another two committees examined By's proposals. They agreed with his estimates, though acknowledging that they were approximate since building conditions were unknown, but reached a compromise on the size of the locks. Locks 5 feet deep, 134 feet long, and 33 feet wide would accommodate the smallest steamers, which could tow bateaux and also accommodate timber sent down through the locks. As a result of this decision, By did not include a towpath such as existed on the Erie Canal, reasoning that steamboats would be used in place of horses to pull the rafts, Durham boats, and bateaux. While he did build four blockhouses to defend the canal, on several occasions he urged the building of further fortifications, since he viewed the canal as a defensive measure and did not feel these would be sufficient.[46]

Construction began in 1827, and the canal opened in 1832, a remarkably short time considering that, even though the route had been surveyed and traversed on more than one occasion, the exact conditions that would be faced in constructing the system were not known. Unlike the usual method for construction by the Royal Engineers, the construction was almost entirely contracted out, and the contracts were controlled by the Commissary General's department, not by Colonel By, leading to endless delays in getting approvals for even minor items. The contractors doing the stone work did a good job, but most of the ones working on the excavation were inexperienced, and either submitted bids so low that they went bankrupt, or failed to complete the work, leading to delays and to work that had to be done over. All work was done by manual labour, whether removing soil by pickax, shovel, and wheelbarrow, or cutting and fitting stonework in the channels. Since local labour on the largely unsettled route was in very short supply, Irish immigrants with no experience were employed in large numbers. In swampy areas, malaria struck and hundreds died while others were laid up for long periods. By came down with the "swamp fever" several times, as well, nearly dying at one point, but persevering in his direct supervision of the work all along the route. Construction accidents caused by the use of black powder for blasting by inexperienced workers were also common.[47]

Among the unique achievements in the course of construction was the erection of a 60-foot dam to raise the height of a portion of a river in order to avoid having to canalize the area. This was the highest dam yet built in North America, more than twice the height of one built earlier on the Erie Canal. A second dam three-quarters of its height was also built. In large, swampy areas, Colonel By also used dams to raise the water level rather than trying to cut a channel. To do work of this magnitude, in such a short time, with inexperienced labour, sickness, and a stifling bureaucracy impeding the project was a great achievement for which By did not receive credit, despite keeping meticulous accounts, being very frugal in spending, and treating his workers with considerable kindness. The terms of the project were that By would spend money before Parliament approved expenditures each year, with the idea that if he overspent one year, he could make it up in another. As costs escalated, a new government in London, which had replaced the pro-canal government (1828–30) led by the Duke of Wellington, balked at the increased cost in 1831. By was not informed of this, and when he indicated the final cost, was recalled to England to explain why he had exceeded the limit set for the project. By and the Ordnance Department, to which he reported expenditures, were able to show that he could not control expenditures which were not approved until after the expenditures were made, and that his actions had been approved at every step, as required. While he could not be faulted on his actions, he was told that he should have kept his expenses down. Had he done so, the project would have taken much longer and it is questionable whether the new government would have allowed continued expenditures on what was the most expensive Ordnance project undertaken in the British Empire to that date. Feeling that he had been unfairly treated, By resigned from the army and spent the last few years of his life trying to clear his reputation. The only recognition that he received was in the naming of the settlement at the mouth of the Rideau where he had built his headquarters, Bytown. Even that disappeared when it was incorporated as the City of Ottawa in 1855.[48]

The Ottawa River canals, though consisting of only three canals, were not finished until 1834, two years after the Rideau, though begun seven years earlier. The Royal Staff Corps had neither the manpower nor the money that By had on the Rideau, and had to cut the Grenville Canal out of solid rock through its entire length. While work on the 5.75-mile canal was completed under the Staff Corps using both civilian miners and men of the Corps, it was decided to contract out work on the two small canals, at Carillon and Chute à Blondeau, to speed up the work. However, given the fact that the yearly appropriations did not increase, progress was still slow. Full use of the canals was not possible until 1843, as a lock was required to allow steamboats to get from the Island of Montreal into the Ottawa, and a private wooden lock in use since at least 1816 was restricted to vessels owned by the same company for a time in the 1830s. Even then, it was not possible to take full advantage of John By's insistence on larger locks on the Rideau. The upper three locks in the Grenville Canal had been built to roughly the same dimensions as those on the Lachine Canal, and despite several recommendations to enlarge them to the same size as all others, this had not been done. The smallest dimensions were 106 feet 8 inches long and 19 feet 3½ inches wide, with a maximum usable depth of 5 feet. Ironically, these canals went over budget by a much higher percentage than had By's, but no problem was seen with this, probably because the work had been stretched out over so many years.[49]

The Lachine Canal, which was the gateway to the Ottawa–Rideau route, had been a subject of interest for some Montreal merchants since the 1790s, but nothing was done until the War of 1812 showed the weakness in the line of transportation to Upper Canada. Ships could make their way around the south side of the island to Lachine, but the passage was difficult and dangerous. At about the time in 1815 that the Ottawa–Rideau was being recommended to the British government, the governor general in Lower Canada asked the lower house of Parliament, the Assembly, to agree to pay for a canal to bypass the Lachine Rapids. This body, unlike the upper house, was dominated by French-Canadian members who represented agricultural interests and had little use for canals which would, in their minds, only benefit English-Canadian merchants. In this case, though, the issue of defence was on everyone's mind as a result of the war, and the Assembly voted to provide the large sum of £25,000 to support the project. Commissioners were appointed to carry out the project, and a survey was carried out by a member of the Royal Engineers, who estimated the cost of a canal capable of handling only Durham boats at almost twice the amount provided in the vote. With the British government shifting its focus to the Ottawa–Rideau system exclusively, the Assembly was not prepared to cover this added cost by itself. In 1819, after extensive debate, this body decided to let a private company, consisting largely of Anglo-Canadian merchants, build the canal. Though the British and Lower Canadian governments bought a significant number of shares in the company, it could not raise sufficient capital and, in 1821, the government of the colony decided to buy out the company and build the canal itself, on the understanding that the British government would contribute £10,000. The £12,000 that the British government decided to contribute turned out to be a good investment, as the canal ultimately cost over £109,000, and, for its small contribution, the British government was allowed free passage of military goods and boats on military service. The canal featured seven locks 100 feet long, 20 feet wide, and 5 feet deep when finished in 1824.[50] The dream of Dollier de Casson more than a century before had been realized, and in almost the same place as he had struggled.

Neither the Grenville nor the Lachine Canal could handle larger vessels, and merchants in both Upper and Lower Canada were anxious to improve the St. Lawrence route to Kingston, which was about 50 miles shorter than the triangular Ottawa–Rideau system and would have considerably fewer locks when finished. In spite of the merchants' dislike, the Ottawa–Rideau was a commercial success. Freight traffic continued to increase on the system until the 1860s even though the first St. Lawrence canals came into full operation in the early 1850s. Traffic picked up again on the Rideau portion after the 1870s, when Smiths Falls, located on the banks of the Rideau, became the service centre for the Canadian Pacific Railway, and large shipments of coal were brought in by barge from the United States. The Ottawa canals saw a steady increase in traffic until the 1880s, with much of it carrying lumber down the river. Upbound traffic also increased over the years and the Ottawa maintained a steady tonnage of cargo from the 1880s until the 1950s and a steady count of boats until the 1930s.[51]

What the merchants of both colonies and the farmers of Upper Canada wanted, however, was an improvement in the direct route to Montreal. The British government had responded to pleas for assistance in attracting more trade to the St. Lawrence in the 1820s and early 1830s by relaxing the rules which imposed high duties on the importation to the colonies of American agricultural products, most notably by allowing American grain shipped to Britain by the St. Lawrence to enter duty free.

These steps did not deal, however, with the inadequacy of the canals themselves. The third canal built in the period shortly after the War of 1812 partly addressed this issue. The Welland Canal, like that envisioned by Dollier de Casson, represented a desire for both transportation into the interior of the continent and power for industry. The man who popularized the idea of a canal between Lakes Ontario and Erie on the Canadian side, William Hamilton Merritt, was another of those early builders who looked to the future. A complex character, Merritt was both a self-seeking entrepreneur and a long-term booster of a St. Lawrence waterway to build up the Canadas. Merritt was born in the state of New York, but moved with his family, including his father who had fought on the British side in the Revolutionary War, to Upper Canada in 1795. He served in the War of 1812, and later claimed that the idea of a canal around Niagara Falls had occurred to him while serving on the Niagara Frontier. Whether or not this is true, it was as a struggling young entrepreneur that he first brought the subject up in public. Merritt owned and ran a sawmill and a gristmill on Twelve Mile Creek, west of the Niagara River, after the war, but because the flow of water varied by season and year, he considered the possibility of bringing extra water from the nearby Chippawa Creek. In 1818, he called a meeting of local residents in the community of St. Catharines and proposed building, not a water channel, but rather a ship canal between Lake Ontario and the Niagara River, using the Twelve Mile Creek and the Chippawa Creek, also known as the Welland River. It was perhaps not coincidental that a report had just been issued by commissioners representing the assemblies of both Canadas, stating that improvements in navigation were essential to the growth of the colonies. However, the petition used the argument that if a canal linking Lake Ontario with Lake Erie and other canals on the St. Lawrence were not built, the Americans would steal the trade of the West. If this canal were built, it would help not only navigation, but also Merritt and his fellow millers on Twelve Mile Creek, significantly increasing the value of their land. The Assembly considered the petition and decided it was a good idea and that a private company should build the canal, but the Assembly took no further action, given that portaging interests at Niagara opposed the idea and a post-war recession had set in.

Merritt and a few supporters, undaunted, abandoned the idea that government would build the canal, and applied to the Legislature in 1823 for the charter of a company to build a canal, as put forward in 1818. They proposed that the company would use a railway to ascend and descend the escarpment, build a tunnel through a high ridge in front of the Niagara Escarpment, and construct a canal that would be four feet deep and would cost only £25,000. As ridiculously small as this amount was, and despite the fact that the chief promoter, Merritt, was a 31-year-old with no experience in this type of enterprise, the charter was granted to the Welland Canal Company in 1824. It was partly the result of Merritt's persuasive powers, and partly due to concern that the Erie Canal, then under construction, would siphon off the trade of the West through New York, that convinced the Legislature to agree. No doubt, the fact that it was a private company that would have to raise the capital, rather than the cash-strapped government of the colony, also influenced the decision, as did Merritt's underestimation of the difficulties involved in such a major engineering project. The lieutenant governor and colonial officials in Britain were horrified that the proposed canal would be built right beside the United States, and thus easily captured, and therefore refused a request by the company for a grant of land to support the project.[52]

Merritt proved time and again that he was not a particularly good businessman, but he was a very successful promoter. When he could not raise enough capital in Upper and Lower Canada, he went to New York and raised a significant proportion of the necessary funds. No doubt some of these investors saw the Welland as a feeder for the as yet unbuilt Oswego Canal, to bring western produce to New York. Merritt had some training in surveying, but there were no engineers with experience in building canals in Canada, except for the military engineers working on the Rideau and Ottawa canals, so Merritt brought in engineers who had worked on the Erie Canal, and employed some American contractors who had similar experience. The American investors pressed for a canal eight feet deep and wider than proposed to accommodate sailing vessels as well as bateaux and Durham boats, and the authorities in London reversed their opposition to the canal and decided that an 8-foot canal would allow gunboats to move between the lakes. This created a curious situation wherein a canal seen as a way to defend against Americans was being built and financed in no small part by Americans.[53]

In early 1825, only a few months after construction began, the company applied for and was granted a new charter which increased the allowable capital investment eight times, up to £200,000, to provide for the larger dimensions and to cover any construction difficulties. The approximately 330-foot climb that the canal had to overcome proved a challenge even to those who had worked on the Erie. The railway section idea was rejected at the beginning as it would force transshipment at two points on the climb up or down, but the tunnel through the upper section of the escarpment was begun, though subsequently abandoned, at some cost, when it became clear that it was not stable. As with the Erie, it was decided that a series of step locks would take the canal up the escarpment. Construction moved ahead quickly, partly because of a new construction device; two wagons on the side of the canal excavation were tied together by a rope that wound around a wheel at the top, and, as an empty wagon went down the slope, it helped to pull a full one up. The project also proceeded more quickly as a result of building wooden locks instead of stone ones, an economy which proved costly before long. Though an eight-foot canal might not seem very difficult to construct, where the canal went through a hill, the channel would be much deeper. In locks there had to be eight feet of water at the upper entrance as well as at the lower, necessitating a lock that was eight feet deep at the lower end, plus the height that the ship needed to be raised to exit at the upper gate, as well as the depth of the lock floor.

Most of the work was done by 1828, despite "marsh fever," sporadic shortages of money as investors reneged on promises, and a shortage of labourers as new immigrants took up available free land rather than work for wages. The Upper Canadian Assembly had loaned the company £25,000 in 1825, and later purchased £50,000 in stock, and the lieutenant governor supported the granting of 13,000 acres of land to the company by the British government. The Lower Canadian Assembly voted to take £25,000 and, when all else failed, the British House of Commons provided a £50,000 loan to help finish the project in return for free passage for ships on British government business. Even the lieutenant governor was prevailed upon to personally guarantee a bank loan. Merritt's persuasive powers were truly amazing.

With a portion of the canal already open and only weeks away from the official opening, a section of canal wall going through the "Deep Cut," the substitute for the abandoned tunnel, collapsed. The high clay banks that were resting on the sand bottom had washed away when water was let in. The engineers' solution was to raise the water level in the canal going through the Cut by bringing in water from a source that was higher than the Welland River, which could not supply a higher canal. Another year was spent digging a feeder canal from the Grand River nearly 21 miles to the southwest. Even when that was finished, more work had to be done, as the dam on the Grand that was erected to raise the water level was quickly and poorly constructed, and was slowly sinking. To celebrate the opening at the end of November of 1829, two schooners, one American and one Canadian, pushed their way slowly through early winter ice, taking more than two days to travel from Lake Ontario to Buffalo.[54]

During construction, work had to be halted on several occasions when money ran out, and when the canal was completed it was deeply in debt. A further provincial loan of £25,000 in 1830 kept the company afloat, but it still had debts, and the outlet to Lake Erie well down the Niagara River from the lake proved to be impractical. The current made

First Welland Canal, lock at St. Catharines.

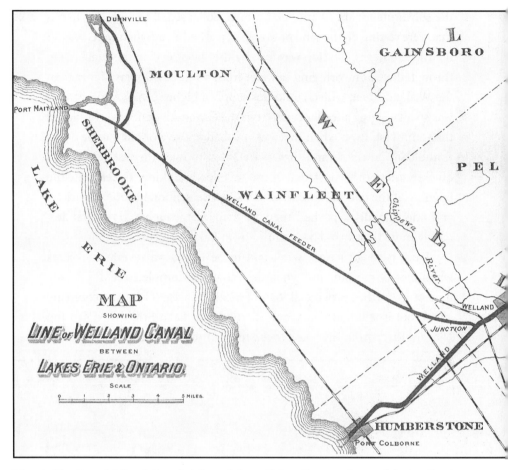

Map 2. The First Welland Canal. Adapted from "Map Showing Line of the Welland

it difficult for boats and ships to reach Lake Erie, and the Niagara River stayed frozen for several weeks after the lake thawed in the spring. In addition, reaching the mouth of the river in Lake Erie required a long detour for Lake Ontario-bound vessels. The directors decided to cut across country directly to Lake Erie, to what became Port Colborne. Again, the province came up with a loan, of £50,000, in 1831 and the canal was finished in 1833. The poor construction of the original canal began to show very quickly, though, and considerable time was lost to lock failures and canal wall collapses. Sometimes, too, the supply of water from the feeder canal proved to be undependable. Finances were a constant problem, and, to make matters worse, members of the Assembly who termed themselves Reformers turned against the canal.[55]

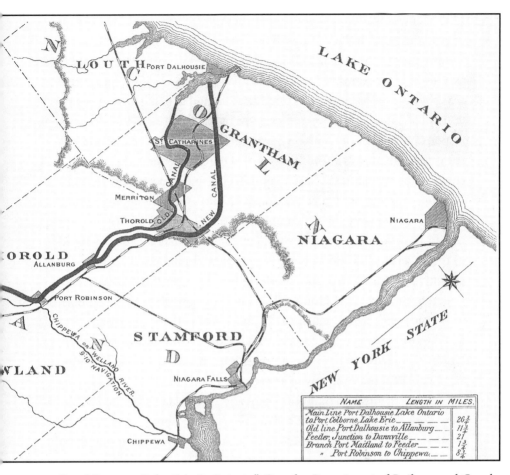

Canal Between Lake Erie & Ontario," Canada, *Department of Railway and Canals, Annual Report, 1900–01*, Ottawa, 1902.

Being a developing colony, taxes were kept to a minimum, and most of the very limited revenues of the province were derived from customs duties collected at Montreal. Many Reformers by the mid-30s saw a large percentage of this money, which could have been used to build much-needed roads, going to a canal that would likely be of more use to Americans near Lake Erie than to Upper Canadians. This perception may have represented a short-sighted viewpoint but it was widely held and was reinforced by the fact that the Reformers' opponents in the non-elected upper house and among the lieutenant governor's advisers, so-called Family Compact Tories, were strongly in favour of the canal and held most of the directors positions, making it a political issue as well. In

1835, an investigation was launched in the Assembly under the leadership of William Lyon Mackenzie, one of the more radical Reformers and one of the directors of the Welland Canal Company appointed by the Assembly as a result of its extensive loans. Mackenzie was more critical than most. He saw the canal as dominated by Americans and as being too connected to political interests that were not elected by the people and therefore not responsible to majority opinion. He was also certain that corruption was rife within the company. The final report of the committee of the Assembly clearly showed that there was a good deal of incompetence in account keeping, wastage, and possibly some favouritism, but no intentional fraud. Unfortunately for the company, Merritt's main American backer was in the process of raising sufficient capital to pay all monies owed to the governments and to turn the company from a public/private co-operative venture into a purely private one. Though this was Merrick's preference, the investigation made it almost impossible. The Assembly, after mid-1836, was controlled by more sympathetic members, and voted more money to the company and allowed it to raise more capital. However, a recession in 1837 and rebellions in both the Canadas in the same year kept the company in a precarious state. Merritt had originally wanted government to build the canal and by the late 1830s he and the New York shareholders were convinced that the only way to save the company, and their investments, was for the government to buy them out. The Upper Canadian government, which already had put up more than half of the money invested in the company, agreed to this, since maintaining the canal was in the public interest, but it took until 1843 for this policy to be implemented.[56]

Despite its imperfections, the Welland provided the vital link in the chain of waterways from Montreal to Lake Huron. At the same time, detractors had been partially right about its limitations. Early traffic was light, nearly all Upper Canadian in origin or destination, mostly flour and wheat, lumber and timber of various types, and pork going out, and salt going in.[57] Throughout the 1830s a significant increase occurred, a good deal being wheat from the United States, but destined for New York, not Montreal. "Of the 264,919 bushels of wheat which passed the canal during 1834, only 18,464 came from Canadian ports on Lake Erie; the remaining 264,555 bushels came from American ports and of these 234,285 were

*William Notman/LAC C-057006.*

William Hamilton Merritt.

consigned to the New York market by way of Oswego."[58] The problem was in the choice of the long Rideau–Ottawa route or the torturous St. Lawrence route versus the more direct Lake Ontario–Oswego Canal– Erie Canal. Although Montreal was closer to Great Britain than New York, the effort and cost of reaching the former city gave New York the advantage. The combined usage of the Erie and the Oswego–Erie routes far outstripped the traffic on the Welland. Merritt and others realized that, until adequate canals were built between Montreal and Prescott, the Canadas could not compete for inland trade.

By the mid-1820s, Merritt had become a believer in a St. Lawrence canal system and spent much of his later career in politics promoting it. Once the Welland was completed, he reasoned, the section between Montreal and Kingston needed to be done. In the 1840s he also campaigned for a new Canadian canal at Sault Ste. Marie, which had not had one on either side of the border since the War of 1812. Substantial iron and copper ore deposits had been found on the shores of Lake Superior and could not easily be transported south on the Great Lakes. While Merritt held shares in one of the mining companies, his actions seem directed, once again, at the public good as much as at his personal profit. He served in the Assembly of Upper Canada for much of the 1830s and then in the 1840s in the Legislature of the United Canadas, actively promoting a system of St. Lawrence canals. After 1848 he was a member of the first "responsible" government, which was allowed to control internal decisions in the Canadas without British government interference. As a member of the Executive Council, the equivalent of the modern cabinet, he promoted the finishing of the St. Lawrence canals, but resigned in 1851, partly because he was upset that large, wasteful government loans were being extended to the newest technology, railroads, while the St. Lawrence maintenance was being ignored. Though he welcomed railways as a supplement to canals, he believed that the future of Canada was in having canals that were adequately sized to accommodate ships of the day, and that they needed to be well maintained.[59]

The concept of a canal or canals around the Long Sault Rapids and the other small rapids west of the Long Sault was first brought to the Upper Canadian Legislature in 1816, and in 1818 a joint commission appointed by the legislatures of the two Canadas recommended that 4-foot canals be built as quickly as possible in this area. Having no eager entrepreneur such as Merritt to take on the task, the recommendations were ignored by both assemblies. At the time, the country was experiencing a post–War of 1812 recession. In concert with this, the merchants of both Canadas, as well as the Family Compact Tories (who controlled the upper house), favoured the scheme, while the majority in the Upper Canadian Assembly (which largely represented the farmers of Upper Canada, then still a frontier province) did not want to take on the debt. In Lower Canada, the Assembly was controlled by representatives of the

French-Canadian farmers, who saw no use in taking on debt to help Anglo-Canadian merchants become wealthier. No action was taken until the Town of Brockville, fearing a loss of trade to the Rideau Canal, paid for a preliminary survey of the route, and pressured the Upper Canadian Legislature to take action. In 1832 the Legislature was more sympathetic to expense on public works than it had been since the war, or would be in 1835 when Mackenzie attacked the Welland Canal Company. Nine-foot canals were approved for the sections where rapids existed, and William Hamilton Merritt introduced a bill in the Assembly allowing money to be borrowed in the London money market for the first time.

The Cornwall Canal was begun in 1834, but construction problems at Long Sault slowed completion. Fill dumped into the river to form the side of the canal was washed away by the current as fast as it was deposited, and the canal had to be cut well back into the shoreline. A similar problem was to plague the builders of the Seaway in the 1950s. The recession of 1837 and the rebellions made it very difficult to sell bonds in London, and the canal was not finished until 1843, after the union of the Canadas. No progress was made on building canals around the smaller rapids west of Long Sault, and Lower Canada studied its section of the rapids, but again chose to do nothing.[60]

The rebellions in Upper and Lower Canada were the product of frustration on the part of a portion of the population which felt that the British government allowed a system of government to exist which was not responsive to the needs of the majority. The risings were poorly organized and supported during their short duration only by a minority, resulting in failure. This set back the course of political reform for several years, as calls for political change were equated in the minds of many conservative citizens with the rebellions. However, it also had major positive ramifications for the St. Lawrence system. Shocked by the rebellions, and unsure what had caused them, the British cabinet decided to send out a representative to study the situation and recommend solutions. The man chosen to do this was one of the most influential and talented men in British politics, Lord Durham. A strong believer in giving the people an expanded role in government, he recommended that a system of "responsible government," in which government would be controlled by a majority of elected representatives, be put in place.

This would ensure that the non-elected upper house and the British governor could not interfere, and would remove the frustration which led to the rebellions. As a radical Whig (liberal) of the mid-nineteenth century, Durham believed that commerce and unfettered free enterprise represented the wave of the future. In his mind, French Canadians, almost all of whom opposed commercial development of the St. Lawrence, were backward and must be prevented from blocking progress. His solution was to propose giving responsible government to the Canadas, but to unite the two colonies so that the votes of the "progressive" citizens of British origins would outnumber those of the French population and give the former control of the Legislature.[61]

Melbourne's government was understandably not willing to give up control of British colonies, especially after they had rebelled, but accepted the idea of uniting the colonies as a way to ensure that French Canadians could not block progress. A new governor was sent out to the colonies, which were united in 1841, with instructions to block any attempt to push for responsible government by retaining control of the legislative agenda, and to make sure that the French Canadians could not gain influence.[62] One way in which he did both was to announce an Imperial loan of £1.5 million when French- and English-speaking Reformers claimed to represent the majority, and demanded responsible government. He made it clear that the Reformers offered only vague political concepts while he offered concrete benefits to the colony. His scheme worked, and the following year the government of the united colonies decided that, since the economy was rapidly improving after the 1837 recession, the loan did not have to be used to pay the large debt run up in the 1820s and 30s, particularly by Upper Canada. Instead, it could be used for new public works, especially canals. A board of works was created to carry out the planning and construction, which it did in a very short time.[63]

Between 1842 and 1848 the Lachine was deepened to 9 feet in the locks and widened to match the Cornwall Canal. The Welland was rebuilt on essentially the same route as the first, with locks either 8.5 or 9 feet deep (the Second Welland Canal) and the number of locks slightly reduced, and the Williamsburg Canals, to bypass the rapids west of Long Sault, were constructed. These latter canals, the Farran's Point, the Rapide Plat, the Iroquois, and the Galops were mainly used by ships going upriver, as

*Alfred Sadham/LAC C-005954.*

Scene on the Welland Canal, *circa* 1840.

most could run the rapids coming down. Several studies had been done in the 1830s and 40s of what could be done to replace the outmoded military canals around the Cascades, Cedars, and Coteau rapids. The final decision was to shift to the south shore, against the wishes of the British military who wanted the canal built as far as possible from the American border. Built between 1842 and 1845 as a single canal, the Beauharnois Canal took a long, winding route inland from the shoreline, some 11.5 miles in length. Dams had to be added later in Lake St. Francis to the west to prevent fluctuations in water levels, also a problem on the Cornwall and Welland canals. All of the canals except a portion of the Welland now had locks 200 feet long by 45 feet wide. Most of the Welland Canal locks were only 150 feet by 26.5 feet, but all locks were rebuilt in stone to eliminate the constant maintenance. The feeder canal from the Grand River was made into a navigable channel of the same width. To do all of this work in so few years, facing the usual range of difficulties, was a testimonial to the abilities of the people working in the new board, and to the politicians, including William Hamilton Merritt, who gave the board support. The Lachine Canal had to be rerouted when landowners asked for too much money for the land to expand the canal. The Beauharnois Canal was only built after a nasty political fight over suggested favouritism in locating the canal, and despite the objections

*Canaux du Quebec/LAC C-063898.*

Beauharnois Canal, lock number 1, looking west from the Lake St. Louis entrance, 1906.

of the British military. Construction problems also had to be overcome. Perhaps fittingly, Merritt died on a ship in the Cornwall Canal in 1862 while coming home from Montreal.[64]

So confident were the politicians that canal traffic, and the trade which drove it, would continue to grow at a rapid pace, that they spent the Imperial loan and went on borrowing money, creating a huge debt. During the same period in the 1840s, Montreal merchants had spent large sums of money building storehouses and mills as traffic through the harbour rose, but more particularly in anticipation of the surge in traffic that would accompany the completion of the canal system in 1848.[65] In celebration of the opening, the governor general, Lord Elgin, offered a substantial prize of £50 in a contest to produce "the best treatise on the bearing of the St. Lawrence and Welland Canals on the interests of Canada, as an agricultural country."[66] At last the St. Lawrence route would be able to compete with the Erie Canal for the trade of the West, with a through ship canal rather than a narrow, shallow barge canal that required transshipment. The year 1849 destroyed these dreams.

# The Age of the Engineers: The Later Canals, to 1932

Overcutting of timber and a worsening economic situation in Britain had led to a glut in the market for timber in 1847–48. Wheat and flour exports through Montreal had dropped by a third in 1848, which was worrying, but there had always been year to year fluctuations, so not too much was made of this. As the shipping season opened in 1849 there was no demand for either commodity. Warehouses in Montreal were still filled with flour from 1848. The 1849 harvest and further cutting of timber would only make matters worse. Those working in milling and warehousing were thrown out of work, their ranks swollen by thousands of impoverished Irish immigrants who had fled their homeland after the disastrous potato famine of 1845. Some businessmen who had invested heavily in new mills or warehouses in the 1840s in anticipation of increased business faced bankruptcy. Who or what was to blame for this situation which had paralyzed the economic life of the city and seemingly ruined the prospects for the new canal system?

In the minds of many in Montreal, particularly in the British-American portion of the population, the villain was Great Britain. Since 1828, the British government had responded to requests from its British North American colonies for trade assistance with a series of acts. These provided lower duties on wheat, flour, and timber entering Britain from the colonies than on those same products entering from other countries. The British duty on wheat was so low in the late 1840s that it was possible to bring American wheat into Canada, pay the duty Canada had imposed as a condition of being given a preferential position in the British market, and sell the flour to Britain as Canadian. This favouring of Canadian products changed dramatically in 1846. The British government had been seriously considering free trade with the world for several years. Conditions in the British Isles speeded up the process. In response to the potato famine in Ireland, with its tens of thousands of starving people deprived of their staple food, Britain removed all duties on wheat and flour from all countries in order to provide a cheap alternative and announced that by 1848 all colonial preferences would be gone. Britain would trade equally with its North American colonies and the rest of the world. Not surprisingly, the business community and out-of-work labourers in Montreal concluded that the loss of their privileged place in the British market was the cause of their suffering.[1]

To make matters worse, the British government had concluded that, as Britain was now going to trade on an equal basis with the whole world, it no longer needed to have the final say in the governing of those colonies in British North America which wanted internal self government. It no longer needed to control them to guarantee they would be secure markets and secure sources of raw materials. Lord Durham's desire to see responsible government in the Canadas came to pass in 1848, eight years after his death. This new policy was extremely unpopular in British Montreal, as the largest group within the Parliament was the united Reformers of Upper and Lower Canada, a group in which French-Canadian members formed a large majority. One of the first acts of the new government, elected in 1848, was to pass a law compensating those people in Lower Canada who had property destroyed in the rebellion there in 1837. Since some of these people would be rebels who had not been identified as such, the British Canadian population of Montreal, who had fought against the rebels, saw this as compensating treason. They appealed to the governor general, Lord Elgin, to refuse to sign the bill, which would make it law. However, Elgin felt that he had to sign as a symbol that responsible government worked, that the majority ruled. The British-Canadian population took this as evidence that they had been abandoned politically by Britain, and the stoppage of trade as a sign that they had been abandoned economically, in spite of their loyalty in 1837. The only answer was to get even.

After Elgin signed the Rebellion Losses Bill his coach was pelted with stones and rotten eggs, a direct insult to the Queen, whom he represented. On the night of April 25, 1849, a mob formed, marched on the Parliament

Building, and forced its way into the building where the Assembly was in session. Parliament was the symbol of French domination and British abandonment. Fuelled by unemployment and hunger, the mob smashed furniture and fixtures and, when a fire broke out, prevented firemen from reaching the building. The building and its contents, including an excellent library and all the government records of the former colonies of Upper and Lower Canada, were consumed. British troops were called out that evening, but arrived too late. They were summoned into the city again the next day, but rioting went on for about a week before order was restored. The business community, which was the preeminent one in all of British North America, was not about to engage in such violent conduct, but it, too, felt abandoned and desperate. The British government repealed the Navigation Acts in June, allowing foreign vessels to enter the St. Lawrence for the first time in the hope of attracting more trade, and the Canadian government passed a law making it possible to have free trade with the United States in non-manufactured goods. But the former action produced no increase and the latter was ignored by the United States government. In October of 1849, after the rest of the shipping season had proved to be just as bad, the business community issued the Annexation Manifesto. This document stated that, since Britain obviously no longer cared about Canada, it should peacefully leave the British Empire and join the United States, a move which would restore economic prosperity. Among the arguments used to prove that annexation would be of benefit to both Canada and the United States was one that pointed out that the United States would gain "the unrestricted use of the St. Lawrence, the natural highway from the western states to the ocean ..."[2]

This call for action was met with indifference, hostility, and only a slight amount of sympathy outside of Montreal. A few businessmen in Kingston, at the other end of the St. Lawrence canals, agreed there was a problem but rejected the solution, and a few supportive documents, signed by a small minority, were issued in other cities. Most French Canadians rejected union with a larger Anglo-Saxon dominated country. Most Upper Canadians felt the economic crisis was not as bad as the Montreal business community felt it was. They also chose loyalty to the mother country over union with a nation which had invaded in 1775 and 1812, had turned a blind eye to raids into Canada after the rebellions there in 1837, and had threatened war if it did not get its way over the Oregon boundary in 1846.[3] The failure of the St. Lawrence canals to bring increased prosperity was largely a Montreal concern.

The truth was that the financial crisis did hit Montreal harder than elsewhere, and it was not to last long. The cause was not Britain's removal of preferential duties, but a combination of overproduction in Canada leading to a glut on the British market, and a recession in the mother country. Also contributing to the lack of trade through Montreal were the American Drawback Acts of 1845 and 1846 that allowed products destined to and from Canada to go through the United States without duties. These acts were designed to counter the opening of the St. Lawrence canals, and they were successful. The situation in Britain began to correct itself by 1850, as the glut was used up and the economy recovered. Larger, faster steamships on the Atlantic and cheaper transportation costs on the new canals also helped. In addition, new markets for Canadian grains and wood developed in the United States. A rapidly increasing population due to immigration meant a shortage of flour and other cereal grains, and the construction boom brought on by this immigration, combined with the depletion of northern forests, led to a huge demand for sawn lumber, including in the Midwest where trees were scarce.

Within a couple of years the economy of the Canadas was doing well again, and things only got better. In response to pleas from British North American colonies, the British government became involved in trade talks with the United States. By 1853 the American Congress was sympathetic regarding lower tariffs. Additionally, it was divided between the Southern states, which looked to a free trade agreement to remove any need for the British colonies to join the United States, and the Northern states, which hoped to use an agreement to bring the colonies into the American federation and bolster the anti-slavery free states. The governor general, Lord Elgin, assisted by William Hamilton Merritt, went to Washington and did his best to extol all the benefits of free trade, both economic and political, to the United States. In 1854, a Reciprocity Treaty brought reciprocal free trade in natural (non-manufactured) products, an agreement which was very much in favour of the British colonies, which already were selling large quantities of these products to the United States. The Crimean War of 1854–56 cut off wheat shipments from Britain's other main supplier, Russia, bringing even more prosperity.[4]

In spite of all of this activity, and the robust nature of the economy in British North America, the use of the St. Lawrence canals did not increase in proportion to the rate of general improvement in conditions. While the short-term use had been a disaster, the longer term use proved to be a disappointment. Despite the fact that American shipping could now use the St. Lawrence, the Erie Canal and the American railways continued to dominate trade to and from the interior. In 1856 the Erie Canal handled more than six times the amount of cargo that the St. Lawrence did. By 1865, Montreal was receiving one-third of the amount of wheat that New York was. By 1869 the quantity of wheat and flour reaching Montreal had tripled the volume seen in 1845, but a government study acknowledged that the system was not doing as well as it should be, thanks to the tactics of its competitors. The Erie had reduced its tolls slightly in 1870 to attract more business, and the railways in both countries were aggressive foes.[5] Although the Erie was being straightened somewhat, beginning in 1834, and deepened to seven feet and widened to 70 feet to handle ever-increasing traffic and to deal with the competition of the St. Lawrence canals, it would not be completed until 1862.[6] But even with these improvements, it was competing with a superior 9-foot canal system. It is not surprising that the merchants of Montreal expected to take back the trade of the West that they had lost when the original Erie Canal opened.

Several factors gave the Erie the advantage. Many shippers had long-established ties in New York and saw no reason to change routes. More importantly, the cost of shipping to Britain was less from New York than from Montreal, even though Montreal had the advantage of the shorter distance to Europe. There were also fewer inbound cargoes going to Canada, meaning that ships had to sail in ballast on the way over; carrying cargoes both ways, which was the norm for ships using New York or Boston, reduced the transportation costs.[7] The fact that Atlantic harbours remained open all winter and were served by the new railways also gave New York an advantage. In addition, the Welland Canal remained a problem for Montreal interests. The original locks were 150 x 26 feet and only 8.5 or 9 feet deep. In 1853, the canal locks were deepened to 10 feet by the simple steps of bolting timbers onto the top of the locks and raising the weirs and some of the canal banks, but they were not widened. The majority of Welland locks were 50 feet shorter than those of the other canals in the system (150 feet versus 200 feet) and narrower (26.5 feet versus 45 feet). As ships had been growing in size, especially the newer steamships, whether paddle wheelers or "propellers," as the newer type of steamship was known, it was often necessary to transship in smaller ships at the Lake Erie end of the canal. Side wheelers could not fit into the Welland because of the width of its locks and larger propellers could not fit in because of their length. By 1860, one-third to one-half of ships carrying grain or flour could not get through the Welland, and nearly three-quarters of propellers were too large. A short-line railway from Lake Erie to Lake Ontario to carry all or part of the cargo of ships that still could not negotiate the canal because of its depth helped somewhat, but many ships could not fit into the length or the width of the locks. Many shippers found it easier to use the New York railways or the Erie Canal at that point. Of the wheat and flour that did enter Lake Ontario, much still went down the Oswego–Erie Canal route to New York. The fluctuating water levels in the St. Lawrence and Lachine canals, whether caused by poor design or by too many mills drawing water out of the canal, as in the Lachine Canal, continued to force some vessels to unload a portion of their cargo in order to pass through them.[8]

The story of the Great Lakes canals from 1850 to the 1930s is essentially one of slow expansion, of the emergence of new rivals for the St. Lawrence canals, and the re-emergence of at least one old rival. Changes in the canals were driven by new technology, both in terms of the increased size of ships and the need in the twentieth century for electrical power, and by the desire of each country to have its own canal system, a rivalry that would exist until the 1950s. Change was brought about by cautious politicians and careful engineers. The era of the entrepreneur and the visionary, the Clintons and Bys and Merritts, was over. Such audacity would not be seen again until the Seaway was being built.

The 1850s saw a flurry of canal activity. The channel leading through Lake St. Peter, east of Montreal, was a shallow one due to silt being brought down the St. Lawrence. In 1838 it was reported that the 31-mile-long channel was only 10 or 12 feet deep. As ocean vessels increased in size, this became a problem for Montreal, as ships had a hard time reaching the city. In 1844 the Canadian Board of Works had begun dredging a straight channel, but ran out of money in 1847, before the work was completed. In 1850 the Montreal Harbour Commission, representing businessmen who were very concerned about the inability of many ships to reach Montreal, gave up on government help and decided to do the work itself, dredging the natural curved channel to save effort. By 1852 the channel had been deepened from roughly 10.5 feet to 15 feet. The commission did not have the resources to do more and prevailed upon the government of the United Canadas to take over. The channel was dredged to 20 feet by 1865 and 22 feet by 1878.[9]

Another potential rival for the St. Lawrence appeared in this period. Canals on the Richelieu River, to join the St. Lawrence east of Montreal to Lake Champlain, had been contemplated as early as 1818, when the Lower Canadian government chartered a company to build a canal around one of the two obstacles on the Richelieu, the Chambly Rapids. The company had been unable to raise funds, and the government, which started the work itself in 1829, moved very slowly. A dam and a lock were built at the other obstacle, at St. Ours, by 1849, and the Chambly Canal was finished in 1843. The latter was inadequate, however, and was rebuilt between 1850 and 1858, with locks of a minimum length of 118 feet, a width of approximately 23 feet, and a depth of 7 feet. The merchants of Montreal had been pushing for these canals so that they could trade easily with New York through the American Champlain canals. This trade never amounted to much, and the canal was largely used to send timber from the Ottawa River to New York markets. At the urging of Montreal merchants, several studies were done between 1847 and 1866 of the feasibility of cutting a canal cross country from the South Shore opposite Montreal to the vicinity of Lake Champlain in order to create a more direct route for trade. Ultimately, the estimated cost of the project doomed the idea. The Richelieu–Champlain–Hudson route remained, though, as a potential alternative route from Montreal to the Atlantic.[10]

To address the problem of insufficient water in the Iroquois Canal, near the end of the Williamsburg Canals, it was joined with the Galops Canal between 1851 and 1856, creating a canal almost eight miles long. At the other end of the Great Lakes, a study by the Board of Public Works was undertaken as to the feasibility of building a canal around the St. Marys Rapids, where no canal had existed since the War of 1812. Nothing was done at the time, although the project was deemed feasible. Shortly thereafter, the United States, and more particularly the State of Michigan, took the initiative away from the Canadians. Copper ore was being produced in Michigan in the early 1840s and iron ore deposits were discovered in the mid-1840s. Without a canal to allow ore to be moved into the lower Great Lakes to be smelted, the mining industry could not expand, as cargoes had to be offloaded and portaged around the rapids before being loaded onto other ships on Lake Huron. The population of the states touching on Lake Michigan and Lake Superior had been increasing rapidly in the mid-century, and transportation of goods both ways was also a problem for them.[11]

Despite pressure from members of Congress from the Midwest, particularly from Michigan, and the forceful arguments of Midwestern representatives at conferences on lake shipping, nothing was done until the early 1850s. The Democratic Party, and particularly the presidents, who had the power of veto, believed that it was not the constitutional role of the federal government to fund internal improvements. These were regional concerns that should be dealt with by the states. Congress passed a bill in 1846 which would have helped to pay for improvements to the shallow, narrow channel from Lake Erie into Lake St. Clair, a necessary step in improving shipping lanes into Lake Superior. President James K. Polk, the same president who fought the Mexican-American war to secure Texas, and threatened war with Britain to secure the present states of Oregon and Washington, insisted that it was inappropriate to use the federal power for national development, which he termed regional development, and vetoed the bill. It was not until Millard Fillmore, a Whig, was president that Congress could act. Interestingly, given later regional divisions, there was substantial support in Congress for measures proposed by Midwest members to develop the route from Lake Erie to Lake Superior. In 1853, Congress agreed to provide 750,000 acres to Michigan so that it could finance the building of a canal around the St. Marys Rapids. Supporters in Congress used a variety of arguments. They emphasized the needs of settlers, businesses, shipping interests, and mining interests in the western region. In addition, they argued that an American canal would avoid the need to use any Canadian canal that might be built at the "Soo," and thus would increase American defence capability, as American warships could reach Lake Superior without entering foreign, possibly hostile, territory.[12]

In the short time of two years, the deadline set by Michigan, a crew of up to 1,600 men built a canal slightly over a mile long, with two locks 350 feet long, 70 feet wide, and 11.5 feet deep. The men were working under the control of the Fairbanks Scale Company, which had extensive mining interests in the area, acting on behalf of a syndicate centred in New York and New England, and supervised by engineers appointed by the federal and Michigan governments. In return, the syndicate received the 750,000 acres, which was carefully selected to contain valuable timber and copper resources. This was another canal project which triumphed over difficult conditions, as had the Rideau. It was very expensive to build, as the canal was in large part cut through rock. Part of the work had to be done in the harshness of a northern winter, and the labourers suffered both from food shortages and from disease, in this case cholera. When finished, the Michigan State Canal (as it was called until 1881, when it was transferred to the federal government for financial reasons) provided a critical link in Great Lakes transportation, one which contained the largest locks on the lakes.[13]

In 1854, a bill which included money to deepen the channel in the St. Marys River and the channel in the St. Clair Flats (located in the St. Clair River at the entrance to Lake St. Clair) passed through Congress with sizeable majorities, but the new president, Franklin Pierce, refused to sign it into law. In frustration, the Buffalo Board of Trade convened a conference of cities on the Great Lakes, all of which felt that opening the channels was critical to trade both ways on the Upper Lakes. A number of the cities agreed to fund the dredging of the channel, and the work was completed that year, 1855, to a depth of 10 feet. This was still not enough, especially as the channel was very narrow, and Congress took up the issue again, passing bills to fund improvements to both channels by large majorities. In fact, when Pierce again vetoed the measures, Congress overrode his veto, so important to the growth of the nation and its trade were these measures considered. Between 1857 and 1859, both channels were improved and some navigational aids were installed. These were only sufficient, however, to keep up with existing traffic. With traffic and the size of ships on the Upper Lakes increasing rapidly, more needed to be done. President James Buchanan, as had his predecessor, refused to agree to fund "local" improvements, and his successor, Abraham Lincoln, was caught up in the Civil War and had little time for improvements on the Great Lakes, even though his party, the Republicans, favoured them.[14]

Finances were an issue for the federal government during the Civil War. They were also an issue for the Erie Canal and for Canadian canals, for different reasons. An acrimonious struggle went on within the government of New York, from the 1830s to the late 1850s, over the assumption of a large debt to pay for the enlargement of the Erie and the building of various tributary canals. This is why the enlargement, begun in 1834, was not completed until 1862.[15] In the United Canadas the large government debt incurred to build the St. Lawrence canals and to expand the Welland Canal in the 1840s was significantly increased in the good economic climate of the 1850s to finance a web of railways across the colony. Despite increasing customs duties three times in the late 1850s to help pay the debt, the government had little financial leeway to fund canals. When the chief engineer suggested increasing the depth of the canals in 1860, to accommodate larger vessels, his recommendation was ignored. The most that the Canadian government would do was to subsidize steam tugs on the St. Lawrence to make it easier for ships to get through locks and more difficult sections of the river.[16] In a clever move to finance the debt, one that did not go unnoticed by the opponents of Confederation in other colonies, the government of the United Canadas was able to unload a sizeable portion of the debt onto the new country, Canada, in the 1867 Confederation agreement. Citizens of the other provinces wound up being responsible for a debt that they had not incurred, but this allowed the new country to help finance further internal improvements through new debt.[17]

The expense for railway building in the 1850s was a result of railway mania, which had hit the United States a decade earlier, moving into Canada. The allure of year-round travel had forced into the background the focus on having the best canal system, in both jurisdictions. There were many short lines built in Canada, but all of the longer ones were in some way connected with U.S. trade. A line from Windsor to Niagara was designed to funnel trade from the Midwest United States to Buffalo.

Another, from Georgian Bay to Lake Ontario at Toronto, was designed to replicate a native portage route and to speed goods from the Upper Lakes to the lower ones, avoiding the longer water route. The longest of all was the Grand Trunk, which ran from the American border at Sarnia to Montreal and then down to Portland, Maine, an ice-free port. As had occurred when the New York railways were built,[18] some well-placed individuals believed that the railways would complement the canals, drawing more trade from the American Midwest. None other than Allan MacNab, who within a short time would be joint prime minister of the United Canadas, argued in 1851 that a railway such as the Grand Trunk would "in conjunction with our magnificent chain of Water Communication secure for Canada a large portion of the Trade and Commerce of Western America."[19] As in New York, the railways proved to be competitors, not allies. In the case of the United States, there was so much going in and out of the western states that both the railways and the Erie Canal were heavily used. Tonnage on the Erie did not peak until 1872. In Canada, however, the underuse of the canals meant that there was less to divide up, and both canals and railways suffered.[20]

One bright spot for the Canadian government, if not always for ship owners, was the sale of surplus water on the canals to manufacturers. Although the desire for power had motivated William Hamilton Merritt in 1818 and de Casson as early as 1689, the focus since the beginning of the 1820s had been on canals for transportation. Beginning in 1847, Canadian canals became identified with both power and navigation, a combination which was to be the basis for much of the negotiations in the twentieth century. Water flowing over dams on the canals, excess water being discharged from canals through weirs (sub-surface dams that maintain water levels, but allow excess water to escape), and water being brought in to regulate the depth of canals could be harnessed to power industry. Over the course of the rest of the nineteenth century, industries large and small congregated along the various canals. Some of the largest industries in Canada located along the Lachine Canal in Montreal, while smaller industries bought water rights along the Welland, where mills were already located in substantial numbers. The smaller size had to do with the fact that the Welland area was more rural and farther from large markets. Some industries located along the Cornwall and Williamsburg

Old Welland Canal (Second) at St. Catharines, *circa* 1880s. Note the mill, powered by water from the canal.

canals, which were not close to markets either, but had the advantage of being close to the railways. Some 19 businesses chose to locate on the Rideau system and a small number leased along the Richelieu. So valuable was this power considered that, when a new Welland Canal was built (the Third), the industries located on the second canal continued to draw power from the abandoned canal. This sale of water rights was not without controversy, though, as industry was often accused of drawing off so much water that the level of the canals dropped, making navigation more difficult. In consequence, industry was banned from the Third Welland Canal.[21]

The fact that the St. Lawrence canals had not succeeded in becoming the method of choice for the transportation of agricultural and mining products out of the interior of the continent and manufactured goods into it was emphasized by discussions in the late 1850s and 1860s, in both Canada and the United States. The government of the United Canadas had engineering reports concerning the feasibility of opening a route by way of the Ottawa River, Lake Nipissing, and the French River done in 1858 and in 1860. This route would allow ships to reach Georgian Bay and all of the Upper Lakes by travelling approximately half the distance of the Great

Lakes route. While the number of canals and locks was small and the total length of the canals was short, the cost of cutting through solid granite was high, so the second report suggested damming the rivers in various places to raise the water level wherever possible. Nothing was done at the time, but this route remained a serious rival for the St. Lawrence, especially after some improvements on the upper Ottawa were made in the 1870s.[22]

In the United States, tensions during the Civil War raised concerns about the safety of American shipping. The government in the Northern states saw the fact that commerce raiders, fast steamships, were built, and in the early part of the war actually armed, in British ports, as a clear sign that Britain sided with the South. British North American newspapers were mostly either in support of the South or critical of the North, a fact well known in Washington. This sympathy was fuelled by several incidents during the war, including the Trent incident, in which a Northern warship stopped the British vessel *Trent* on the Atlantic and forcibly removed Southern political agents. Northern anger increased when, in a desperate move to save itself in 1864, the South sent agents to Montreal, from where they carried out a raid on St. Albans, Vermont. Having robbed the banks and killed one man, they retreated to Montreal, hoping that this would be taken as a sign of British support for the South and cause a war between Britain and the North. Their arrest, and the seizure of the very large amount of money that they had stolen, briefly mollified the North, but the Confederate soldiers were let off on a technicality at their preliminary hearing. Then someone at the bank where the money was being held handed it back to them while the bank was closed. While this did result in anger, threats, the cancellation of the Reciprocity Treaty, and tightening of the border, from both sides, it did not achieve the desired effect of provoking a war. However, it did further emphasize the danger of having all of the ship canals east of Lake Superior in British hands.[23]

Various solutions were proposed and these were echoed in Congress. Some supported the idea of a separate American canal around Niagara Falls. Others insisted that an Erie Canal, enlarged to take ships from Lake Erie to New York, was the answer. Still others were supporters of a new rival for the St. Lawrence. Between 1836 and 1848, Illinois had constructed the Illinois and Michigan Canal to link Lake Michigan at Chicago to the Illinois River, from which the Mississippi and the Gulf of Mexico could be reached. Sixty feet wide and six feet deep, it allowed barges to go from Chicago to the shallow Illinois River, where dams and constant dredging of sandbars kept a channel open. Proponents of this canal, which had made Chicago a growing transportation hub, wanted it to become the chief medium for carrying the farm produce of the West to Europe. Although it was deepened in 1871, largely to flush the notoriously odious Chicago sewage into Lake Michigan, it remained mainly an avenue for agricultural production going out through the Great Lakes, rather than being the gateway to the Gulf. In the difficult years of the Civil War and Reconstruction, Congress had little inclination to spend what would be very large amounts of money on these ventures. Besides, in contrast to the general support of the Soo Canal a few years earlier, and as a precursor of what was to happen in the negotiations over a possible seaway in the twentieth century, supporters of each of these proposals spoke against the other ones. Regional rivalries made it difficult for Congress to favour any project.[24]

Not everyone in the northern portion of the United States was fearful of using the Canadian canals. Representatives from Midwestern states from time to time noted the advantages of the Canadian canals. After the war was over, they became quite vigorous in their demands for negotiations with Canada for permanent access to the St. Lawrence canals. The abrogation of the Reciprocity Treaty in 1866 had meant that the United States no longer had access to the canals, although the Canadian government had not enforced the exclusion for several years, while unsuccessful negotiations for a new reciprocity treaty went on. Despite pressure from the Midwest, the American Congress would not concede reciprocity in return for use of the canals.[25] Commissioners appointed by the government of Illinois to deal with Canada wrote the Canadian government in 1863, explaining that American railways and canals could no longer handle the volume of agricultural products, with "more than 100 million bushels of grain," "vast numbers of cattle and hogs," and "immense quantities of other provisions" coming out of the Midwest, and expressing a desire to use the St. Lawrence canals, "a natural outlet to the sea."[26] Finally, the matter of the canals was lumped in with other issues to be discussed by Britain and the United States in Washington in 1871. The bulk of the issues to be discussed had little to do with Canada.

The most pressing issues were left over from Britain's perceived support of the South in the Civil War. Unfortunately for Canada, the young nation had recently begun excluding American fishing vessels from the Atlantic inshore fisheries, as it had a right to do, but had not done until then, although the American right of access had expired with the Reciprocity Treaty. Some American fishing vessels were seized for violating the ban. The American government threatened reprisals to protect its fleet and, fearing a war, Britain and the United States added the fisheries to the issues to be settled. The American government saw this as a way to get both access to the fisheries and access to the canals.[27]

The third member of the three-person British negotiating team was John A. Macdonald, prime minister of Canada. However, the need to settle the very contentious American claims for damages done by British-built commerce raiders led the other representatives to give up ground that Macdonald wanted to hold. There would be no reciprocity treaty, but instead the Americans would get permanent use of the St. Lawrence and the use of the fisheries for at least 12 years, in return for permanent use of three rivers in Alaska and the use of Lake Michigan for at least 12 years. The American delegates pressed for deepening of the St. Lawrence canals as well, agreeing that American shipping would pay a toll to help defray the cost as long as Canada did not discriminate when setting those tolls, but none of this was included in the treaty. The channel through the St. Clair Flats was guaranteed to the Canadians, and Britain was to urge the Canadians and the United States government to pressure the states to open other canals near the Great Lakes to the other country's vessels on terms of equality with its own citizens. Losing the fisheries as a bargaining tool, getting little in return for use of the St. Lawrence, and not achieving reciprocity was humiliating for Macdonald, who had the unenviable task of getting the Canadian Parliament to accept a treaty which did little for Canada and much for the United States.[28]

The canals were enlarged, as the Midwestern representatives wanted, but not because of American pressure. In 1870, the Canadian Minister of Public Works called the attention of the government to the inadequacy of the St. Lawrence and Welland canals and the necessity of using the American canal at Sault Ste. Marie. A royal commission was established to study the future of the whole Canadian canal system, with the intent of determining "the best means of affording such access to the sea-board as may best be calculated to attract a large and yearly increasing share of the trade of the North Western portion of North America through Canadian waters …" Hugh Allan, who controlled a very successful line of steamships engaged in trade with Britain out of Montreal, was selected as its head. The commissioners solicited input from interested parties in both Canada and the United States, receiving replies from several American cities around the Great Lakes. This study could be said to mark the modern age of canal building as the result of the commission's report in 1871 was the creation of the system which served until the Seaway was built in the 1950s. The major recommendation of the commission was for uniform locks on the Welland–St. Lawrence route 270 feet in length and 45 feet wide, with a depth of 12 feet. Locks on the Richelieu–Champlain route needed to be only 200 feet long, 45 feet wide, and 9 feet deep (essentially matching the scale on the Ottawa), as the canals were used mainly to transport lumber to the United States market.

The report also called for the clearing of channels through the rapids in the St. Lawrence from the Long Sault to the Lachine to 8 feet, and later to 14 feet, so that freight as well as passenger ships could descend the rapids and avoid having to use the canals. At that time passenger ships could descend all the rapids, and one line of ships did every day, while freighters could descend only through the upper ones. Improvements to the Lachine Canal and Montreal Harbour were also urged so that ocean-going ships could easily enter the lower portion and manoeuvre. The commissioners called for a second entrance to the harbour, a deeper basin with docks, and an enlarged entrance to the canal. The commission further recommended the building of a Canadian canal at Sault Ste. Marie. This was of particular concern because the American government, at the urging of Michigan, had refused to allow Canadian and British troops to use the American canal in 1870. The troops were on their way to the recently acquired Canadian territory at Red River (now Winnipeg), where there had been armed resistance to the Canadian takeover of the area. Of all the canals mentioned in the report, priority was given to the Welland–St. Lawrence system, as this was seen as the most useful. The commissioners once again found the proposed Georgian Bay Canal to be shorter than the St. Lawrence route, but impractical because of the high cost of construction.

The report also acknowledged that it would be necessary to build up more of a two-way trade with Europe in order to be competitive with American seaboard ports such as New York, Boston, and Portland, instead of relying on the one-way shipments of bulk goods to European markets.

In beginning their recommendations, the commissioners cautioned that the canals should be built only large enough to handle existing shipping, or construction would lead to higher costs, higher tolls, and increased time to fill and empty the locks, slowing shipping. A deeper set of canals and channels would not work anyway, they claimed, as Great Lakes harbours had not been deepened. Additionally, a young country could not afford such a great expense as a deeper system would entail. This idea of building to handle only ships of a current size had previously been the practice, and was to continue to bedevil canal construction right up until the Seaway was built. Each time the system was enlarged, the increasing size of ships fairly quickly made it obsolete. On the basis of the report, Parliament authorized contracts for work on a new Welland Canal and for the start of work on expanding the Lachine Canal at the beginning of 1873.[29] Nothing was done, however, as the government was forced to resign over an election scandal. It was discovered that the government had accepted large sums of money from Hugh Allan during the election of 1872, while negotiating with him to build a trans-Canada railway. The government had committed itself to a railway during negotiations with British Columbia for that British colony's entry into Confederation. Completing the railway became almost an obsession for the Conservative leadership, leading to John A. Macdonald's unethical dealings with Allan, the only individual who seemed capable of financing the building of it.[30]

In office, the Liberals, led by the frugal, rigid Alexander Mackenzie, had no great interest in rushing the canal enlargements, to which they were committed, despite continued pressure from American and Canadian interests. In further negotiations over a new reciprocity treaty, the American negotiators pushed for enlargement on the basis of the desire of western states. Shippers and ship owners and even American competitors from the Oswego and Chicago boards of trade recognized the superiority of the St. Lawrence system, if it were enlarged. The general consensus seemed to be that 12 feet was not enough and that the canals should be 14 feet deep.[31] Mackenzie's natural disinclination

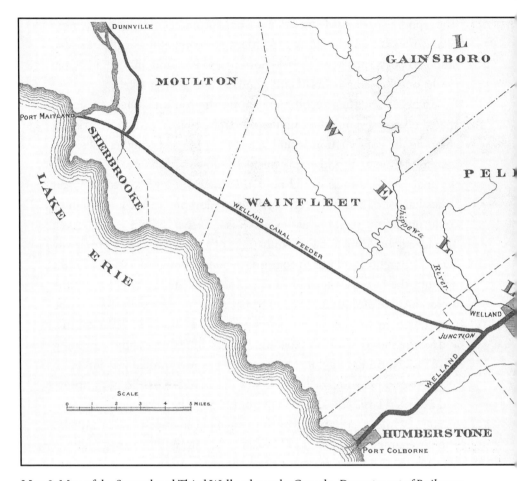

**Map 3**. Map of the Second and Third Welland canals. Canada, *Department of Railways*

to spend government funds was reinforced by a severe recession that set in shortly after he took office. The government raised its money largely from customs duties. With the serious decline in trade, funds to support the Pacific railway project as a government venture, the as yet incomplete Intercolonial Railway from Quebec to Halifax, Nova Scotia, and canal construction, were very limited. Mackenzie saw canal construction largely in terms of providing work in hard times, and in terms of doing just enough to satisfy the demand in Canada that the canals be improved.[32] Contracts for some of the work were given out in 1875, but little was done. Finally, in 1877, the government gave in to the very strong pressure for a deeper system and ordered that all enlargement not already covered by a contract would be done to a depth of 14 feet. The Welland

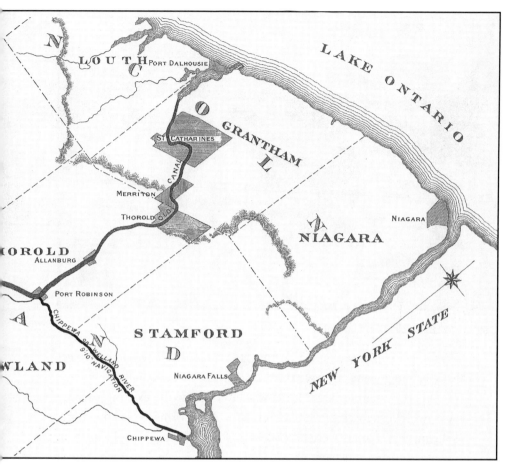

*and Canals, Annual Report, 1900–01,* Ottawa, 1902.

was completed to 12 feet, except for one aqueduct, in 1881 (the Third Welland), with locks 280 feet long and 46 feet wide. It reached 14 feet in depth in 1887, 14 years after the first contract was signed. The Third Canal followed the route of the Second Canal, except for the northern section, where the Twelve Mile Creek was relegated to local traffic and the supplying of water power, and a direct cut was made across country from Thorold to Port Dalhousie on Lake Ontario.[33]

Other construction was carried out at an even slower pace. The Conservatives returned to office in 1878 and the recession lifted, but their main concern was finishing the Pacific railway. Work on the St. Lawrence canals and the canal at Sault Ste. Marie was not finished until 1905, nine years after the Conservatives again were defeated, and 14

Public Works Canada/LAC C-002859.

Lachine Canal, lock at St. Gabriel, 1903.

years after John A. Macdonald, whose government had begun the project in 1870, had gone to his reward. The major work was actually completed by 1900. A system of larger locks was built beside the existing Lachine locks, which themselves were rebuilt later. The Cornwall Canal and the Williamsburg Canals were all widened, while keeping the old locks in operation during construction and for future use by smaller ships. As well as deepening the canals and building up the walls, some of the entrances were extended to protect shipping from eddies caused by the rapids. One interesting feature added was a lock seven miles up the Galops Canal. All ships that could traverse the Iroquois and Cardinal rapids, which were really just very strong currents rather than true rapids like the Galops, could avoid having to use the canal on the way upriver, except for the last 4,000 feet past the Galops Rapids. This would relieve congestion on the canal and save time going upriver. A 17-foot channel was dredged through the Galops Rapids so that downbound ships could avoid using the canal, and a new 17-foot channel was cut on the Canadian side of the river, from below Prescott almost to the Galops Canal, replacing a longer, winding 9-foot channel on the American side. Two large 800-foot locks were installed in the Farran's Point and the Galops canals, so

Cardinal in April 1959. Although the nine-foot canal has been breached in places, and has been flooded by construction of the Moses–Saunders Power Dam, it is still visible on the St. Lawrence side of the town, and the 14-foot, with its swing bridge can be seen at the back of the town.

that standard-length tow groupings could enter the lock without having to be separated.[34] With the new 14-foot canal, the village of Cardinal, which was located on a point of land, became an island. The 9-foot canal had skirted the community on the river side, but the new one cut across the rear of the village to the north, making it necessary to install a swing bridge to connect with the "mainland." Italian workers were brought in and the deep V-shaped cut was lined with large cut-stone blocks.

A repetition of earlier conflicts involving Irish Catholic labourers on the Rideau Canal and Irish labourers from different counties on the Welland Canal occurred when Canadian labourers on the Galops Canal fought with the Italians. Ethnic, religious, and regional conflict involving immigrants seems to have been a fact of life in nineteenth century canal construction. Irish labourers were usually the poorest of the poor, often working without their families present. Disdained by the largely Protestant communities in which they lived as crude and illiterate, and often exploited by contractors, they worked hard, drank heavily, and fought over the smallest slight. During the construction of the Rideau Canal, Irish workers who were accused of illegally cutting timber on a settler's land fought with the local sheriff and his deputies who had come to arrest them, resulting in the calling out of the county militia. Irish workers on the original Cornwall Canal, in the mid-1830s, committed two murders, which resulted in British troops being stationed in Cornwall for a brief time. Ten years later, labourers from the rival counties of Cork and Connaught fought with each other on the Welland, resulting in the use of police or militia troops, at various times, to keep the peace. In 1876, Irish and Italian workers on the Third Welland staged a bloody riot. By the 1880s, the Italians had become the main immigrant group working on the canals and were viewed as the main danger to the public, meaning Protestant, peace.[35]

One final step in work on these canals involved the building of a dam in the river near the entrance to the Galops Canal to prevent cross-currents pushing ships off course and to maintain an adequate water level in the canal (1904). The other step was the installation of electric winches in the Cornwall Canal to pull ships through the locks and thus speed up passage through the long canal (1905).[36] This was quite an innovation given that the electrification of cities was only beginning at that time. The final stage in the development of the St. Lawrence canals as a whole was the building of the Soulanges Canal. Between 1872 and 1891 there was considerable debate in government circles as to whether the Beauharnois Canal with its long winding waterway, tight turns, and tendency to operate at less than a 9-foot level of water should be expanded, or a new route selected. An alternate route was surveyed in 1872–74, but not adopted until 1891. The new canal was built on the north shore, where the British military had wanted the 9-foot canal built in the 1840s out of concern about a possible American invasion. The Canal Commissioners' report of 1871 had suggested that there was still pressure to build it on the north shore based on military concerns. The decision in 1891 was not made for defence purposes, but instead because an almost straight canal could be built for the approximately 14 miles from Lake St. Louis to Lake St. Francis. Finished in 1899, the canal had only five

*Canaux du Quebec/ LAC C-063868.*

Soulanges Canal, Lock 3, looking east, 1910.

*William James Topley/ LAC PA-008503.*

Western end of the Soulanges Canal.

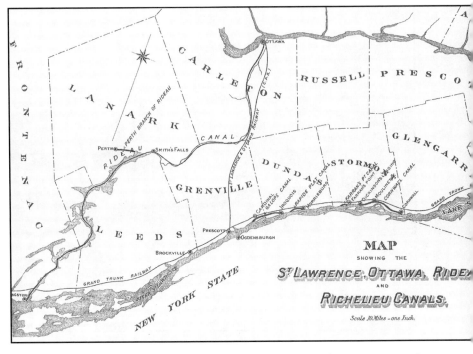

Map 4. The St. Lawrence, Ottawa, and Richelieu canals. Canada, *Department of Railways and Canals, Annual Report, 1900–01*, Ottawa, 1902.

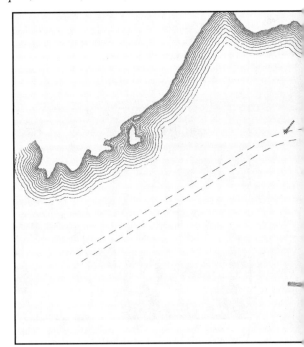

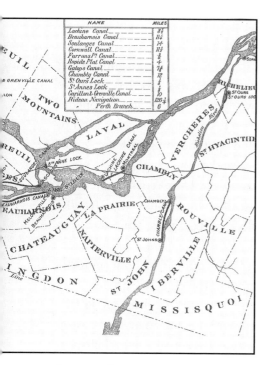

| NAME | MILES |
|---|---|
| Lachine Canal | 8½ |
| Beauharnois Canal | 11½ |
| Soulanges Canal | 14 |
| Cornwall Canal | 11½ |
| Farrans Pt Canal | ⅜ |
| Rapide Plat Canal | 4 |
| Galops Canal | 7¼ |
| Chambly Canal | 12 |
| St Ours Lock | ¼ |
| St Annes Lock | ¼ |
| Carillon & Grenville Canal | 10 |
| Rideau Navigation | 126¼ |
| „ Perth Branch | 6 |

Map 5. The Canadian and American canals at Sault Ste. Marie. Canada, *Department of Railways and Canals, Annual Report, 1900–01*, Ottawa, 1902.

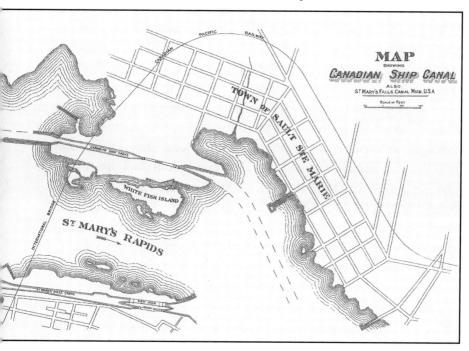

locks to raise ships 82.5 feet, the greatest difference in height on the St. Lawrence. It covered the same ground as had the old engineer canals of the eighteenth century, actually cutting across and obliterating a large section of the Cascades Canal. Water was diverted from the canal at a point approximately halfway along the cut and dropped a short distance down to the St. Lawrence, enabling the generation of power to electrify the machinery and to light the canal with arc lamps. Together with two range lights at each end of the canal, which, when lined up, allowed easy access in the dark, these lamps enabled the canal to be used both day and night. With work on the canals completed, the Canadian government abolished tolls on the canals, temporarily in 1903, and by legislation in 1905.[37]

Work on the connecting channels was continued by both countries from the 1860s to the end of the century. The channel through Lake St. Peter below Montreal was gradually dredged to a depth of 35 feet. The American government continued work on the channels between Lake Erie and Lake Superior. The Detroit River had a natural channel 13 feet deep but, as ship sizes and traffic increased, this had become a hazardous passage. The easiest way to increase the depth and width was on the Canadian side of the boundary, but Canada refused to allow this. Work was then begun on the American side of the boundary in 1876, but after a few months it was discovered that measurements were incorrect and the work was actually being done on the Canadian side. Another approach to the Canadian government resulted in an agreement that work could proceed on the Canadian side, resulting in a 20-foot-deep channel. After a trip sponsored by House and Senate members from Michigan for members of appropriate committees, Congress voted in 1891 to create a channel 20 to 21 feet deep throughout the Upper Lakes. This was achieved by 1897. By 1894, the St. Clair Flats channel had been dredged to 29 feet. The channel through the St. Marys River was dredged to a depth of 16 feet for most of its length when the decision was made to abandon the existing winding channel in favour of a more direct one. In 1894, the new 20-foot-deep channel was opened. It was later widened, and lights were added to make night navigation possible.[38]

The Michigan-owned St. Marys Canal was deteriorating by the 1870s, and the rapidly increasing population of the Midwest and rapidly increasing iron and copper production led to more traffic and larger ships. At the urging of government officials, and with the consent of Michigan, which could not afford needed repairs and expansion, Congress voted to take over the canal, repair it, and build a second, larger lock beside the old one. Finished in 1881, the year that the United States government took over the existing canal, the new lock was 515 feet long by 60 feet wide and was 17 feet deep, with a 16-foot channel on either side. The canal was constructed by the Army Corps of Engineers, who were to maintain their role of constructing canals for the American government. The canal was only recently finished when Major Godfrey Weitzel, who was in charge of the construction, was recommending the urgent construction of a larger canal with a larger second lock in place of the old Michigan canal. His successor, General Orlando Poe, took up the cause in the mid-80s, and Congress voted money to begin construction in 1886, but Canada finished an even larger canal before the American construction was finished.[39]

Despite the international co-operation shown in the matter of the St. Clair River channel, suspicion and competition still existed between Canada and the United States. In 1883, to deal with the looming enlargement of the St. Lawrence and Welland canals, New York had abolished tolls on the Erie Canal. The Erie was gradually becoming obsolete as new, larger ships on the Upper Lakes found it increasingly inconvenient to transship their cargoes into 300-ton barges. But until the new St. Lawrence and Welland canals were completed, the Erie Canal and, increasingly, the New York railways were the most convenient methods for many shippers to get their cargoes to the Atlantic. Canada responded in 1884 to the abolition of tolls on the Erie by providing a rebate of half the toll on goods shipped through the Welland and St. Lawrence canals to Montreal or beyond, increasing this to a 90 percent rebate the following year. The Americans responded with a duty on the St. Marys Canal equal to the one they had to pay on the Welland. This was resented in Canada as much as the rebate was resented in the United States, and was perhaps the deciding factor in the Canadian government's decision to go ahead with a Canadian canal at Sault Ste. Marie. The earlier refusal by the United States to allow British and Canadian troops to use the canal in 1870, and a growing population on the Canadian prairies which led to an increase in wheat production, also contributed to the decision.[40]

The Canadian canal was begun in 1886, the same year that construction on the new American canal was started. Several design changes during construction led to a straighter and deeper canal than originally envisaged. The single lock was 900 feet long, 60 feet wide, and 22 feet deep (though less when the water level dropped), the largest in the world at the time. Able to handle multiple ships end to end, it was also the first to operate its gates by electricity, which it generated on-site. As of 1895, Canada was no longer at the mercy of the United States when it came to getting ships into and out of Lake Superior. She was also in a position to service the growing population on the Canadian prairies. Population growth, too, was a factor in the decision to build the new American canal, which was finished a year later. The other factor was the discovery of the huge Mesabi iron ore field in northeastern Minnesota in 1890. Traffic going through the American canals had reached 690,826 tons in 1870.

View of the Canadian canal at Sault Ste. Marie with steamer *Northwest* in the foreground, 1906.

*William James Topely/LAC PA-009450.*

Ships in the American "Soo" Canal.

By 1885 it was 3,250,000 tons, and by 1894, 13,200,000 tons. Work was speeded up on the canal as a result. It featured what became known as the Poe Lock, which had dimensions of 800 by 100 feet by just over 20 feet deep, but less at the lowest water level. In spite of the construction of the three new locks, all were almost at capacity by the turn of the century as a result of the continued rapid growth of western areas in both countries. A Canadian government report of 1898 noted that ships were getting larger, with a few drawing 18½ feet of water, making the 18¼-foot channel leading to the Canadian lock a problem.[41]

The building of the canals on the St. Marys River put pressure on the Erie Canal and the canals along the Welland–St. Lawrence route, which could not handle ships coming from the Upper Lakes. None felt this pressure more than the Erie, which, by 1900, was a canal from another era. Even the Welland–St. Lawrence canals could handle small ships, while the Erie was still a barge canal. The state engineer recommended, in 1884, that New York build a ship canal 18 feet deep. The following year the New York City Board of Trade put itself behind a move to improve the state canal system. By that time, the railroads were diverting a considerable amount of trade to other cities on the Atlantic coast, and New York saw its preeminent position slipping. The solution, the board of trade believed, was to improve the canals as an alternative to the railroads.[42]

National and international discussions also influenced what the State did. In the period 1889–92 there were discussions in Congress about building both a ship canal to the Atlantic and an American canal at Niagara. Several surveys and estimates for possible routes were undertaken in the 1890s and early 1900. Midwestern states, which were upset at the monopolistic practices of the railways in transporting goods to and from the West, began at this time to call for larger St. Lawrence canals. After an International Deep Waterways Convention in Toronto in 1894, which included delegates from Canada and Midwestern states, called for the enlargement of the St. Lawrence canals, Congress authorized the creation of an International Deep Waterways Commission. The Canadian government agreed to participate and, in the report of the America members of the commission in 1897, the commissioners recommended that a canal 28 feet deep be built on the American side at Niagara, and that the Canadians use the St. Lawrence route to reach the Atlantic, while the Americans should deepen either the Oswego–Hudson route or the Champlain–Hudson route to 28 feet to reach the ocean.[43]

In New York State, a constitutional convention in 1894 called for a 9-foot canal. A popular vote in 1895 approved this, and also the spending of nine million dollars to build it, an amount which ran out in 1897 with only about one-third of the work done. At almost the same time as the convention endorsed the depth of 9 feet, the state engineer, in response to these national and international discussions of ship canals, called for a deepening to 20 feet on the Oswego–Hudson route. This canal would be much less expensive to deepen than the Erie to Buffalo, but the suggestion did not have the support of western New York, which backed the Erie, and the cost was deemed to be too great. Federal backing for a ship canal did not come about either. Although Congress authorized studies of the Niagara and New York ship canals, a subsequent report claimed that the St. Lawrence route was best, and that a New York canal would unfairly benefit New York over other parts of the country. The report warned though that, if the St. Lawrence canals were enlarged, it would be commercial suicide for the state.[44]

In New York, pressure mounted for a deeper canal as the St. Lawrence canals neared completion, and the governor (1899–1900), Theodore (Teddy) Roosevelt, appointed advisers who recommended deeper barge canals, but felt that a ship canal was a matter for the federal government, not for New York. Roosevelt supported this latter recommendation in 1900; however, the Legislature had earlier overwhelmingly rejected the idea of turning over the canals to the federal government, a move which might have meant federal funding for a deeper canal. During the following three years, Roosevelt's endorsement of a deeper canal was questioned, including by his successor, Benjamin Barker Odell (governor, 1901–04). In a similar situation to that which preceded the enlargement of the Erie in the mid-nineteenth century, a vigorous and protracted debate began in the early years of the twentieth century, in the Legislature of New York State, as to whether to spend the huge sums of money necessary to enlarge the canal beyond nine feet.[45]

Anti-canal forces, which included, among others, those in rural areas and others far away from the canal (the same interests as had opposed the Erie Canal enlargement of 1835–62) were purportedly heavily financed by railway interests. Among the arguments used, aside from the cost, was the idea that a railway built in the bed of the canal, once drained, would be superior to an increase in size. Pro-canal forces coalesced around the New York Board of Trade and included among their leading figures legislator George Clinton, grandson of De Witt, builder of the Erie. Reports at both the federal and state levels concluded that it was cheaper to transship into barges at Buffalo and at New York than to build and operate ocean-going ships on the Great Lakes using canals suitable for ships, thereby strengthening the case for the pro-canal forces. Those who saw expansion as the only salvation for the Erie, which had done so much to build the state and New York City, ultimately won, and in 1903 the Legislature voted to build what would become the 12-foot New York Barge Canal, including the Erie, the Oswego, the Champlain, and the Cayuga–Seneca (linking the Erie with Lakes Cayuga and Seneca) canals. Begun in 1905, construction went on until 1918. The Erie Canal was rerouted to take advantage of rivers and Lake Oneida. It had been too difficult to canalize sections of rivers such as the Mohawk, Oswego, Seneca, and Genesee during earlier construction, but modern construction techniques allowed these to be used. The result was that, particularly in the middle section, communities such as Syracuse that had been created as a consequence of the original canal route were no longer on the canal. Now 75 feet wide at the bottom and 12 feet deep, with provision made to easily increase the width, and capable of handling vessels exceeding 1,000 tons, the Erie was prepared to continue its rivalry with the St. Lawrence canals. However, if the Welland and St. Lawrence canals were considered inadequate by shippers at 14 feet in depth, the Erie, at 12 feet, was going to continue to struggle to keep traffic. Before construction began, a majority of the Canal Board rejected the idea, advanced by New York City interests, of increasing the lock size to match that on the St. Lawrence, although the state engineer and the advisory board agreed with it.[46] Traffic did increase when the Barge Canal began operations, but it was a temporary increase.[47]

In addition to its struggle with the St. Lawrence system, the Erie had to face a new challenger for the trade of the Midwest at the turn of the century, in the form of the Chicago Sanitary and Ship Canal, also known as the Chicago Drainage Canal. The decision to create a new canal to supplement the Illinois and Michigan Canal (a portion of which was incorporated into the new canal) was made after a massive storm in 1885 drove sewage well out into Lake Michigan, close to the city's water intake pipes. Engineers decided that it would be possible to reverse the flow of the Chicago River and flush Chicago's sewage into the Mississippi River system. This had been partially successful when sewage had been pumped into the Illinois and Michigan Canal in the 1860s, and more successful when the canal was deepened in 1871 by cutting a deeper channel through the divide between the Great Lakes Basin and the Mississippi Basin, which lay only a few miles from Lake Michigan. The flow south was intermittent, however, and Chicago's sewage problem had been increasing. Pollution plagued both branches of the Chicago River, but was worst on the South Branch. The south fork of this branch was home to the Union Stockyards, which discharged so much offal that the water appeared to be a solid surface, broken in places by dead, bloated animals. The fork was known as Bubbly Creek because the decaying offal on the riverbed created a frequent discharge of gases from decomposition. Rather than recommending the treatment of the sewage, engineers suggested that dilution and flushing into the Mississippi system would solve Chicago's problem. In a massive project, which trained some of the engineers who later worked on the Panama Canal, between 1892 and 1900, a 28-mile canal was dug from the Chicago River to the Des Plains River, 25 feet deep and between 160 and 300 feet wide. Downriver states complained, and Missouri took Illinois to court over perceived pollution, but lost, and Illinois continued to increase the water flow of the canal, adding new water inlets from Lake Michigan in 1910 and 1922.[48]

Chicago businesses saw this as an opportunity to use the Sanitary and Ship Canal to increase the flow of goods from Chicago to the Gulf of Mexico, again hoping to become the hub for transportation of goods between the Upper Lakes and Europe, as they had when the Illinois and Michigan Canal opened. They were encouraged in this by the formation of the Lakes–to–Gulf Deep Waterways Association, founded in 1906, which garnered substantial support among congressmen and presidents. Whether this was ever a possibility, especially after federal engineers rejected a proposal in 1909 to canalize the Mississippi to 14 feet, from St. Louis to the Gulf of Mexico, is difficult to assess. Downriver states must have thought so, as Missouri, Tennessee, and Louisiana reversed themselves in 1926 and supported the diversion. A number of bills were discussed in Congress after 1916 to improve the Chicago to the Gulf route, but nothing came of any of them. Newspapers in other Great Lakes states often claimed in the 20s and 30s that building the Sanitary and Ship Canal was carried out to facilitate Chicago's navigational interests, at the expense of other states and provinces on the Great Lakes. This feeling existed despite the fact that traffic on the canal began to decrease in the 1920s and consisted largely of regional traffic. Certainly the canal was one of the reasons that there were mixed feelings within the Chicago business community regarding the St. Lawrence canals, until the Seaway was built. The Sanitary and Ship Canal also became a source of controversy and repeated legal action, both among Great Lakes states and in Canada, because it diverted water from the Great Lakes, actually lowering the water level, especially in Lake Michigan.[49]

An old rival of the St. Lawrence made another appearance at the same time as the Erie was being rebuilt. Discussion of the much shorter Ottawa River–Lake Nipissing–French River route to the Upper Lakes had been very limited since the 1860s, but the Canadian Parliament authorized another survey and costing in 1904 as part of a general assessment of transportation needs, given the rapidly growing wheat production on the Prairies. The report submitted in 1909 suggested that a 20-foot-deep canal was feasible, and the government of Wilfrid Laurier promised to build this project and also carry out a rival project of enlarging the Welland Canal. Nothing was done, however, before the defeat of the government in 1911.[50]

Given the strong pressure that was building in both the United States and Canada, due to a rapidly increasing population in western areas of both countries, the massive increase in wheat production, which the railways could not handle,[51] and the high cost of railway transportation, it would seem logical that Canada would respond by enlarging the St. Lawrence canals. This conclusion is reinforced by the fact that neither of the rival systems, the Erie nor the Mississippi, was particularly appealing to shippers. Several factors worked against such a decision. Although canals were recognized as a less expensive means of transporting bulk goods than railroads, the latter were the transportation technology of the late nineteenth and early twentieth centuries and the canals were of an earlier era. Railroads were built by private companies, though with government assistance in Canada, and were thus less expensive for taxpayers. While neglecting to act on proposals to enlarge the Welland and to build the Georgian Bay Canal, the Laurier government provided financial assistance to companies building a second and a third transcontinental railway, even building a portion of one of the routes and leasing it to the company. Shortly before being defeated, the government authorized the building of another railway, a short route into the West, from Winnipeg to Hudson Bay. This railway was the dream of many on the Canadian prairies, as it would provide a much shorter route for Canadian grain going to Britain. In addition, what was regarded as a very efficient system was developing in Canada. As an alternative to shipping by train from western Canada, wheat was transported in large ships from the head of the lakes as far as the Welland, where it was transshipped into specially built 14-footers, small ships designed to use as much space within the canal locks as possible, for the remainder of the trip to Montreal. Alternatively, wheat was shipped from the head of the lakes to ports on Georgian Bay from which it went by train to Kingston, or more often to

Prescott on the St. Lawrence, where it was loaded into the 14-footers. In later years, after the Welland was enlarged, ships could come all the way to Kingston and Prescott before transshipping. The government built a large grain elevator at Prescott to facilitate the transfer. Increasingly, American shipping chose the St. Lawrence route as well.[52]

The one concession that Canada did make was to enlarge the bottleneck of the Welland Canal. The choice for the government of Robert Borden was either to pay for two expensive projects, the other being the Georgian Bay Canal, or to choose just one. The choice was between an expensive new canal serving the Upper Lakes and a less expensive, existing canal serving all of the Great Lakes. In addition, pressure was exerted by the Winnipeg Grain Exchange, which handled sales of western wheat, by the Dominion Marine Association, representing ship owners, and by numerous other boards of trade and similar organizations, to enlarge the Welland. Construction was begun in 1913. From Lake Ontario to the Niagara Escarpment the route was a new one, with a new entrance to the east of the existing one. From the escarpment to Lake Erie, the old route was used, with some minor straightening, necessitating careful scheduling so that traffic was not interrupted. The First World War resulted in a halt in construction from 1917 to 1919, and the post-war recession slowed work, but the canal was finally finished in 1931. It was built on a scale unprecedented on the Great Lakes. The number of locks was reduced from 26 to 8. Seven of them were 859 feet long, 80 feet wide, and 30 feet deep. The eighth, which served as a guard lock at the Port Colborne entrance, was 1,200 feet long. This guard lock was designed to make small adjustments in the difference between the level of Lake Erie and the level of water in the canal. Three of the locks were step locks, or flight locks, at the escarpment, and these were twinned with matching locks beside them, allowing simultaneous traffic in two directions. Most lock gates, to provide for an unusually high 46½-foot lift, had to be 83.4 feet high. While the channels were only 25 to 27 feet deep, the 30-foot lock depth allowed for easy deepening of the canal when needed. Engineers from numerous countries studied the engineering firsts of the canal, including the high-lift locks. The official opening of the canal was postponed until 1932 so that delegates to the British Empire Economic Conference in Ottawa could attend and be impressed by the facilities

View of the old (Third) Welland Canal, *circa* 1913, with the beginning of construction of the Lock 6 pond of the Fourth Canal, which would provide water to the flight locks, in the background.

Locks 4, 5 and 6 of the Fourth Welland Canal at Thorold (the flight locks) under construction, July 1916.

Gate lifter on the Welland, lifting a gate leaf (one-half of a gate), April 5, 1933. When built at Collingwood, Ontario, in 1930, it was claimed to be the largest crane of any type in the world, and was capable of raising 500 tons.

S.S. *Lemoyne*, the largest ship on the Great Lakes, at Lock 6 the day of the official opening, August 6, 1932.

available to ships of the world. The first ship through, the S.S. *Lemoyne*, was the largest ship operating on the Great Lakes, its passage emphasizing that the Welland bottleneck was no more. Now wheat, coal, and iron ore could be conveyed without interruption into Lake Ontario.

While the First Welland was built largely with picks, shovels, and wagons, a few plows and the odd American scraper, steam-driven machinery, especially the steam dredge and the steam crane, began to appear during the building of the Second Welland. Steam shovels were a feature of the construction of the Third Canal, though there was still much work done with traditional tools. By the time that the Fourth Canal was built, most work was done with steam machinery, including steam drills and steam trains, which were used in the canal bed to move materials. Black powder, and its volatile successor, nitroglycerine, had been replaced by dynamite. By the time the canal was finished, modern construction machinery was also employed, driven by gas, diesel, or electricity, including

Long Sault Rapids from the Cornwall Road, *circa* 1820.

Lock at the Cascades Rapids (likely Rocher-Fendu/Split Rock), *circa* 1820.

Durham Boat in the Lachine Rapids, 1843.

Long Sault Rapids with lumber dram, 1849. Note the Cornwall Canal in the background.

A lumber dram in the Lachine Rapids, *circa* 1920s.

A timber from a timber raft recovered from the St. Lawrence; skilled axemen left almost no marks when squaring it.

Entrance to the Rideau Canal at Bytown, February 1839.

Kingston Mills Locks on the Rideau Canal, *circa* 1832.

The nine-foot canal at Cardinal; see also the epilogue.

The 14-foot canal at Cardinal; see also epilogue.

The western entrance to the old Beauharnois Canal, used to moor pleasure boats, about one-fifth of what is left; see also the epilogue.

Sault Ste. Marie Rapids from the United States canal, 1860.

Inside one of the step locks of the Second Welland Canal today, showing about two-thirds of the lock; see also the epilogue.

The Third Welland today. Notice the step-up at the far end of the lock, which represents the distance that a ship would have to be raised to clear the upstream end of the lock; see also the epilogue.

Samuel McLaughlin/LAC C-000771.

The Great Western/Grand Trunk Railway Tunnel under the Third Welland. Built when the canal was constructed, because trains on bridges interfered with ships in the canals and vice versa, it was soon replaced for most traffic by a bridge and abandoned during the First World War.

Photo by the author.

The tunnel today. It is still intact, down to the railway ties in the floor of the structure, but the canal above it is dry, the flow of water now being on the other side of the weir (dam) visible in the first photograph; see also epilogue.

*Clifford M. Johnston/LAC PA-056507.*

C.S.L. *Rapids Prince* in the Long Sault Rapids, 1929. Passenger ships regularly ran the rapids until the Second World War; this line, which included the *Rapids Prince, Queen, and King*, was dedicated to running the rapids.

*Notman & Sons/LAC PA-166130.*

S.S. *Corsican* in the Lachine Rapids, *circa* 1889.

caterpillar tractors, electric cranes, and large concrete mixing towers. At the same time, mules pulling scrapers and dump wagons, the predecessor of the dump truck, were employed until the end of construction.[53]

There were continued improvements in the Great Lakes canal system prior to the building of the Seaway in the 1950s. Alterations were made in the Soo locks, with two new locks being built on the American side in the period of the First World War, both 23 feet deep and 1,350 feet long. Channels leading to these two locks had to be deepened to 24 feet beginning in the early twentieth century to accommodate larger ships. Another was added in 1945, 29½ feet deep and 1,800 feet long. All were 80 feet wide. Only the original Poe Lock survived, to be rebuilt after the Seaway was opened. The Canadian channel was deepened to 21.5 feet after the First World War. Montreal Harbour was taken over by the Canadian government and improved, and other harbours, such as that at Toronto, were also made accessible to ships that could traverse the Fourth Welland. The national governments put money into improving about 90 American ports and a number of Canadian ones. Channels were improved by dredging or removing rocks so that larger ships could use the system, except for the St. Lawrence canals. Lighting was installed on various parts of the system. By 1932, when the new Welland opened, only the set of canals on the St. Lawrence stood in the way of the Great Lakes welcoming ocean-going ships in large numbers. The Erie was no longer a serious challenger, and the Chicago Sanitary and Ship Canal had never lived up to the expectations of the Chicago business community. Backers of the two canals may not have realized it at the time, but their dream of dominating the trade of the Great Lakes was over. The railways were carrying a large amount of western wheat by this time, but farmers in both countries desperately wanted a cheaper alternative. Though the Churchill Railway to Hudson Bay had been completed in 1931, it was to prove a great disappointment for Canadian farmers, as the shipping season on the bay was, at best, a few weeks in the summer. Yet it would be more than 20 years before anything was done to remove the last barrier to efficient bulk transportation by water.[54]

# Whose Dream? Negotiating the Building of the Seaway

Those who were alive in the early 1950s probably remember the negotiations to construct the Seaway in terms of Canada asking the United States to jointly build the canal system. When the United States declined to participate, Canada announced that it would do the work itself, building an all-Canadian route along the St. Lawrence. After at first refusing to believe that Canada would undertake such a mammoth project by itself, the Americans came to the realization that the Canadians were serious and that, if the United States did not participate, Americans would be in the embarrassing position of depending on a foreign country to move American goods in and out of the Great Lakes. Such a scenario contains a good deal of truth with regard to the period just before the agreement was signed, but is a distortion of the real negotiating process. The concept of building a substantial ship canal along the St. Lawrence had been discussed by the two countries since the 1890s, and the delay in agreeing to build it as a joint project was the result of each government being more or less enthusiastic about the project in inverse proportion to the enthusiasm of the other government.[1]

Within the United States there was very strong opposition throughout much of the country and, even in the one state that stood to gain from the project, New York, there was far more opposition than support, as backers of New York City trade far outnumbered the sparse population of the area bordering the St. Lawrence. In Canada, the areas bordering the St. Lawrence, Ontario and Quebec, were characterized by indifference or outright hostility for much of the first half of the twentieth century, and the farmers of the Canadian prairies saw their salvation in terms of the Hudson

Bay (Churchill) Railway for a large portion of the time. The impetus for the Seaway and its most ardent boosters came not from the St. Lawrence region or from the national governments, but from the American western end of the Great Lakes, an area that would not be exploiting the St. Lawrence to control the trade of the Lakes, but rather one that saw its future prosperity in terms of being able to get sea-going ships into its harbours.

While there had been calls within both countries for an improved St. Lawrence both before and after the 14-foot canals were begun, the Canadian government was not prepared to pay for such an expensive project, given that existing canals did not pay their way and the alternative, privately owned railways, was in place. However, resentment of monopoly railways, owned by eastern business interests, was intense in the western regions of both countries. As a result of this feeling, congressional representatives from Minnesota, Wisconsin, and Michigan applied pressure to get a joint study of the issue done by Canada and the United States. In 1892, lawyer John Lind of Minnesota introduced a resolution in Congress calling for a joint study of possible improvements of the water route from the head of Lake Superior through the St. Lawrence to the Atlantic. Lind was a constant foe of eastern railways, and saw canal enlargement as an alternative to his failed attempts to control freight rates on the railways. That same year, Colonel Frederick Charles Denison, the member of Parliament representing West Toronto, put forward in the House of Commons a motion calling for a Great Lakes canal system 20 feet deep, able to handle ocean-going vessels. Denison was a member of a wealthy and prominent old Toronto family. He rose to a senior rank in the militia, and achieved celebrity status in 1885. Using his company of Canadian fur trade boatmen, native canoemen, and lumbermen, which had been assisting the British Army to ascend the Nile River, he was largely responsible for evacuating, under threat of imminent attack, the British Army force sent to rescue Major General Charles "Chinese" Gordon from Khartoum in the Sudan. As a member of Parliament in subsequent years, he generally said very little, except on military matter. The canal issue was one exception about which he seemed to feel strongly.[2]

In 1894, the Toronto Municipal Council called an international Deep Waterways Convention, which was attended by delegates from Canada and from eight states in the American Midwest. An ongoing recession and a drop in the price of wheat, combined with the slow progress in deepening the St. Lawrence canals to 14 feet, made the need for less expensive transportation even more acute, and Toronto was anxious to benefit from increased shipping on the St. Lawrence. The delegates discussed various transportation routes and schemes, but focused a good deal of attention on the St. Lawrence, and endorsed Lind's resolution for a joint Canadian–American study of the issue. Out of the convention came an International Deep Waterways Association, with Oliver A. Howland of Toronto as president, Lyman E. Cooley of Chicago and James Fisher of Winnipeg as American and Canadian vice-presidents, James Dunham of Chicago as treasurer, and Frank. A. Flower of Superior, Wisconsin, as executive secretary.

This was a formidable executive. Howland was a lawyer and a member of the provincial parliament of Ontario (1884–98). He later served as a member of the Canadian Parliament (elected 1897) and as mayor of Toronto (1901 and 1902), as well as president of the League of Canadian Municipalities, an organization of mayors and municipal politicians. Cooley was the Chicago engineer behind the Sanitary and Ship Canal. His participation, as a believer in canals (he later backed a possible canal through Nicaragua), was seemingly at odds with the later opposition of Chicago business to improvements in the St. Lawrence. James Fisher was a lawyer and a member of the Legislative Assembly of Manitoba (1888–99). As a lawyer, he was solicitor for the Northern and Northern Pacific Railways, and as an MLA was a very vocal proponent of the proposed Hudson Bay Railway. He was also president of an international organization, founded in 1893 in Midwestern states and western provinces, devoted to promoting reciprocity (free trade) between the two countries. Most of the chief Midwestern advocates of enlarged St. Lawrence canals were also members. As with Cooley, his involvement with rivals to the St. Lawrence did not preclude a general interest in assisting the farmers of the West in getting their crops to market. Captain James Dunham was a wealthy ship owner who operated a fleet of tugboats out of Chicago, through the Chicago Towing and Wrecking Company, and a fleet of transports on the Great Lakes through the Chicago Steamship Company, as well as being involved with other Chicago companies. His work on Great Lakes shipping policy would get him elected president of the Lake Carriers Association in 1898. Frank Flowers was a journalist and amateur historian whose fervent belief in the cause led him to become the chief publicist for the Deep Waterway concept.[3]

The convention urged the Canadian and American governments to create a joint commission to study the common financing and operation of a channel to the sea 26 feet deep, with 21-foot canals. Flowers took the ensuing year off work and devoted himself completely to lobbying and publicizing, supported by private contributions. By the time of the next convention, in Cleveland in September of 1895, the United States Congress and the Canadian cabinet had agreed to participate in a joint committee. In the United States, it was the efforts of Midwestern members of Congress, backed by lobbying on the part of the association, which influenced the decision. In Canada, a delegation sent by the association and led by MP Frederick Denison was able to persuade the cabinet and the prime minister of the value of the joint investigation. The American commissioners included Lyman Cooley and the Canadian included Oliver Howland, an auspicious indication that the association had the ear of both governments.

This, the first joint lobbying on behalf of a deep waterway to the Atlantic and the first co-operative study by the two governments, proved a great disappointment to its supporters. Opposition, much of which would continue until the Seaway was built, appeared as fast as did the association's campaign. Opponents included east–west railways, east coast ports, owners of lake ships which could not sail on the oceans and feared competition from those which could, existing transfer cities such as Montreal and Buffalo, those who supported other waterways, especially the Erie, and many who saw the canal idea as a needless extravagance or an unaffordable dream. The old concern about national self-reliance and defence also played a part. While the association managed to get the commission appointed with its campaign, the commissioners could not totally ignore this competition.[4]

In addition, there was some divergence of opinion among the American backers of the deep waterways concept. The conference of 1894, called by Toronto, had originally intended to concentrate on the discussion of the St. Lawrence, but so many delegates were eager to come from the Midwestern states that the discussion had been broadened to include other possible routes. Thus, the issue for the commissioners was how best to reach the Atlantic by water, all factors considered. Even the central figure in the publicity campaign, Frank Flowers, rather aggressively told a *New York Times* reporter in 1895 that, "New-York may not want us to come down to tidewater with our unbroken cargoes [i.e. not transshipped] of grain and merchandise, but New-York does not always know what is best for herself. We believe that what is good for the West is good for New-York, and we propose to come."[5] In so doing, he was suggesting that the coastal terminal for the deep waterway might be the city of New York.

As mentioned in chapter 2, the American commissioners agreed that the St. Lawrence was the best route for the Canadians, but supported an all-American route around Niagara Falls, and suggested that the best method to reach the Atlantic from there was down one of two routes to the Hudson and New York. They argued that most cargo was domestic in nature and that the St. Lawrence was too far north to serve the recipients on the eastern seaboard. The separate Canadian report recognized that there was a strong nationalistic feeling among the American commissioners, but hoped that they could work together to develop a St. Lawrence–Richelieu River–Lake Champlain–Hudson River canal system to New York, and that the Americans would share in the cost of the Canadian improvements.

The Canadian commissioners advocated spending Canadian funds to survey the Canadian portion of the Richelieu–Champlain–Hudson route, if the Americans were prepared to embrace that route. However, in response to the American commissioners' report, the American president, Grover Cleveland, and Congress authorized the Army Corps of Engineers to survey the possible routes to the Atlantic for either a 21-foot or a 30-foot series of canals. Not surprisingly, the engineers rejected the St. Lawrence as too far north to be of use to American commerce, but they also spoke less enthusiastically of the Lake Champlain option than the Oswego–Lake Oneida–Mohawk–Hudson option. Combined with a new American canal at Niagara, this would create an all-American route. With the United States flexing its international muscle in the Spanish-American War and with the Great White Fleet, symbol of the United States' wealth and power, then under construction, and with relations with Canada often strained, an Army report was very unlikely to advocate any scheme that required passage through foreign (Canadian) territory.[6]

When this report was prepared, Canada and the United States were locked in a diplomatic confrontation over the Alaska boundary. At issue was the Alaska Panhandle, the sliver of territory which occupies almost half of the coastline of the Province of British Columbia. After acquiring Alaska in 1867, the Americans had occupied the old Russian whaling stations such as Wrangell and Sitka and laid claim to a wide swath of territory along the coast, without protest from either Canada or Britain, which controlled the area until 1871. With the discovery of gold in the Yukon in 1897, the Canadians realized that the only easy access to the area was through the Panhandle, and insisted that the United States was entitled only to a narrow band of territory, a claim which would allow access to the Yukon without having to go overland through American territory. After some forceful diplomatic exchanges, President Teddy Roosevelt agreed to arbitration, having been assured that the Canadian government did not expect to win but only wanted to save face. The certainty of a favourable decision hinged on the judgment of the British member, required by the fact that Canadian foreign policy was still controlled by Britain. The American government privately let him know that the Americans felt strongly enough about their case to use the army, if necessary, to draw the correct border. While the American case was very strong, especially since Canada had not protested the American claim for almost 40 years, the fact that the British member awarded two of four small islands at the bottom of the Panhandle to the Americans, when Canada expected to get all four, caused a protest from the Canadian government. Plans to terminate a new trans-Canadian railway at an inlet behind the islands were altered out of concern that any shipping would have to pass American-held territory to reach the open sea. As long as Britain and Canada on one side and the United States on the other had doubts about each other's motives and intentions, co-operation on an international waterway would be very difficult.[7]

While the Army engineers' report suggested that 21-foot canals were the best option, on the basis of cost and the current design of vessels, Congress showed no interest in financing any scheme.[8] Undoubtedly the forces of opposition in that body, both regional and financial, played a large part in this, as did the announcement in 1903 that New York would enlarge the Erie Canal, and that the 14-foot St. Lawrence canals would be completed at about the same time. Few realized that, by the time the New York State Barge Canal would be completed in 1918, lake ships would grow in size to the point that transshipping to barges would be an unpalatable option for many shippers, or that the Welland and St. Lawrence canals would soon prove to be a bottleneck to water commerce. Consistently throughout the history of the building of Great Lakes canals, governments built for present needs, not for future ones.

With Congress losing interest, so did the members of the International Deep Waterways Association, and this first attempt at international co-operation to provide an adequate outlet from the Great Lakes to the ocean came to an end. Shortly thereafter, though, the issue of power generation on the St. Lawrence canal system added pressure and support for a seaway. This was not water power, which had contributed to the attempt to build de Casson's canal in the seventeenth century, to the building of the Welland in the nineteenth, and to the partial funding of canals through the sale of industrial water rights in the same century. This was electrical power, the generation of which was in its infancy.

Hydro power had been generated at Niagara Falls since the early 1880s, though long distance transmission was not practical until some 30 years later. In the meantime, the Pittsburg Reduction Company, soon to be known as the Aluminum Company of America (Alcoa), which needed large quantities of power to produce aluminum, located at Niagara and at Massena, New York, where a short canal brought water from the Long Sault Rapids to a powerhouse near the plant, and then into the Grasse (also Grass) River. Not long after building a plant in 1902, the company began buying up land on the American side through a subsidiary, the Long Sault Development Company, and on the Canadian side through the St. Lawrence Power Company, another subsidiary. That these two subsidiaries were acting on behalf of Alcoa was intentionally not divulged. Only when engineers arrived on Barnhart Island, in the middle of the St. Lawrence near the foot of the Long Sault Rapids, and began testing the riverbed did it become clear what the purpose of the land acquisition had been. Even then, it was not clear who was behind the effort or what the plans were. In 1907, the Long Sault Development Company asked the New York Legislature for the right to build a dam from the American side to Barnhart Island, and to generate power. The

St. Lawrence Power Company asked the Canadian government for the same right on the Canadian side.

The New York Legislature quite willingly gave the company the right to exploit the American side of the St. Lawrence. This was subject to congressional approval, since construction of power facilities would affect navigation, and navigation on rivers and lakes was controlled by the federal government. The area of New York near the project, being largely undeveloped compared to other areas of the state, gave the project strong support.[9] The request to the Canadian government met with a strong public protest. The fight to have publically owned power had been a hard fought one in Ontario and the proponents were not about to see new private generating facilities approved. Canal proponents were concerned that construction would make it impossible for ships and timber rafts to shoot the rapids, forcing them into the canals, and make it impossible to enlarge the canals in future. Local residents worried about the effect on the area. As it became likely that there would be a large power pool behind the dams, residents of towns and villages worried about being flooded out of their homes and businesses. Others feared that the decrease in water flow would lead to winter ice jams which would cause further flooding. Some who distrusted the United States were concerned that power generation and navigation would be controlled by a "foreign country." Montreal shipping interests and its board of trade and the Shipping Federation of Canada joined the chorus of protest. Any support lay in towns outside the affected area which might benefit from cheap power.[10]

The Canadian government did not take a stand until 1910, when the St. Lawrence Power Company applied for an exemption to the rule that a licence was required to export power to the United States. In a turbulent debate, during which claims of Alcoa bribery of certain members were made, the House of Commons rejected the request and voted to prevent construction work on the St. Lawrence by the company. Congress rejected the original proposal of the Long Sault Development Company in 1907, as the Company would not be obliged to do anything to improve navigation on the St. Lawrence. A revised proposal, which included a provision to improve navigation, was presented in 1911, but strong opposition, including from Canada, led to its defeat. Even Premier Whitney of Ontario, told that the bill was likely to be defeated if a strong enough protest was made, sent a message of protest. The New York Legislature cancelled the Long Sault Development's charter two years later, after receiving a legal opinion that it was not within New York's constitutional power to grant such a charter.[11] Though Alcoa's plan failed, it did raise important issues. Power development could not be carried out without considering navigation. Canal improvements could be made without considering power development, but the two would be easier to carry out if done in tandem. Power development, if done in concert with canal improvements, could be used to pay for such development. Each of these ideas would now be considered every time a new scheme for St. Lawrence improvements was considered.

A major step in international co-operation was taken in 1909 with the signing of the Boundary Waters Treaty by Britain and the United States. It was negotiated at a time of increasingly good relations between the two nations. The document, which covered all lakes and rivers shared in common by Canada and the United States, plus Lake Michigan, and all canals connecting them, set out certain parameters for their use. It also created an International Joint Commission to deal with all boundary water issues, and more. This six-member commission was to do much invaluable work in coming decades. The treaty guaranteed equal access to both parties to all waters covered by the treaty, though tolls could be charged if one or both parties wished to do so. If any diversion of water not already agreed to (such as the Chicago diversion) took place in either country, which affected the other, the affected country was given the legal right to compensation. Neither country was allowed to build obstructions which would affect water levels in the boundary waters, or to pollute waters in the other country. Though the commission was created under the Boundary Waters Treaty, any other matters affecting the common frontier could also be referred to the commission by either or both countries. The commission would render a decision that was provided as advice to the two countries, which would take political action.[12]

During this period of greater co-operation, another attempt was made to have the St. Lawrence route approved in Congress by the areas of the United States that supported a deep waterway to the Atlantic. In Canada, an attempt was made to acquire St. Lawrence power and improve canals. Even though it had only been a few years since the last attempt, a new group of leaders was promoting the project. In the United States, Senator Charles E. Townsend of Michigan was the most vocal supporter. A lawyer, and former member of the House of Representatives, Townsend served in the Senate from 1911 to 1923. He was appointed as a member of the International Joint Commission after his defeat in 1922. In 1911, and again in 1913, he put forward resolutions calling for negotiations with Britain or Canada on improving navigation in waterways which could be used in common by the United States and Canada. In Canada, the cause was embraced by Daniel B. Detweiler. The president of a boot and shoe manufacturing company, Detweiler was a man of immense enthusiasm who put himself behind numerous projects to benefit the public. He was one-third of a partnership which built a power generation facility in 1900 to provide mines north of Lake Superior with electric power. The partners became convinced that the industrial centre of Ontario, around Detweiler's home city of Berlin (now Kitchener), needed public power, which would be much cheaper than private power. A mixture of municipal reformers seeking inexpensive power for the people and industrialists seeking cheap power for industry, stretching from southwest Ontario to Toronto, took up the cause. Detweiler became the chief publicist of the movement, riding his bicycle from town to town to convince municipal leaders of the need for municipally controlled power distribution of power generated at Niagara Falls. He also came to believe that power should ultimately be generated on the St. Lawrence.

Among those who took up the cause was Adam Beck, who had become wealthy as a manufacturer of high-quality boxes, mainly for cigars, and other related paraphernalia. As the mayor of his home city of London, Ontario (1902–05), and as a private philanthropist he was a crusading and popular urban reformer. Elected to the provincial parliament in 1902, Beck came to believe that provincial rather than municipal control was necessary to ensure efficient operation. Thanks to his bullying of cabinet colleagues after joining the new Conservative cabinet of Premier James Whitney in 1906, Ontario became the first jurisdiction in the world to embrace public ownership, creating the Hydro-Electric Power Commission of Ontario. Beck became its chairman, while retaining his seat in parliament. His aggressive campaign to distribute public power in Ontario, against all efforts of private power interests to discredit him, made him immensely popular with the citizens of Ontario, but a thorn in the side of every government until his death in 1925, as he refused to be accountable to the politicians and spent lavishly on his power projects. In terms of energy and single-mindedness, Beck's subsequent development of public power was, in many ways, a match for Robert Moses's devotion to the development of the Seaway and power production in the 1950s.

When Canada was toying with the idea of the Georgian Bay canal in the later years of Laurier's years as prime minister, Detweiler turned his enthusiasm to enlargement of the St. Lawrence canals and the Welland, which he believed to be a superior plan. In 1912, Detweiler brought together municipal politicians and businessmen from south central Ontario, many of whom he had worked with in the hydro campaign, to discuss an improved water route with a 32-foot depth. In proposing the idea, he suggested that incidental development of power generation could be used to pay for the improvements in the St. Lawrence. The meeting created the Great Waterways Union of Canada, with Detweiler as president, to promote the enlargement. This project, the union claimed, would rival the Panama Canal, which was under construction at the time, in terms of its importance as a deep waterway. Boards of trade across Ontario endorsed the union, as did Senator Townsend and Horace C. Gardner, a leading figure in the Chicago Association of Commerce. The following year, the union claimed at least partial credit for the Canadian government's decision to deepen the Welland Canal instead of building the Georgian Bay canal, and to deepen it to 25 rather than to 22 feet. The union also claimed credit for federal funding to deepen the Toronto harbour to 30 feet.[13]

In 1911, Senator Townsend took up the idea of creating a power pool behind a dam on the St. Lawrence as a way of producing deeper water for navigation as well as the concept of using St. Lawrence power to pay for canal construction, ideas borrowed from Alcoa, and presented them to President Taft. Townsend then took them, first to the House of Representatives, and subsequently to the Senate, after his term there started. The Taft administration had embraced reciprocity (free trade) with Canada, a policy that the Canadian electorate subsequently rejected, and was meeting opposition from Midwestern farmers. Townsend argued that support of the Seaway could offset the failure of the reciprocity negotiations in farmers' eyes, and won Taft over. However, Townsend's efforts in Congress to have the government initiate negotiations with the Canadians went nowhere. Once work on the Welland had been approved in Canada, and the Canadian government had suggested to the Ontario Hydro-Electric Power Commission that it look into the possibility of developing power generation in conjunction with enlargement of the St. Lawrence canals, Townsend thought it an auspicious time to try again in the Senate. This time (1913) the Senate voted unanimously to support negotiations, and President Woodrow Wilson seemed supportive. A delegation representing Midwestern commercial interests visited Secretary of State William Jennings Bryan to urge quick action. Not too long after, Adam Beck led a delegation of 2,000 hydro supporters to Ottawa, to press the government for support for hydro expansion, including improvement of the St. Lawrence. Unfortunately, Canada was slow to respond to a request from the Americans to put a series of questions about improvements in navigation in the Great Lakes system before the International Joint Commission. These included ones dealing with issues of water diversion, the health of the Great Lakes fisheries, and the generation of power. Prime Minister Borden was concerned with the cost of railways then under construction and the possible political consequences of funding a project which would principally help Ontario. Both the companies building the new transcontinental railways were in financial trouble and begging the government for assistance. While recognizing that the St. Lawrence would need to be improved to match the deepening of the Welland at some point, the government had already rejected the added expense of the Georgian Bay canal. After a few months' hesitation, the opportunity abruptly vanished. The First World War broke out and Canada was preoccupied in Europe. With the coming of the war, the Great Waterways Union, which had drawn much of its energy from Daniel Detweiler, gave up the struggle and faded from view.[14]

The issue of co-operative development of the St. Lawrence did not, however, disappear from the public agenda for long. During the First World War, the St. Lawrence Power Company, an Alcoa subsidiary company, applied to the War Department for permission to build a submerged dam, or weir, from Long Sault Island to the American shore, to divert more water into the Alcoa power canal. The need for more power to produce aluminum for the war effort was given as the justification. When Canada objected, claiming that such a dam could impede the full development of the St. Lawrence, the company indicated that the weir would be temporary. The War Department gave its support but required that the International Joint Commission give its approval. The State of New York objected on the basis that the weir would violate the rights of the state in the St. Lawrence. The Canadian government sent senior government representatives to Washington to protest and to offer to discuss the joint development of power in the St. Lawrence. When the International Joint Commission approved the temporary dam in 1918, which, as a member of the Canadian cabinet said, in reality, "would never come out," the government sent another note to the American government. In it, the Canadians again suggested joint development of the St. Lawrence. The Canadians recognized that "navigation is the paramount national and international use of this great highway of commerce," but "that the subordinate and incidental but important use of these international boundary waters for power purposes" would be less successful if done through "a haphazard series of unrelated enterprises," than if undertaken by the two governments. Just as the Canadian government had not responded to the American initiative in 1914, the Americans did not reply to this offer, merely acknowledging receipt. Since no reason was ever given for the lack of action of the American government, the rationale is a matter of conjecture. It may have been a result of opposition in Congress. It may have been because of a report by the United States Army Engineers in December of 1918 suggesting that there was no point in deepening the St. Lawrence canals when other portions of the St. Lawrence and the Great Lakes were not of a comparable depth, and that the system was adequate for current needs. Perhaps having met the needs of Alcoa was enough for the American administration, especially now that the war was over. What is known is that within the space of four years each government had urged joint development of the St. Lawrence on the other, and each government had rejected the other's proposal.[15]

The 1920s and early 30s provided the best opportunity yet to build a seaway. The first step was the creation of new organizations devoted to deep waterways, one in each country. The stronger of the two, the Great Lakes–St. Lawrence Tidewater Association, came into being at Washington in February of 1919, and the sister organization, the Canadian Deep Waterways and Power Association, some nine months

Charles P. Craig, 1926.

later, in Windsor, Ontario, beside the Detroit River, an integral part of the Great Lakes waterway. Their creation had followed an international deep waterway conference in Minneapolis in January 1918, at which Daniel Detweiler was asked to speak, but had to decline because of ill health. Involved with both organizations, and the driving force behind the first of these, was Charles P. Craig of Duluth, the city that was still the centre of the drive for a deep waterway to the Atlantic. Craig was a wealthy lawyer who had made his money by investing in the growing city, and one of those who supported the ongoing campaign to reduce freight rates on the railways. He was described as a "gentleman of the old school, reserved, genteel in voice and manner, very high principled." In forming the Tidewater Association, Craig was careful to consult most of those who had been involved before, or were currently involved. These included prominent Duluth native S.A. Thompson, who never missed an opportunity in the 1890s to appear before congressional committees to urge the building of a deep waterway to the sea, to the point that he was referred to as "Deep Water" Thompson in the press. Also consulted were Senator Charles Townsend, who had pushed the project before the war, Daniel Detweiler, Horace Gardner from the Chicago Association of Commerce, and Frank Keefer, Conservative member of the Canadian Parliament from Port Arthur, a major grain-shipping port.[16]

The president of the new organization was Horace C. Gardner, engineer, member of the Chicago Association of Commerce, and a benign conciliatory figure in the movement. The driving force was Craig, part-time executive director and strategist. His concept was of an organization of states, not of individuals, each of which would contribute funds each year to pay for the Tidewater Association's extensive work to publicize its goals. According to his ideas, the association would not endorse any party, take a stand on public versus private ownership of power generation, or trade off support for other projects in return for support for a seaway. It would simply push for the building of a deep waterway from Lake Superior to the Atlantic. Seven Midwestern states joined in the early months of its existence, and the executive was drawn from this area, but within the year, the number of states had doubled and continued to grow until 21 states on the Great Lakes, on the Plains, and in the Rocky Mountains were members. This membership brought in a very large amount of money each year, but also contributed personnel and propaganda to the cause.

Craig was at the formative meeting of the corresponding Canadian organization. Detweiler had died, but many of those who had worked with him previously were there, as was Frank Keefer, now undersecretary of state for foreign affairs in the Borden government. Keefer was a lawyer, grandson of George Keefer, first president of the Welland Canal Company, and counsel and adviser to the wartime Food Board. The meeting chose Oscar Earnest Flemming, wealthy Conservative and the former mayor of Windsor, as its president. Though this organization was not financially supported by the same method as was the Great Lakes–St. Lawrence Tidewater Association, it used the same techniques to publicize the cause. One of the early supporters was Adam Beck. Although his main goal in life, now that he had greatly expanded the transmission system and defeated the private power interests, was to get more power out of Niagara Falls for the Ontario Hydro-Electric Power Commission, his secondary goal was to have the commission be given the right to develop the power capacity of the Long Sault Rapids. At the founding meeting, Beck advanced the argument that St. Lawrence power could pay for the construction of the seaway. Before his death in 1925, Beck had a falling out with the Deep Waterways and Power Association and wrote a stinging criticism of the group, which he saw as a mouthpiece for the Tidewater Association and that organization's desire solely for navigation improvements. During the time he supported it, however, he contributed much needed energy, for the Deep Waterways and Power Association did not have the same drive that Craig brought to the American organization.[17]

What followed was a torrent of newspaper and magazine articles and interviews, speeches, pamphlets, conferences, and letters to politicians, arguing the justice of the cause. The opponents of the two associations, who were many, responded in kind. Interested individuals not connected to either side, including engineers, economists, academics, and other "experts," felt the need to weigh in on what became within a few years a major public issue. Both groups used not only the popular press but also spoke to interested groups such as engineers, bankers, and shippers. It would be difficult today to examine the papers of a prominent politician of the post-war period without finding material relating to this propaganda war. Few academic libraries or archives lack a supply of the publications on the issue of the seaway. Even the Internet is a good location to examine the arguments of the two sides.

The opponents included the same interests in the United States that had opposed the project for a good portion of a generation, plus one or two new ones. Most of New York, as well as the New England states, were opposed because a seaway would draw business away from their ports. New York residents tended to support the Barge Canal or the railways, or did not want to see the St. Lawrence area have tax money spent on it instead of on their area. The Lakes-to-Gulf Deep Waterways Association, devoted to the Chicago Diversion–Mississippi route, was created in the period of the Boundary Waters Treaty. Gulf of Mexico states and some states in the Mississippi Valley could be counted on to oppose any east–west route, even though an unfavourable 1909 report by the Army Engineers had convinced the government that the Great Lakes to Gulf project was not viable. The Gulf states still hoped that the Chicago Drainage and Ship Canal–Illinois River–Mississippi route would bring shipping their way.

Along with New York, the most vigorous opponents were the east–west railways, which stood to lose lucrative business, and which heavily bankrolled the opposition. Railway unions added their voices to those of the other critics. A new opponent was private power interests in New York, which feared the possibility of publically owned power generation and transmission, as Adam Beck was aggressively pushing in Ontario. Opposition from private power interests also appeared in Quebec, which feared competition for export sales from Ontario. Some ship owners in both countries worried about competition from ocean-going ships.

In Canada, most of the people of the Prairie provinces (Alberta, Saskatchewan, and Manitoba) were counting on the Hudson Bay Railway, being built from Winnipeg to Churchill, but as yet only partially completed, to bring lower freight rates and a shorter distance to markets. The Province of Quebec was opposed because the business community had much to lose. Quebec City, and to a much greater extent Montreal, feared losing the economic benefits of the transshipment business. Private power interests that had been allowed to develop power generation on the rapids west of Montreal and on the abandoned Beauharnois Canal did not want to lose market share to Long Sault power. A large share of Quebec power was going to Alcoa at Massena. The Maritime provinces, especially New Brunswick and Nova Scotia, were suffering from a declining economy, partly due to the ending of the dependence on wooden sailing ships, which comprised the majority of the large Maritime merchant fleet, and partly due to conditions which emerged at the end of the war. Lumbering interests suffered from competition from timber coming from British Columbia by way of the newly opened Panama Canal. Fishing, mining, and manufacturing suffered from changes to import duties in Canada and the United States and from changes in freight rates, both of which made it difficult to compete in the markets of central Canada and to sell to the United States. The ports of Halifax and St. John could not compete with their American counterparts in New England and New York; though excellent ports from the standpoint of their size and shape, their facilities were outmoded. During the war, Britain had directed ships to both ports, but with the war over, shipping went elsewhere. The newly government-owned Canadian National Railways had a well-equipped port at Portland, Maine, which it advertised heavily. Feeling that the Canadian government did not care about their economic situation, the provinces opposed improvements to the St. Lawrence, a competitor for Atlantic shipping.[18]

The arguments used for and against a deep waterway were mostly ones that had been employed in previous attempts. On the pro-seaway side, proponents suggested that transportation costs for grain would drop considerably, that every port on the Great Lakes could become a seaport, generating wealth for the community, that the problems caused by a shortage of freight cars could be alleviated, that St. Lawrence power could pay for the seaway, and that new sources of power were necessary for industrial growth. There was no point in completing the enlarged Welland Canal, it was asserted, unless the St. Lawrence canals were also enlarged. It was pointed out that the Treaty of Washington of 1871 gave Americans the same rights to use the St. Lawrence as Canadians had, making it, in effect, an international waterway which should be developed. On the opposing side, questions were raised about the safety of large numbers of ships using the St. Lawrence River, where they were subject to fog and ice, about the enormous cost of building not just enlarged canals but also deeper channels, about whether the system would ever be able to pay its costs, and whether there would be sufficient return cargo to justify use of the canals by ocean-going ships. National and regional arguments were also used. Opponents in various parts of the United States and Canada questioned funding a project which would harm the interests of their particular part of the country. Canadian critics asked whether it was wise for Canada to fund a project which would be used more by American than Canadian shipping, and American foes warned that it was not wise for the United States to depend on a system which ran through a foreign country, especially in times of war. Critics on both sides of the border insisted that there was no foreseeable need for more power.[19]

What gave the pro-seaway forces a slight edge was the fact that they had the ear of government on both sides of the border at the beginning of the 1920s. Through senators from Wisconsin and Minnesota, the Tidewater Association had an amendment added to the Rivers and Harbors bill of 1919, asking the International Joint Commission to investigate what would be necessary to make the St. Lawrence west of Montreal useable by ocean-going ships, and to recommend co-operative steps for Canada and the United States to take to carry out the improvements. This was supported by President Woodrow Wilson. At the same time, Craig sought out his fellow Duluth citizen and ardent seaway supporter Julius Howland Barnes who, along with Horace Gardner, had been involved in the Midwestern delegation that prodded Secretary of State Bryan to enter negotiations with Canada after the 1913 congressional vote. Barnes had started as an office boy in a Duluth grain brokerage company and had rapidly risen to be its president. By 1915, the Barnes-Ames Company was reputed to be the largest grain exporter in the world. It had offices in Duluth and New York City, and controlled grain elevators and a shipping fleet. To this Barnes added numerous other businesses. During the First World War, Barnes' shipbuilding firm, McDougall-Duluth Shipbuilding (later Barnes-Duluth), produced cargo ships for the war effort. A multi-millionaire, Barnes was asked during the war to become president of the United States Food Administration Grain Corporation (1917–19), which managed distribution of wheat, flour, and other foodstuffs during the war. He also served as president of its successor, the U.S. Grain Corporation, until it dissolved in 1920. In this position, he became friends with Herbert Hoover, who was highly regarded by Americans for his work as a private citizen evacuating American citizens from Europe at the start of the war, organizing massive relief in occupied Belgium, and as head of the United States Food Administration after America entered the war. Hoover also served as chairman of the various subsidiary organizations, including the Grain Corporation. Following the war, Hoover served as head of the American Relief Administration in Europe, returning to the United States

NEMHC, S2386.

Herbert Hoover gives a banquet at the Commodore Hotel to thank Julius Barnes for his work with the Grain Corporation. The two remained close friends, and seaway supporters, for the rest of their lives.

in 1919 as a hero. Barnes approached him about support for the seaway and Hoover agreed to endorse the project. In the following presidential election, Hoover ran but, seeing he had little chance, threw his support behind Warren Harding. As a reward, Harding made him secretary of commerce, putting a supporter of the seaway in close proximity to the president. Hoover proved to be one of the most dynamic members of Harding's cabinet and the rather lethargic president tended to go along with Hoover's recommendations. Harding was soon supportive as Craig, Hoover, and Barnes planned how best to advance the project.[20]

The wording of the amendment to the 1919 River and Harbors bill and a note asking for Canadian approval were sent to the Canadian government through British diplomatic channels. Several of the prime minister's advisers urged him to agree to participation. Among them was Frank Keefer, Undersecretary of State for Foreign Affairs, who was active in the pro-seaway movement. It would be hard to ignore the request, Borden was told, given Canada's recent attempt to get the United States to co-operate in developing power generation at Long Sault. As grain production increased, Canada would soon see the kind of rail bottlenecks that the United States was experiencing unless something was done, and Canada did not have the resources to act alone. Besides, there was considerable pressure from private interests to develop power generation on the St. Lawrence, and they could not be denied indefinitely. With American involvement, these resources could be developed by government. An added benefit would be that the use of St. Lawrence power would remove the necessity to import large amounts of coal each year for industrial use. Weighing the benefits against the drawbacks, which included opposition from Quebec, from nationalists who were still suspicious of the United States, and from the hectoring Adam Beck, who constantly harped on the need to let the Ontario Hydro-Electric Power Commission develop the power capacity of the Long Sault, Borden decided to acquiesce in the American request. The two governments created a two-man engineering board and the IJC held hearings on the development issue. At the hearings, the usual arguments were used by representatives of both sides, but there were more presentations in favour than opposed to the scheme. This may had had something to do with the fact that Craig arranged for groups to testify in whichever cities hearings were held. What was clear from the hearings was that the most opposition in the United States came from New York State, and the most enthusiasm in Canada was to be found in Ontario. Regarding the issue of power development, Quebec companies strongly opposed development, fearing competition from public power. American companies supported public development of power generation, believing they would be given the power to distribute, in keeping with current practice.

The engineering board reported that a 25-foot channel with locks 30 feet deep was both practical and sensible, and that the development of power generation at Long Sault would facilitate navigation. The IJC decided that weight of evidence was in favour of development of the St. Lawrence and recommended that the Welland enlargement be completed and treated as part of the whole project.[21] Harding received the report early in 1922 and the State Department opened negotiations with Canada, preliminary to sending the matter back to Congress. Unfortunately for the seaway supporters, the Conservatives in Ottawa had lost power to the Liberals late in 1921. The new prime minister was William Lyon Mackenzie King, a man who built his long career as prime minister on taking strong action only when absolutely necessary and on pursuing policies which were designed to offend the smallest number of people. Only when fearful of losing substantial numbers of votes to more radical opponents would he endorse radical proposals. In 1922, he was one seat short of a majority and depended on a new western party, the National Progressive Party, to hold on to power. The Progressives were more interested in lower railway freight rates and lower import duties than in canals. Additionally, during the First World War most English-speaking Liberals had joined the Conservatives in a union government which introduced conscription and left Quebec, with a large Liberal majority, isolated. King had become leader of the Liberals by sticking with Wilfrid Laurier and the Quebec Liberals. He was not about to go against Quebec, whose premier, Louis-Alexandre Taschereau, was utterly opposed to the idea of a seaway and to Long Sault power. Sixty-five of King's 117 members were from Quebec, and much of the powerful Montreal business community was also antagonistic to the seaway. To make matters worse, a post-war recession had recently begun and the country had a large war debt. For a cautious man, large expenses would have to await better times. In addition, King could never forget that Wilfrid Laurier had been defeated in 1911 by trying to sign a treaty with the United States regarding free trade. In these circumstances, King indicated that the time was not right to undertake negotiations, without indicating when it might be more auspicious.[22]

While King ignored the issue and the pro and anti forces continued their war of words, Ontario elected a new government in 1923, headed by Conservative Howard Ferguson. The new premier decided that enlargement of the St. Lawrence canals would only interfere with the important task of developing power facilities. It was ironic that Ferguson lured Frank Keefer, strong supporter of the seaway, from federal politics to the Ontario government, after the federal government went Liberal in 1921, because Ferguson became a leading foe of federal development of the canals. It was public knowledge that Ontario was short of power. The mining areas of Northern Ontario were feeling the shortage, industrial expansion would soon come to a halt, and eastern Ontario was plagued by an inadequate supply for homes and businesses, and by frequent outages. In 1918, Adam Beck had made a submission during the IJC investigation of the Alcoa proposal for a submerged dam on the St. Lawrence, arguing in favour of having Ontario develop power in the area. When Ferguson came to power, the unrelenting Beck discussed St. Lawrence power with him. Though the tough-minded political infighter that was Ferguson was a match for Beck, and put limits on his activities at Hydro, he completely agreed about the need for St. Lawrence power. Beck then made a formal proposal for development in early 1924. Ferguson's cabinet approved the proposal for a dam at Morrisburg, which then had to go to the federal Department of Railways and Canals, which controlled navigation, for approval.

There were two problems with this proposal. For one, the Americans would have to be involved, as the dam would span the river in the International Section. More importantly in the immediate situation was the fact that the federal government laid claim to power developments on the Ottawa River and on the St. Lawrence, because of its control of navigation. The Canadian constitution was ambivalent on the issue of which jurisdiction had the right to control power development and King's government was adamant that it controlled both navigation and related power development. Beck led a delegation from 350 municipalities to Ottawa early in 1924 to try to persuade King of the need to allow Ontario to develop power generation on the St. Lawrence. King's reaction was to suggest to the American government that, in keeping with the American request for negotiations, an expanded engineering board be created to study further the issues involved in canal and power development. To Ontario, King announced that he could not deal with the application for a power dam at Morrisburg while the broader issues were being studied, effectively putting the matter on hold until some unspecified later date and putting off Ontario's request to develop power generation facilities.

To Ferguson, King's claim to jurisdiction raised the issue of whether the federal government would use revenues from power to pay for the seaway project, driving up the cost of power for Ontario taxpayers, or give out licences on the Ottawa and St. Lawrence rivers to private companies, in competition with public power. Either possibility was totally unacceptable.[23] The result was an unlikely alliance. In the late nineteenth century, Ontario and Quebec had co-operated in a successful struggle to gain more control over what the provinces could do, in what had been a highly centralized federal state. This alliance had been weakened in the 1890s by a campaign centred in Ontario to base Canada on an Anglo-Saxon, British culture. The partnership was then destroyed during the First World War by the division over conscription for overseas service, which left Quebec isolated politically, and by the debate over actions of the Ontario education ministry which issued Regulation 17 in 1912. This regulation largely limited teaching in French to grades one to three. Seeing the war as a British war, since Canada was not being attacked, caused French Canadians to be regarded as disloyal in a country where heavy recent British immigration and general pride in the British Empire created a climate of fervent pro-British feeling. Many French Canadians from Quebec saw Regulation 17 as a betrayal of the Quebec–Ontario partnership in the 1860s to create a country for both cultures. Ferguson, a fervent and proud believer in the unifying effect of having only one language outside Quebec, English, consistently defended the regulation. Ferguson also saw Quebec, with its private power companies and its surplus of power, as a direct competitor with Ontario in attracting new industries to the province.

Premier Taschereau of Quebec, though smarting from the insult of Regulation 17, came to recognize that the two provinces had a common foe. The premier felt that if the federal government developed the canals, ships would bypass Montreal and hurt all those businesses there which depended on the shipping industry. In addition, capital would flow to the United States, where the shipping would now go. If St. Lawrence power were developed by the federal government, at least half would go to the United States. Tachereau wanted power to be used in Quebec, to create more industry and thus more jobs for French Canadians. Ottawa River power, if developed by the two provinces instead of by the federal government, could be shared between the two. This would forestall any move by Ontario to develop the St. Lawrence and its canals, which would harm Montreal interests. Just as King stalled Ontario with the claim that nothing could be done while the engineering board studied the St. Lawrence, he stalled Quebec by promising to consult before signing any licences for the export of power. After meeting with Taschereau, Ferguson set up a commission to investigate the use of French in Ontario, and in 1927, Regulation 17 was replaced by a compromise system based on the commission's recommendations. Though the need for co-operation with Quebec was only one factor in the decision, it went a long way toward removing the barrier to co-operation. The hard-nosed Protestant lover of Canada's British heritage and the patrician Catholic descendant of a line of public servants allied themselves against the claims of Mackenzie King.[24]

Ontario was able to negotiate a deal with Quebec companies to buy power, ending the immediate need for St. Lawrence power. At an interprovincial conference in 1927, Ontario and Quebec won the support of the other provinces for the contention that Ottawa did not control water power on navigable rivers, only navigation. King had not done well in elections in 1925 and 1926, and this may have increased his willingness to compromise. He offered to send the issue to the Supreme Court for settlement and, after trying to have the federal government frame the questions, gave in to pressure from the two provinces and made a joint submission. The decision of the court in early 1929 was inconclusive. King suggested that a conference of the three leaders could sort the matter out, but three meetings failed to come up with a statement satisfactory to the two sides. Although King had earlier informed the Americans that Canada had studied the matter of the St. Lawrence and was ready to negotiate, subject to delicate negotiations with the two provinces, nothing could be done, as neither King nor the two premiers would budge.

Two steps were taken, however, that favoured the St. Lawrence. In 1927, after a public outcry against private power, the Parliamentary Committee on Railways and Canals rejected the application of the company that had applied to develop the Georgian Bay canal and the coincidental power development on the Ottawa, ending the federal government's attempt to control power development on the river, but leaving the issue of which level of government had jurisdiction over such development in the St. Lawrence undecided. An attempt in 1927 by the Department of State to get Canada to work with the United States in deepening the channel through the Thousand Islands as part of the total development of the St. Lawrence failed to get an agreement on the whole project. However, it did result in the two nations dredging the Thousand Islands section to 25 feet. When the Welland was finished in 1932, Upper Lakers were able to reach Ogdensburg and especially Prescott, where the federal government built a large grain terminal to facilitate transshipment, giving the Canadian port an advantage over the American one.[25]

Ontario did negotiate even more power from Quebec companies. One of these was the Beauharnois Light, Heat and Power Company. It was licensed by Taschereau's government to divert all St. Lawrence water not being used for other purposes in the Lake St. Louis to Lake St.

*Northway-Photomaps Inc./AO C30 ES12-374.*

Beauharnois powerhouse and channel with Seaway canal in the background, *circa* 1958. The powerhouse had been expanded twice (notice the different section of the roof), but the channel appears as it was excavated in the late 1920s.

Francis section west of Montreal through power facilities it would build on the South Shore. The Quebec government believed that this would bring electricity prices down in Montreal, where all electricity sales were controlled by one company. The company offered to build a combined power channel and canal with locks for ship traffic, and easily won swift approval from the federal government. This was a radical departure from current ideas regarding this section of the river, as other companies had been turned down and the IJC plan for the seaway called for a ship canal on the north shore and power development in the river. It turned out that investors in the company had a great deal of money to spread around, which they happily did among Liberal politicians in Ottawa. Several of the Liberal supporters of the project were tied closely to the men behind the Beauharnois scheme, though it was unclear how much influence the latter had on the decision. The ensuing scandal caused embarrassment for governments in Ottawa and in Quebec City, though no actual penalties. At the same time it provided an agreement to build a power channel deep enough for ocean-going ships, and to provide land on which to build a canal beside the channel, rather than the original offer of a canal. Completed in 1932, and enlarged twice, the Beauharnois powerhouse was so massive that special carts were developed to transport working employees from one part of the station to another. Charles P. Craig visited the site of the development in 1929 and was told by the head of the company, an engineer by the name of R.O. Sweezey, that the company would also build an enlarged Lachine Canal. Craig was ecstatic, and reported to the new president, Herbert Hoover, who felt that all that was left to do was to build the International Section of the seaway.

In fact, the seaway cause had been doing much better in the United States than in Canada. In the optimistic economy of the mid to late 1920s, contributions of member states poured in to Craig's organization, and he had tens of thousands of dollars to spend each year, spreading the word about the benefits of a seaway. He was also able to send financial support to the sister organization in Canada, which did not have adequate resources. In 1922, the headquarters were moved from Duluth to Washington, and Craig devoted all his time to the organization. Numerous "experts" were willing to speak on behalf of the cause in the United States, including a number of ex-governors and several senators. The Great Lakes–St. Lawrence Tidewater Association not only generated publicity material and attempted to get its message into the press, but also became the resource for people and organizations in the United States and in Canada seeking information on the seaway concept.[26] Warren Harding, who found the job of president daunting, and tended to leave much of the work to his cabinet, gave support to Hoover's enthusiasm for the seaway. With Harding's sudden death in 1923, his vice-president, Calvin Coolidge, took office. A great believer in a minimal role for the president, he, too, gave his cabinet a large measure of power, and supported Hoover's desire to have the seaway built. Coolidge once commented somewhat sarcastically about Hoover's influence: "That man has offered me unsolicited advice for the last six years, all of it bad."[27] From 1925 to 1929, Frank A. Kellogg of Minnesota, a long-time supporter of the Seaway, was secretary of state, giving the project another supporter close to the president. When Coolidge decided not to run for another term in 1928, Hoover put himself forward as a candidate and easily won the election. This was largely thanks to his handling of flood relief after serious flooding on the Mississippi in 1927, and the fact that his opponent, Al Smith, former governor of New York, was a Catholic at a time when Catholicism was regarded as an evil foreign influence in parts of the United States. At this point, the pro-seaway forces had an ardent supporter and good friend to Craig in the White House. When Hoover moved to negotiate a treaty with Canada, he appointed the current president of the Tidewater Association, Henry J. Allen, outspoken former governor of Kansas, as special adviser on the issue.

At the same time, the outlook for the route to New York deteriorated. In 1925 and 1926 a forceful attempt had been made by supporters of an all-American route to have the Great Lakes–Hudson River route developed, but an engineering report of a special board created to study the Great Lakes–Hudson route concluded that it was not financially viable. After this, an advisory committee to the American half of the Joint Board of Engineers, headed by then Secretary of Commerce Herbert Hoover and with Charles P. Craig as executive secretary, made up primarily of pro-deep water interests, strongly rejected the Hudson route. Both of these actions gave supporters of the St. Lawrence route a clear field, subject to Canadian approval.[28]

Behind Hoover was the Tidewater Association, and its tactics were almost entirely controlled by Craig. When association president Horace Gardner of Chicago asked that the issue of Chicago seeking the right to divert more water from Lake Michigan be downplayed, Craig refused, insisting that nothing annoyed the Canadians more than the diversion, which lowered the level of the Great Lakes and thus reduced the amount of cargo ships could carry. When Gardner insisted that, as president, he was in charge of what the association did, Craig had the executive committee remove him in 1926. The same fate awaited the next president, Governor W.L. Harding of Iowa, when he campaigned for Hoover in 1928–29, identifying himself as president of the association, in violation of its principle of neutrality in politics. In fact, Craig was right on both accounts. During the 1920s, both Canada and Ontario complained about the volume of water that Chicago was diverting. Canada insisted, against strong opposition from Secretary of Commerce Hoover, that the matter of the diversion be included in the Joint Engineering Board's study of the St. Lawrence.[29]

Nothing would hurry King. The American minister in Ottawa made a speech in 1927, assuring Canadians that power was secondary and that the United States only wanted a seaway, in order to get the contentious power issue shunted aside, but this speech caused denunciations of American interference in Canadian affairs. Craig had warned Tidewater Association members not to speak on Canadian matters out of concern that such actions would rekindle Canadian sensitivities, but the State Department did not report to Craig. Realizing that the speech had been a mistake, and after waiting some months to let agitation in Canada subside, Kellogg pleaded with the Canadian government to act while he was still secretary of state, warning that when he was gone there might be a move to build an all-American canal. When King responded that he was moving as fast as he could given internal opposition, the American minister in Ottawa attempted to play on Mackenzie King's fears. In his election campaign of 1928, Hoover had discussed aid to the farm sector, hit by low prices, and the possibility of higher tariffs to protect the same sector. King expressed concern to the minister that higher tariffs would offend Canadians and make it even more difficult to sign a treaty. The minister in turn warned King that something had to be done soon for the farmers, and that either cheaper transportation costs through the building of a Mohawk–Hudson River system or higher tariffs to protect American agriculture were the alternatives to building the St. Lawrence canals. King was concerned about the effect of increased tariffs, but was also concerned about the Liberals' position in Quebec.

Early in 1929, the question of trading action on the St. Lawrence in return for the American government holding the line on tariffs was raised by newspapers on both sides of the border, on the basis of an "anonymous" tip in Washington, giving the Conservative opposition the opportunity to attack the Liberals for thinking of giving in to American pressure. This made it even more difficult to begin negotiations on a treaty.[30]

King's continued insistence that he was moving as fast as he could was a reflection of his deeply political nature. He recognized that eastern and western Canada were indifferent to the seaway project, that Quebec was opposed, and that Ontario was primarily interested in power development. There was some pressure in Ontario for an all-Canadian route, and signing a treaty with the Americans would not be popular with its supporters.[31]

Just how adamant King was about federal control of power in the rivers is very difficult to assess, but certainly prolonging negotiations with Ontario and Quebec kept all other issues at bay. Only when the threat of a high protective tariff emerged was there pressure to settle the St. Lawrence question. As Ontario, Quebec, and Ottawa continued to negotiate in early 1930, after the Supreme Court's inconclusive decision, the pressure to trade tariff status quo for the development of the St. Lawrence disappeared. Congress responded to Hoover's call for a protective tariff by approving an even higher tariff than the president suggested. King was now boxed in. He had to call an election by 1931, but the deteriorating economic situation after the stock-market collapse made him decide to call one in 1930. He had hoped to keep both the tariff issue and the issue of St. Lawrence development out of the public eye until after the election, but now had to face both, plus the accusation that he had not done enough to deal with the economic slowdown. The leader of the Conservatives, R.B. Bennett, attacked King on all fronts. In the election campaign he claimed that by raising Canadian tariffs, Canadians would "blast a way into the markets that have been closed to you."[32] On the issue of the development of the St. Lawrence, Bennett played down the position that the party had adopted at a convention in 1927, that the seaway should be developed as an all-Canadian route, and played up the Liberal's lack of action on the American request to negotiate a treaty. Clearly the 1927 position was one of convenience, adopted to please the Conservatives' traditional power base, pro-British Protestants who were suspicious of the United States. One of its biggest supporters had been Howard Ferguson. Bennett, however, was prepared to play politics. A self-made millionaire with a strong sense of purpose and a large ego, he treated issues exactly the opposite way to how Mackenzie King operated. Where King held long, painful cabinet meetings to let his ministers come to some agreement on policy, Bennett often made policy without consulting his colleagues, or bullied them into agreeing with his point of view.[33]

King had underestimated the widespread concern about job losses, reductions in exports, and the clearly weakening economy. The tariff issue rather than the seaway question played the largest part in this, but Ferguson did engage in a public debate with King during the election as to which one of them was to blame for the delay in negotiating a treaty, arguing in his usual blunt terms that King was stalling and was intending to sell out Canadian sovereignty to the United States. King announced that he had had enough of Ferguson's stalling and would proceed with the Seaway as soon as the election was over.[34] When it was over, King could not show that he was a man of his word. The Conservatives won 136 seats out of 245. Internal politics in Canada had delayed consideration of a treaty for eight years, while an impatient American executive committee had regularly prodded Canada to begin negotiations on the basis of uniformly positive engineering reports. Now there was a prime minister committed to the seaway by his statements in the election. The replacement of the retiring Ferguson by the more pro-seaway George Henry in Ontario further smoothed the way. Only Premier Taschereau continued to insist adamantly that Quebec had to approve any prospective treaty. For a couple of years, while moving cautiously toward negotiating a treaty with the Americans, Bennett negotiated with him, but, not depending on Quebec as did King, and having Ontario onside, ultimately Bennett decided to ignore Taschereau. In July of 1932, Ottawa and Ontario signed an agreement giving Ontario the right to use water from the International Section to generate power while the federal government would build enlarged canals. The agreement divided the costs between Ottawa and Ontario, with Ontario paying the cost of power development and the majority of the cost of joint power-navigation facilities and Ottawa paying for the navigation aspects of the development.[35] In late March, when this agreement was nearing completion, Bennett informed Taschereau. The latter reacted angrily to the betrayal by Ontario, which would now have access to cheap power without having to rely on Quebec. Bennett answered politely, but his true feelings are to be found in an unsent draft letter. He angrily denied all Taschereau's charges and insisted that "no province in Canada will more greatly benefit from its [the Seaway's] development than the Province of Quebec".[36] After that, Bennett ignored Taschereau's repeated demands.

The inquiry into the Beauharnois power scandal, negotiating with Tachereau, and dealing with the onset of the worst of the Great Depression, including dealing with tariff issues, caused Bennett to be in no hurry to negotiate a treaty. The poor state of the economy and a series of vexing issues between the two nations, one of the most annoying being the continued draining of large quantities of water through the Chicago Diversion, were also factors. He met with Hoover in January of 1931, but, despite Hoover's repeated urgings that negotiations begin, they did not take place until late summer of 1931 and were not concluded until mid-1932. Ultimately his belief in the need for the seaway, and his belief, shared by Hoover, that the seaway would create badly needed jobs in the depth of the Depression, as well as his election promise, must have encouraged him to move ahead. According to Bennett, speaking in the House of Commons, the threat of an American canal linking to the Hudson and fed by the soon to be completed enlarged Welland Canal made negotiation of a treaty critical.[37]

During the negotiations, Hoover had problems as well, problems which made it difficult to conclude a treaty in 1930–31. In the early 1920s, power companies controlled by General Electric, Alcoa, the Du Pont family, the family of Andrew Mellon, secretary of the treasury, and the law firm of Henry Stimson, who would succeed Frank Kellogg as secretary of state, tried to get the right to develop power in the St. Lawrence from the State of New York. The then governor, later presidential candidate, Alfred E. Smith, an advocate of publically owned power generation facilities, out-manoeuvred them at the time. After Smith was succeeded by Franklin Delano Roosevelt, another Democrat, the various private power interests amalgamated in the Niagara Hudson Corporation, which also included J.P. Morgan, a massive and very powerful company. Roosevelt, like Smith, fought for public power against a vigorous public relations campaign waged by the power interests. Equally adept at public relations, Roosevelt capitalized on the Depression in explaining to the people that public power would be inexpensive power. Concerned citizens all over the state, and especially in the St. Lawrence area, organized to pressure the politicians. The leading figure in Massena, merchant E.B. Crosby, who was to play a key role in the struggle for 20 years, was in charge of a committee that pressured local state and federal senators. With the help of Republican congressman Bertrand Snell, who represented the St. Lawrence area of New York, and public opinion, Roosevelt in turn pressured the Republican State Legislature to create a public body, the Power Authority of the State of New York, the first of its kind in the United States, to develop St. Lawrence power. In fending off the Niagara–Hudson interests, Roosevelt had to concede that the power might be distributed by private interests, which meant the Niagara Hudson Corporation.[38]

This development posed a problem for Hoover, who like King believed that the federal government had the right to control development of power in the St. Lawrence, and was a strong believer in private rather than public power. He also worked closely with Mellon and Stimson. Negotiations between the two governments went on from 1931 until the treaty with Canada was signed in July of 1932, without any resolution. When New York asked to be included in the negotiations with Canada, Hoover insisted that the issue of who would build and who would operate the power dam was a domestic issue, not an international one, and refused Roosevelt's request. The two men had a broader disagreement than the question of which level of government would develop power in the St. Lawrence. Hoover wanted the seaway built, and had no particular interest in power development. Roosevelt's main concern was power; the canal was secondary. When Charles Craig approached Roosevelt about the latter's seeming lack of concern about how quickly the canals would be built, Roosevelt indicated that he favoured a Lake Ontario–Hudson canal, which had considerable support in New York State, as much as he favoured the St. Lawrence. The situation became even more confused as Roosevelt was, as expected by many, chosen as the Democratic candidate for president in 1932.[39]

With Ontario now supporting the deep waterway, or seaway concept, as it was becoming known, Quebec's and New York's objections being ignored, and the two national leaders ready to proceed, the project had the best chance of success that it had enjoyed since it was first brought forward in the 1890s. Relations between the two countries were also the best that they had been. Canada had traditionally been seen as a subsidiary of Britain, since the latter country legally controlled Canada's foreign policy. In the First World War, Britain's declaration of war had automatically committed Canada. Since that time, Canada had arranged to negotiate a fisheries treaty with the United States in 1923 without Britain's participation. Then, in 1926 (unofficially) and in 1931 (officially) Canada had been given the freedom to look after its own foreign relations. Negotiations were not difficult, since both sides based their case on the recommendations of their engineering boards. The treaty was favourable to Canada, though neither nation received all that it wanted. The terms reflected a political settlement, taking into account the divergence of opinion between the two engineering boards, and the insistence of the Canadian government on certain points. The waterway from the head of the Great Lakes to Montreal was to be 27 feet rather than 25 feet as the United States engineers suggested. The Canadians also got their way with regard to the number of power dams. The United States had concluded that a one-stage (i.e. one power dam) arrangement, with a dam at Barnhart Island, west of Cornwall, would be sufficient and less expensive. The Canadian plan for a two-stage arrangement was accepted. The second dam, at Crysler's Island several miles west of Barnhart, as well as generating power for both countries, would control the level of Lake Ontario, an issue which was of particular concern to Montreal, and would ensure that there would be less flooding in Ontario than the single stage plan would cause. Since there was a much larger riverfront population in this part of Ontario than in the comparable portion of New York, this was another important issue for the Canadians.

The United States would be responsible for finishing all of the channels from Lake Superior to Lake Erie and the Canadians for the work between the International Section and Montreal. Canada was credited with the cost of the completed Welland Canal enlargement, but not for work done previously in Quebec. In consequence of this, the United States agreed to pay most of the cost of construction on the Canadian side of the International Section except for the canal and lock, though Canadian firms were to do most of the work. Two canals would be needed to get ships through this section, one on the Canadian side, by the upper dam, and one on the American, by the lower dam. The two countries agreed that the development of the seaway should be supervised by a joint commission made up of five members from each country, rather than by the governments. Each country would get half of the power, but how that power was to be transmitted was very intentionally left out of the treaty.

A substantial portion of the draft treaty dealt with water diversion, at the insistence of the Canadian government. The Chicago Diversion was limited in the volume of water that could be drawn from the Great Lakes. It could only divert the amount of water allowed by a decision in 1930 of the Supreme Court of the United States resulting from a complaint from several Great Lakes states. The required reduction had to be done by the end of 1938. Any emergency increase would have to be approved by an arbitration panel if Canada objected. The United States and Canada were required to construct "compensation works" in the Niagara and St. Clair rivers, to restore the level of the western lakes which was reduced as a result of the Chicago Diversion and by power generation at Niagara. To head off objections from Chicago, the State of Illinois, and some of the Mississippi Valley states, Hoover had General Douglas MacArthur, Army Chief of Staff, explain that Army engineering studies showed that the treaty allowed enough water to be diverted to the Mississippi to meet all the needs of Chicago and the states to the south.[40]

Just days before the draft treaty was signed, Roosevelt telegraphed Hoover offering to meet to settle the issue of how much New York would have to pay as its portion of the cost of developing the St. Lawrence, even if he had to interrupt an imminent cruise. He reaffirmed his claim that New York owned the rights to power, explained that he wanted to distribute that power through a state agency, and, in the opening salvo of the election campaign of 1932, stated that "I am deeply interested in the immediate construction of the deep water way as well as in the development of abundant and cheap power." This telegram was published, putting Roosevelt clearly on the side of inexpensive public power and the seaway project. An annoyed Hoover telegraphed back that it would not be necessary to interrupt the cruise, and that such questions would have to be settled by Congress after the treaty was ratified. He concluded: "Having ardently advocated for over 10 years the great work of completing this shipway from Duluth and Chicago to the sea, I am glad to know it will meet with your support." While Hoover had put Roosevelt in his place, and shown his long-standing support for the seaway, Roosevelt had made the point that he stood for both the seaway and inexpensive power for the people. How committed the presidential candidate was to the seaway project, given his lack of enthusiasm only a year before, Roosevelt never revealed, but he was now publically in favour of it.[41]

When the signing of the treaty by the two countries was made public a few days after it was done, there were celebrations and expressions of excitement at what was to come in many places on the Great Lakes. Massena, the modest little town that had hoped to grow on the basis of the power to be generated in the nearby river had waited almost 30 years while engineers poked and prodded the riverbed over and over again. Now its citizens and those from surrounding areas had a grand outdoor party to celebrate. In what could not be called a case of false modesty, Bertrand Snell announced to all those assembled that he was "the only man in public life today in the State of New York who has supported this project from the very beginning." At the other end of the Great Lakes, the City of Duluth declared a public holiday. Other cities dreamed of the wealth that would come when they became seaports on the Great Lakes. Perhaps the only communities that were not in a mood to celebrate were the towns and villages along the Ontario shore that would be flooded. The sentence that had hung over their heads as long as the prospect of prosperity had tantalized the southern shore of the river seemed about to be applied.[42]

Unfortunately for Hoover, and for the expectant communities, the negotiations among the various governments had taken too long. The session of Congress had ended and the presidential campaign was underway. Hoover would have to wait until after the election to see his long-held dream become a reality. When the election was over, however, the reality was a very different one for the president. While Hoover had been seen for almost 15 years as a champion of humanitarian causes, in the depth of the Depression his fundamental belief in the ability of the individual human spirit came across to the voters as an inability or unwillingness to use the full power of government to assist the unemployed and the desperate. Instead of being identified with aid, he was identified with Hoovervilles, those tarpaper shantytowns that had grown up on the outskirts of cities and towns, home to the dispossessed. It was Roosevelt, the recent convert to the seaway, who had to take the treaty to Congress. Before he left office, Hoover accepted the new reality of a Democratic regime in Albany and another in Washington, and with the approval of the Senate, allowed Army engineers and the Power Authority of New York to work out an arrangement for the joint development of power and navigation on the St. Lawrence. The agreement was essentially the same as that between Ontario and Ottawa, except that it did not make a decision as to whether New York would build the power works or the federal government would, and bill the state. The treaty was passed by the Senate Committee on Foreign Relations, but there was not time to take it to Congress before Hoover's term expired, and Roosevelt took his revenge for Hoover's earlier refusal to meet with Roosevelt, refusing to meet with Hoover to discuss measures to deal with the economy. The agreement between Washington and Albany passed the House but failed in the Senate on the basis that the treaty should be considered first.[43]

A concerned Charles Craig tried to reach the new president. The Great Lakes–Tidewater Association, despite trying to remain neutral in politics, had a strong Republican flavour, and had worked closely with Republican regimes for over a decade, since it was created. Allen, the president of the Tidewater Association, had worked closely with Hoover on the president's two campaigns. Dealing with a Democratic executive would be difficult. Using intermediaries, Craig urged Roosevelt to push the treaty through the Senate. In addition, he organized a conference of Midwestern governors at which 16 governors signed a letter urging the president to take action on the treaty. Eight Midwestern senators urged the president to put the treaty forward as a part of the economic stimulus package that formed the centrepiece of his "100 days" program. Roosevelt seemed in no hurry, though. He did not include the treaty in the economic stimulus package, despite the fact that it would have produced thousands of jobs. When asked by reporters if he would put the treaty forward, his answers were evasive, despite his support during the election campaign. Few understood that Roosevelt often danced from one measure to another in his career, favouring first one and then the other, without any outward logic. In this case, he probably thought that there was not enough support to get the treaty through with ease and he did not want to overuse the goodwill that new presidents generally received. In a clever move, he left it to one of the senators backing the bill to persuade the Senate leaders to put the treaty before the Senate, which the senator could not do.[44]

It was not until various government economic studies were done of the seaway, at the request of the Senate, that the president submitted the treaty in January of 1934. By this time opponents had had sufficient time to mobilize a very strong campaign against it. All the usual foes were involved, plus new ones. The strongest opponents were the railways and the interconnected financial and private power interests, which never let up in their opposition, the east coast port states and the Gulf states, and much of New York State. Lake carriers who felt their smaller ships would not be able to compete with ocean-going vessels still objected. In addition, the Depression caused some supporters to switch sides and other interests to join the opposition. The eastern railways had worked on the western ones, which had been onside with the Tidewater Association. Now they were opposed, at a time when business was depressed. Chicago, which had provided some of the leading figures in the pro-seaway movement, had always been quite divided because the business community included railway interests as well as shipping companies. It now came out in opposition, as did the Plains states, which again looked to the Chicago River–Mississippi route as a potential salvation. One huge reentry to the ranks of the opponents was the railway unions. The railways played on their fears of unemployment, and in the harsh economic climate of the mid-1930s, it did not take much to win their support. Hundreds of thousands of workers could be found, even in the Midwestern states, who previously had been behind the deep waterway movement for much of a generation. Coal interests, which had always been minor players among the opponents, stepped up their efforts, worried that increased electrical power in Canada meant less reliance on coal for power, at a time when sales were already down. Wherever possible, business interests opposed to the concept put economic pressure on businesses that favoured the seaway.[45]

At the same time, the Great Lakes–Tidewater Association, one of the strongest lobbying organizations ever created in the United States, was in serious trouble. Aside from defections such as Illinois and Missouri, it suffered from a massive drop in financial support. In the hard times of the 1930s, contributions to the association were a luxury. Charles Craig opened a Chicago office to counter bad feelings over inclusion of the Chicago Diversion in the treaty, but was forced to close it for lack of funds. In the critical weeks before the treaty came to a vote, only volunteer help from northern New York and the Midwest kept the Washington office functioning.[46] For his part, the president verbally twisted a few senators' arms, generally without success, and sent a message to the Senate, urging ratification. In the message, Roosevelt explained that the channels were clear as far as the International Section of the St. Lawrence and the Beauharnois locks would be easy to construct. Only the International Section needed just two locks, which Canada could build herself if the United States did not take part in the project, leaving Canada totally in charge of the St. Lawrence. He also insisted that the seaway would not

… injure the railroads or throw their employees out of work, that it will not in any way interfere with the proper use of the Mississippi River or the Missouri River for navigation. Let us be wholly frank in saying that it is better economics to send grain or other raw materials from our Northwest to Europe via the Great Lakes and St. Lawrence than it is to send them around three sides of a square — via Texas ports or the Mississippi, thence through the Gulf of Mexico, and thence from the southern end of the North Atlantic to its northern end…. I am satisfied that the treaty contains adequate provision for the needs of the Chicago Drainage District and for navigation between Lake Michigan and the Mississippi River…. This river is a source of incomparably cheap power located in proximity to a great industrial and rural market and within transmission distance of millions of domestic customers.

He pointed out that New York had already passed legislation to make it possible to work with the federal government to distribute power as a part of a "national policy." Should the United States not want to do this, Canada could develop "a huge block of power at the other rapids." In both navigation and power, it was better to co-operate with Canada than to let Canada go it alone.[47]

This was a good argument to offer to a disinterested individual, but was hardly likely to win over those senators who were opposed to the treaty. Roosevelt chose not to put his prestige as president on the line to win over those who were sitting on the fence, and Democratic leaders in the Senate had little to say in what was a very protracted debate. Clearly, Roosevelt did not feel this was a critical issue, though he quipped to the press that the seaway would be built at some point "just as sure as God made little green apples."[48] The vote was 46 for and 42 against. Even several Democrats voted against it. Since a treaty needed a two-thirds majority to pass, the measure failed. The best chance in over 30 years to build the seaway was gone.

It is easy in retrospect to criticize the opponents as standing in the way of inevitable progress, as Roosevelt did at the time. Certainly the railways and related interests had worked long and hard to ensure that their profits were protected. However, with millions either unemployed or struggling to earn enough to live on and many businesses on a shaky financial footing, states, businesses, and unions can hardly be faulted for defending their interests against what they believed was a venture that would either make matters worse for them or, as with the Gulf and Plains states, deprive them of the opportunity to improve their economic condition. Had political conditions in both countries been as favourable as in the more prosperous 1920s, the treaty might well have had a better reception in the Senate.

Conditions were to worsen for those who promoted the seaway concept, but Roosevelt remained committed to it. In fact, the defeat of the treaty may have made him more determined to get approval for the project, in a treaty which would be his, not Hoover's. His comment, when asked if the treaty would go back to the Senate again, was, "It will go back in some form. How soon, I don't know, but it will go back as soon as it can."[49] The failure of the treaty left Charles Craig open to attack for not doing enough. A rival organization, the Great Lakes Harbors Association, created to fight the Chicago Diversion, but, since it won its case in the Supreme Court in 1930, devoted to promoting the seaway, was critical of Craig's leadership. He tried to bring the two organizations together, with William George Bruce of Milwaukee, a member of the executive of both organizations, as executive director, but a bitter struggle broke out between the Democrat-dominated Harbors Association and the Republican-dominated Tidewater Association. During the struggle, funding for the Tidewater Association shrank even further and Craig not only had to forego his salary, but also had to put his own money into the operations of the organization. In late 1935, he made another of his many speaking tours. Before he was to speak in Tacoma, Washington, the tireless worker for the Seaway, had a heart attack, and two days later was dead at age 77. More than any other member, he had built the Great Lakes–Tidewater Association into the powerful organization that it had been, and had been responsible for its program of applying political pressure through state governments as well as local organizations. He had twisted arms to ensure senior members did not step outside the bounds that he had created for the organization's activities and had personally logged many thousands of miles delivering the seaway message to audiences around the country. His campaign to get the seaway message into print over and over again had been most effective. His death, at a time when the association was already struggling, was a serious setback to the organization. Although he was a wealthy man when he took on the job, his exertions on behalf of the cause left him almost penniless when he died.[50]

The weakened Tidewater Association struggled on, becoming just one of a number of pro-seaway organizations in a new National Seaway Council, formed at a Seaway Conference in Detroit, in March of 1936. Warned that the conference might attack the government for inaction, Roosevelt dispatched the chairman of the Senate Foreign Relations Committee to the conference, to tell the attendees that the president was working on a new treaty proposal which would deal with both power and navigation. Instead of criticizing the administration, the delegates praised it. Included in the Seaway Council were the Great Lakes Harbors Association, the Great Lakes–Tidewater Association, the National Grange, and several regional organizations — the Ohio Lake Ports Association, the West Michigan Legislative Council, the Minnesota Arrowhead Association, the Northern New York Federation of Chambers of Commerce, the Champlain Valley Council, and the Power Authority of the State of New York. At the head of it was John C. Beukema, secretary of the Muskegon, Michigan, Chamber of Commerce, who had been active locally in support of the seaway, in Michigan, since the early 1920s. Known as a clever negotiator, Beukema was skilled at reconciling quarreling factions. E.B. Cosby of Massena, New York, vice-president of the Northern Federation of Chambers of Commerce, became vice-president and, at a later time, treasurer. The Seaway Council did its best to press for action from the administration, but it was hampered by lack of funds, resulting from the shrinking support, even in the Midwest and in the Great Lakes area, where the Depression continued to take its toll. It did hire Raymond G. Carroll, a well-connected journalist, to be the council's lobbyist in Washington. Reputedly he came recommended by Roosevelt, for whom he had done some work. Carroll was effective at his job, but did not have Craig's outgoing character. He refused to deal with seaway supporters beyond Beukema and a few others, and made no attempt to give speeches or travel to other areas of the country outside Washington. The Tidewater Association, no longer the central

*Muskegon Area Chamber of Commerce.*

John C. Beukema, *circa* 1950s.

organization in the struggle, was even poorer than the council. In 1939 it was forced to close its office in Washington and move back to the Midwest where it had begun. It had gone home to die. In Canada, the always weak Deep Waterways and Power Association, deprived of the financial support of its American counterpart, simply faded away.[51]

Support for the seaway also declined in Canada. When asked to accept revisions to the treaty that might make it more acceptable to the Senate, Bennett refused, fearing a backlash if he appeared to be giving in to the Americans. In 1934, Ontario elected a new premier. George Henry, the steady, competent Conservative lost out to the flamboyant Mitchell "Mitch" Hepburn. Governments everywhere were susceptible to charges that they did not do enough to relieve the Depression. Hepburn was a federal backbencher, one of those interchangeable members of Parliament in Mackenzie King's government in the 1920s. Unhappy in that role, he had impressed Ontario Liberals with a lively speech and had essentially been handed the provincial leadership in 1930. He was able, with his folksy, humorous style, to label the Conservatives as uncaring fat cats, driving around in their black limousines while others suffered, and to win a sizeable majority in the election. While his early months pleased people, as he sold off the limousines and unilaterally cancelled the power contracts with Quebec power companies, which Ontario did not need in the hard times of the 1930s, he proved to be more than some people had expected. Erratic, impetuous, and vicious with those he saw as opponents, he drove his federal counterparts to distraction. He had no use for the St. Lawrence power project, as he believed Ontario did not need more power, and did not want to pay for any national project. As he said, Ontario would not be the "milch cow" for the rest of Canada.[52]

In 1935, his leader, Mackenzie King, was re-elected. Bennett, like Hoover, was blamed for the Depression suffering. Labelled as a hard-hearted millionaire because of his belief that everyone who really tried to get a job would, he was memorialized in Bennettburgs, the Canadian equivalent of Hoovervilles and in Bennett Buggies, cars pulled by horses because farmers could not afford repairs or gas. The Conservatives won only 39 of 245 seats nationally, while the Liberals won 171. Hepburn had no use for King, whom he felt was a weak, overly cautious leader. This feeling only intensified his opposition to federal undertakings. In Quebec, a new leader, Maurice Duplessis, leading a new party, the Union Nationale, was elected in 1936. Like his predecessor, Taschereau, Duplessis defended Quebec business interests that would suffer if the seaway were completed, but more than Taschereau he used defence of French Canadians in Quebec against incursions by the federal government as a way to win and to keep support. The cautious King was not about to move on the seaway with the two most populous provinces in Canada opposed to the idea of a seaway and power development. He also was concerned for the health of the two national railroads and the livelihood of railway workers, both already suffering from the Depression.[53]

After the 1935 Canadian election, with the New Deal experiment well underway, Roosevelt met with King in Washington to discuss revisions to the treaty, as he had discussed with Bennett, but then decided to seek a more comprehensive agreement regarding the Great Lakes. He requested the American minister in Ottawa to try for a new treaty. In February of 1937, Roosevelt sent a draft treaty to King. Aside from containing much of the content of the Hoover draft, it gave Hepburn much of what he wanted, the right to divert water from rivers flowing into Hudson and James Bay into Lake Superior. It also granted to New York the right to divert more water at Niagara to generate electricity. In addition, to satisfy Hepburn's concern about excess power, it would allow Ontario to delay the power generation portion of the Seaway project until power was needed. Hepburn had wanted these concessions separate from any discussion of the seaway. Relations between the premier and the prime minister had been deteriorating, and Hepburn flatly rejected the scheme, although it gave him all that he wanted. When King's government rejected diversion of a river into Lake Superior, and rejected Ontario's proposed sale of surplus power to the United States — power resulting from a possible settlement of the court case initiated by Quebec over Hepburn's cancellation of power contracts with Quebec — Hepburn attacked King. The two refusals, he claimed, were the result of a Roosevelt–King plot to force Ontario to accept the treaty. Both Hepburn and King released their correspondence, showing that King was not plotting; Roosevelt, however, was. He decided to link what Hepburn wanted to the seaway, by refusing to allow the diversion or to accept Ontario's surplus power.

Conditions changed dramatically in 1939–40. Premier Duplessis, entering a provincial election, once again used the federal whipping-boy to generate support. He claimed that the federal government was dragging Quebec into a foreign war which had nothing to do with Canada. This was his only mistake in a political career that lasted till his death in 1959. The federal cabinet ministers from Quebec, led by King's Quebec lieutenant,

Ernest Lapointe, as tough-minded a politician as was Duplessis, campaigned for the Liberal opposition in the province. These men explained to the voters that the war was a just one, and if Quebec felt otherwise, it should vote Union Nationale, and all the federal ministers would resign, leaving Quebec without representation in cabinet. The provincial Liberals, who worked closely with their federal counterparts, were elected, and Quebec's opposition to the seaway was blunted. The Liberal premier, Godbout, agreed to support the project under certain conditions, and the Quebec government bought out the Beauharnois power facility. Hepburn ran a provincial election campaign which was critical of King's lack of adequate preparation for war, but, because of a strong sense of patriotism, Hepburn soon let King know that he would do whatever necessary to help the war effort, including supporting the seaway. Besides, Ontario was likely to need more power to pursue the wartime industrial production.

Roosevelt asked for a delay until after the American presidential election in 1940, but he allocated one million dollars of defence funds for engineering studies, since the Canadian and American governments agreed that the seaway project would begin in the coming spring. When he was told that this appeared to be an election ploy, Roosevelt dispatched the army engineers to begin work near Massena. After the election, the engineers disappeared, and a new version of the treaty was negotiated. To sidestep opposition in Congress this was to be an agreement between the two countries, not a treaty. As such, it would require only a simple majority in the Senate. The Ontario Hydro-Electric Power Commission was worried about wartime power shortages, so the agreement allowed Canada to build the power facilities first, if necessary. As in the previous draft, Ontario would be able to exceed the amount of water diverted at Niagara set by the 1909 Boundary Waters Treaty, and to divert water into Lake Superior. The United States would pay a larger portion of the cost of construction in the International Section to compensate for previous Canadian expenditures on the Welland. The biggest differences from the previous draft treaty included the provision that there was to be only one power dam, the American preference. A second dam near Iroquois would only be used to control water levels in Lake Ontario. This was a compromise proposal made by the Canadians in 1939. The canal around this second dam would be on the American side rather than on the

Canadian, as had been specified in the 1932 draft treaty. The agreement was signed in March of 1941. Quebec and Ontario signed agreements regarding their parts in the construction of the seaway and Hepburn agreed to Ontario's share of the cost. Hepburn gave as much enthusiasm to the project as he had in opposition to it. He endorsed it in a radio broadcast heard in both countries. King made public a statement from Roosevelt explaining that the seaway was part of United States efforts to assist in the defence of the British Commonwealth. Everything seemed to be in place in Canada to assure the success of the agreement. King, being the cautious man that he was, waited for the United States Senate to pass the agreement before he took it to Parliament.[54]

Pro- and anti-seaway forces once again gathered for the new battle. Hepburn's radio address from Oswego, where he had arrived with 400 members of the Detroit Chamber of Commerce, led by the governor of Michigan, was one of the first new efforts on behalf of the seaway. The Seaway Council, still weakened by the Depression, managed to collect enough money from its remaining supporters, Michigan, Wisconsin, and the St. Lawrence area of New York, to publish a pamphlet aimed at railway workers in the Midwest. Edward J. Noble, wealthy chairman of the board of Life Savers Corporation and originally from the St. Lawrence Valley, put together a Seaway for Defense Committee, composed of influential men from business, labour, philanthropy, and the media. Among them was David Sarnoff of the Radio Corporation of America and Julius Barnes, still very active in the movement that he had joined before the First World War. Barnes, always available to speak on behalf of the seaway concept, had begun putting his own money into the movement as other sources dried up. Several Midwestern cities created seaway committees and the Superior, Wisconsin, Chamber of Commerce contacted every chamber and farm organization in nine Midwestern states urging them to pressure congress. Carroll, Beukema, and others, such as Edward Crosby from Massena, lobbied hard in Washington. Even the Chicago city council came onside in another demonstration of its uncertainty as to what project would best serve its interests.[55]

On the opposition side, all of the former foes, except for Chicago, united in the National St. Lawrence Project Conference, and chose a very capable and well-connected Washington lawyer to speak for them. Their chief argument was that the project was not needed for defence, which was Roosevelt's main argument for the agreement. In a message sent to a pro-seaway conference in Detroit in December of 1940, the president attempted to prove that both the seaway and power were necessary for defence, that the critics were wrong, and that the project would also provide major beneficial results for the country after the war:

> The United States needs the St. Lawrence Seaway for defense. The United States needs this great landlocked sea as a secure haven in which it will be able to build ships in order to protect our trade and our shores.
>
> The United States needs, tremendously needs, the power project which will form a link in the Seaway in the International Section of the St. Lawrence River to produce aluminum and more aluminum for the airplane program which will assure command of the air.
>
> Selfish interests will tell you that I am cloaking this great project in national defense in order to gain an objective which has always been dear to me. But I tell you that it has always been dear to me because I recognized its vital importance to the people in peace and in war.... What would we not give today, we who are responsible for the country's supreme defense effort, if the great St. Lawrence turbines were already in place, steadily revolving under the drive of St. Lawrence waters now running to waste, producing every hour of the day 1,000,000 horsepower to supply our essential defense industries.... Seacoast shipyards are already overtaxed with uncompleted construction. Shipyards on the Great Lakes, with access to the ocean, yet close to the sources of supply of labor, raw materials, further removed from possible attack, may be a vital factor in successful defense of this continent. They will build the ships which will bring back commerce to the harbors of the Atlantic coast.
>
> Opponents of the project have pointed out that it takes four years to build this seaway. They know, but

fail to mention, that it takes at least that long to build a battleship. They also know that this project will cost the United States less than three battleships and that the power project will be self liquidating.... The need for the seaway is coupled with an increasing demand for power. Already our defence industries in the Northeast have been required to import huge blocks of electric power from Canada. They are asking greater imports and Canada can agree to supply this power only temporarily. A new source of cheap power for national defense must be developed immediately.

Along with its benefits to national defense, this project will contribute to the peace-time welfare of a multitude of laborers, small businessmen, home owners, and farmers.... It means more industries, both defense and domestic, thriving on the cheapest power in history. It means more comfort in the homes of many cities and rural areas. It means more work for the ordinary citizens in shipyards, factories, and other transportation services connecting the centre of this continent with this great highway to and from our national and international markets ...

Roosevelt also repeated the 1936 claim that the seaway would not hurt the Gulf or the Atlantic ports.[56] This was a far superior argument for the project than Roosevelt had used in 1936, appealing as it did not only to those concerned about defence, but also those who wanted jobs and inexpensive power. It tried to put the critics in the National St. Lawrence Project Conference on the defensive.

Everywhere, the backers of the project expected success. The leadership of the Seaway Council felt they had a good chance of succeeding. On both sides of the St. Lawrence, planning was underway for the building of the seaway. In the Ontario government, for instance, the ministers responsible for various departments that would have to deal with issues that would arise because of the flooding: compensation of municipalities for flooding, the flooding of highways and provincial lands, the need to look after cemeteries and other entities which had no boards to look after them, and any unexpected issues, were warned to make preparations. The local government of the areas to be flooded, though they recognized that the project would be of benefit, asked to be consulted about the very issues raised within the Ontario government. The Canadian government hired an engineer to study the effects of the anticipated flooding and to recommend actions to alleviate the consequences. In August of 1941 the American government even began construction of a government-owned aluminum plant at Massena, in anticipation of the new power. In the fall, the government was forced to build a transmission line to the south, to draw power from steam power plants. Despite the optimism of many, the project passed a committee of the House of Representatives in August, but got no farther. The opposition had been effective, with its claims that the war would be over before the seaway project could be completed in 1947, and that it would consume needed resources of manpower, materials, and machinery. Even when completed, the seaway could easily be crippled by one bomb. The usual claims that Canada would control the entrance and could cut off access at any time, and the appeals to regional prejudice also carried great weight. Large amounts of money were available from railway and power interests to publicize the anti-seaway cause.[57]

Even the attack on Pearl Harbor did not improve the chances for the agreement, and Roosevelt had to concede that it would not pass. Faced with the many needs of a country at war, congressional leaders decided not to push projects such as the seaway. Refusing to give up, in June of 1942 the president decided to try to build the seaway as a war measure, an area over which he had been given control. Unfortunately, because it was estimated that the project would take three to four years and it would require vital war materials, the War Department recommended against it and Roosevelt gave up. There would be no seaway while he was president. The United States did build a naval base in the interior of the continent, Sampson Naval Base, on the deep Lake Seneca, in the Finger Lakes of New York. Safe from attack, one of the largest naval bases in the United States at 2,535 acres trained sailors throughout the war, some 411,429 of them. One of the easiest ways of sending them out to the ocean was by way of the New York Barge Canal. However, ships could not be built in the Finger Lakes and sent to sea the way it had been proposed for the

Great Lakes. Small corvettes, which would fit in the existing canals, were built on the Canadian side of the Great Lakes and a small number of ships were built on the American side, and sent with difficulty down the Illinois–Mississippi River system and the Minnesota–Mississippi River system. Only about 2 percent of the 60 to 70 million tons of ships built in the United States had been built on the Great Lakes, and 60 percent of the raw materials to build all of the ships had come from the Great Lakes area. Most of the heavy materials such as iron had to be transported by rail when they could have been sent by ship if the seaway had been built. After extensive hearings on the proposed agreement with Canada, and recognizing that war was a very distinct possibility, the House Public Works Committee had concluded in August of 1941 that the power was required for defence purposes, that shipbuilding on the Great Lakes of both civilian and military vessels was necessary for defence, and that the Lakes would provide an additional safe transportation corridor for United States shipping, and would reduce congestion on other routes. The subsequent failure of the agreement meant that what could have been a tremendous asset for the Allied cause went to waste.[58]

With the recognition early in 1942 that the agreement would not pass, the forces backing the seaway fell apart. What had held them together and given them a last surge of energy after the hard times of the Depression years was the belief that they were on the verge of victory. During Roosevelt's attempt to get the agreement through Congress, he had on several occasions let it be known that he was willing to postpone the building of canals, and concentrate on his long-time goal of power development. Although the pro-seaway forces put pressure on him to build the combined project, his attempts helped to accentuate the existing divisions in the movement. Once it was clear that the agreement would fail, the various factions began to quarrel. There were those who wanted power, those who wanted navigation, and those who wanted both. Among power supporters there were those who wanted publicly owned power and those who wanted private power. Without a common goal, they began to quarrel, and to blame each other for the failure. The nadir came with the sudden death of Carroll in December of 1943. Carroll had lived beyond his means when he no longer was free to work as a journalist, and especially after his salary was cut because of the lack of funding for pro-seaway forces, but he gave little consideration to his financial welfare and concentrated on the cause. Like Craig, he died broke.[59]

Within a few months of his death, the remaining disorganized pro-seaway forces were faced with the need to support another attempt to build the seaway. The seaway was often mentioned by public bodies as a project that would assist the economy in the transition from war to peace. After discussions with the Power Authority of the State of New York, Senator George Aiken of Vermont, a state which along with New York was running short of power, put forward a bill to build the seaway as a post-war reconstruction measure. Those who were still with the movement organized a National St. Lawrence Association and persuaded Julius Barnes to be president. Barnes was now 70 years old, but still as committed to the cause as he had been 30 years before. He had begun to divest himself of some of his business interests, but still had his shipping line and several other businesses, and was quite a wealthy man. Though not an organizer, he was a skillful strategist, was well connected in business and government, having served as president of the United States Chamber of Commerce from 1921–24 and as chairman from 1929–31, was known as a kind man who had nothing bad to say about anyone, and had a very evident enthusiasm, which tended to influence others. As one friend put it, he was "as infectious as smallpox." Beukema was still involved, as was Crosby from Massena. Dr. N.R. Danielian was put in charge of the Washington office and would soon become vice-president of the organization. His full name was Noobar Retheos Danielian, but he only used his initials. A brilliant economist who graduated from Harvard and taught there from 1929 to 1935, he had written, among other works on corporate control of public services, a muckraking account of the rise of AT&T, published in 1939, that is still used today. A frequent contributor of articles on the economy, he had published an influential article in September of 1929, a month before the stock market crash, on the theory of consumer credit as a possible cause of recession. He had most recently worked for the United States Department of Commerce, from 1939 to 1943. While with the department he had directed a seven-volume study, published in 1941, of the commercial, navigational, power generation, and defence potential of the St. Lawrence. All of these qualifications, plus an acute political sense, made him the ideal organizer. The new organization

Julius H. Barnes, *circa* 1937.

hoped to raise money from business for the first time, because of Barnes' connections, but wound up raising money largely from Barnes, who backed up his fervent belief in the seaway with his personal fortune.[60]

Though Roosevelt gave his endorsement to Senator Aiken's bill, once again he did not go all out for it, probably because it had little chance of success. Even its sponsor recognized that it would fail, as strong opposition in the Commerce Committee held the bill up for well over a year. The war ended with no seaway, or commitment to one. The United States Congress had provided for the construction of a huge lock at the Soo, the MacArthur Lock, to facilitate the transportation of iron ore for the war effort, but large ships still could not get in or out through the St. Lawrence. By the end of the war, both New York State and Ontario were short of power, as the Ontario Hydro-Electric Power Commission had predicted for the province.[61]

Between 1945 and 1948, supporters of the navigation-power project in Congress tried twice to get approval for the scheme. The first time the session concluded without a vote being held. The second attempt saw supporters advocating tolls on the system to pay for the construction, in order to blunt criticism from the railways about subsidized transportation, and to win over senators who were worried about the large cost of the project. No longer was there the idea that power generation would pay for navigation, an idea Canada had already abandoned with the 1932 agreement between Bennett and George Henry of Ontario. In answer to a query from the Department of State, Canada agreed to the idea of tolls on the seaway. After a long debate, during which the railroads insisted that the tolls could not cover both the capital and operating costs, the second attempt was sent back to the Senate Foreign Relations Committee. Ironically, its powerful chairman, Arthur Vandenberg of Michigan, one of the few prominent Republicans to support Roosevelt's efforts to get the 1932 treaty approved, had been behind the tolls idea. Some hoped that sending it back would kill the attempt to get the resolution through. Julius Barnes actually encouraged this move in the hope it would allow the resolution to come back to Congress at a later date, when conditions might be more favourable. Unfortunately for supporters of the bill, this did not prove to be the case. As in the earlier attempt, testimony at committee hearings brought out all the old arguments, plus a few about defence, and the bill went nowhere.[62]

Both Ontario and New York were increasingly short of power and increasingly frustrated by the lack of action by their national governments. Governor Thomas E. Dewey of New York, a supporter of both power and navigation, but principally of power, consulted the head of the American section of the International Joint Commission and concluded that Ontario and New York had the right to built the power generation facilities under the Boundary Waters Treaty of 1909, subject to the approval of Ottawa and Washington. Dewey approached the premier of Ontario, George Drew, in 1948, and had an enthusiastic response. The Power Commission and the Power Authority quickly worked out the details, and each of them, together with the State government, applied to the appropriate federal departments for permission to proceed with an application to the IJC. The Ontario application caused consternation in Ottawa, which felt that approving a power-only scheme would make it more difficult to get approval from Washington for the navigation features and more expensive to build the canals as separate structures. It would also jeopardize the tens of millions of dollars in credits that had been offered in two previous proposals as compensation for money spent on the Welland. The Canadian government stalled, informing the head of the Ontario Hydro-Electric Power Commission that it should not file an application with the International Joint Commission unless the United States agreed, because it would violate the 1941 agreement. The matter was then discussed at the American Federal Power Commission. Supporters and opponents of the seaway were divided over this idea, with Midwestern advocates believing the scheme would make it more difficult to get support for the canals and power-hungry eastern states favouring Dewey's idea. Some power interests began to change sides when Dewey indicated that he would allow private distribution of the power if rates were kept reasonable.[63]

President Truman, who was soon to face Dewey in the 1948 presidential race, came out strongly against the project, insisting that the combined canal-power dam version must be built. As a senator, he had been one of the very few Mississippi Valley representatives who voted in December of 1944 for the Aiken's bill to build the seaway.[64] Though considered a nonentity as vice-president because Roosevelt almost totally ignored him and gave him no role, and a weak president when he took over after Roosevelt's sudden death in 1945, he confounded many of his critics. They saw him as a local politician from Missouri, who had been brought to national prominence by a corrupt state political machine and who had neither the intelligence nor the talent to be president. Though it took him some time to learn how to deal with Congress, and he did make the odd misstep, Truman proved to be tough, smart, and capable of developing and managing a complex national agenda.[65] From the beginning he was strongly committed to the seaway and to federal control of power distribution. It was not until two years later, in 1950, that the Federal Power Commission turned down New York's application and recommended that the United States and Canada build the combined project. Dewey was furious and attempted to go ahead anyway, but the FPC refused to hear a second application. Truman was now unencumbered in trying to persuade Congress to endorse the seaway.

Each year he included in his annual economic report, in his budget message, and in various other messages to Congress a request that Congress begin work on the seaway. In 1950, though, he also asked congressional leaders to the White House to urge them to approve it. There was additional evidence to back up his plea in 1950, consisting of iron ore. In his annual budget message to Congress on January 9, which followed a more general plea in his State of the Union address of January 4, Truman delivered the unequivocal statement: "I repeat most emphatically my previous recommendation for approval of the St. Lawrence waterway and power project. Authorization of the seaway, with its related power facilities, is a matter of urgency for our peacetime industry and our national security. In particular, each succeeding year reduces further our domestic reserves of iron ore, and increases correspondingly the importance of the seaway as a means of economical access to proven ore deposits in Quebec and Labrador." Truman tried one more time to impress Congress with the need for action when, in May, he transmitted a new treaty with Canada regarding the diversion of further water at Niagara for the purpose of generating power. Acknowledging that the new power would be a help to both countries, he added, "The St. Lawrence project is urgently needed, of course, not only as a source of additional power, but equally as an additional avenue of transportation. Considered from the power point alone, however, both the Niagara and St. Lawrence sources are badly needed. The national security and economic growth of this part of the country require that additional sources of low cost power should be rapidly developed". Even more than the two previous presidents, he kept up the pressure on Congress.[66]

Experts had noted as early as the 1930s that the iron ore in the great Mesabi Range in Minnesota was running out and steel companies had begun looking for major new sources. During the Second World War the Hollinger Company of Canada began looking for ore in Quebec and Labrador. Soon it was joined by the M.A. Hanna Company of Cleveland, which had large holdings of iron ore around Lake Superior, and later by five American steel companies. The combined company, known as the Iron Ore Company of Canada, discovered extremely large concentrations of high-grade ore close to the surface in the rocky, forbidding Labrador wilderness. A railway was gradually built to the St. Lawrence, but the logical market, the steel mills of the Great Lakes, would not be easy to reach because of the bottleneck caused by the 14-foot canals. Truman stressed both the defence benefits and the ease of access to new ore deposits of the projected seaway. The former issue became more important with the beginning of the Korean War later in the year.[67]

The pro-seaway forces also saw that they could take advantage of the iron ore situation. They worked on George M. Humphrey, president of the M.A. Hanna Company, through Joseph Winterbotham of the Champlain Valley Council, who was his close friend, and gradually Humphrey and the steel companies that were part of the Iron Ore Company came around. This caused a split in the Lake Carriers Association, as the steel companies owned some of the ships, and it brought Cleveland to the pro-seaway side. Other steel-producing areas began to waver. In Canada, opinion was changing, as well. The Hudson Bay Railway had not been a boon to the West as had been expected, and both British Columbia and Lake Superior ports looked more attractive. In Ontario, with extensive industrial development during the war, and a rapid population increase after it, there was a desperate need for more power. Quebec also needed more power because of industrial growth and it saw the advantage of a seaway now that Labrador ore would provide economic benefits for the province, and Premier Duplessis promised to be neutral, since he would not approve of any federal government project. Montreal business interests were beginning to think that the loss of transshipment business would be offset by increased traffic on the St. Lawrence.[68]

Barnes and his associates were once more energized by the possibility of mustering enough support to finally get the 1941 agreement through Congress. The National St. Lawrence Association was in bad financial shape, and the executive had been losing members. It had never been able to recover from the desertion of member states and the loss of both business and farm support as hard times and relentless pressure from the railways, the railway unions, and interests allied with the railways had made many wary of giving support. In May of 1949 the always optimistic Barnes and Dr. Danielian called a meeting of interested parties in Washington to launch a new organization, the Great Lakes–St. Lawrence Association. It was smaller than previous groups, but had essentially the same people running it as the National St. Lawrence Association. The New York Power Authority was not there, as it had abandoned the idea of joint power–navigation development, and many regional bodies that had previously been part of the movement were not represented. Most of the money that the association raised was from business sources now, principally the iron ore and steel companies. Barnes was to be honorary chairman, and the chairman of the executive committee was Lewis Castle, a Duluth bank president who was brought in by Barnes. Danielian, who became executive vice-president, provided much of the energy in the organization. He kept the Canadian government apprised of developments in Congress and advised that pressure be applied to the United States. He was also a skillful practitioner of the art of arranging the trading of votes in Congress, a policy which his predecessor Craig had always disliked.[69]

Members of the association met with Truman to urge him to do more. He replied that he supported them but could not even control his senator from Missouri. Julius Barnes urged action and said that the association would deliver 50,000 votes in northern New York if he put the seaway across. Truman smiled and said, "I didn't do badly there last time, did I?" It was very clear despite the light-hearted comment, that the president was very knowledgeable about, and very committed to, the seaway. Proponents of the seaway in Congress also continued to press for action under Truman. In April of 1950, the House Committee on Public Works held hearings on a seaway resolution brought forward by a Michigan representative. Appearing before the committee, Major General Lewis A. Pick, Chief of Army Engineers, spoke in favour of a 30-foot channel in endorsing the project. In Senate hearings three years before, when the extent of the Labrador find was not yet known, he had shocked the Foreign Relations Committee by insisting that the United States was in danger of becoming a secondary nation without the seaway to bring Labrador ore to the steel mills of the Midwest. At the House hearings in

1950, George Humphreys of M.A. Hanna warned that, with the Mesabi Range nearing depletion, except for low-grade ore, the best source for the future would be Labrador. Without a seaway, the cost of transportation by other routes would be excessive. What was also needed, he explained, was a secure source of iron ore in times of national emergency, and other major sources were too far away. Other witnesses emphasized the needs of national defence, in essence echoing Humphrey. After hearing all the witnesses, the committee terminated its discussions of the resolution, claiming that the information about the iron ore made it important that the Senate deal with the seaway issue. This move echoed House action in 1949, when the House had also refused to deal with several seaway bills because the Senate showed no interest in the subject.[70]

At the beginning of 1951, Truman again slipped references to the seaway project and the power project into both his Annual Economic Report and his Annual Budget Message, though not to the same extent as in the previous year.[71] However, later in January, he went further and invited congressional leaders to the White House to ask them to support the power–navigation project. Shortly thereafter, a bill authorizing the approval of the 1941 agreement was introduced into the Senate, but the head of the Foreign Relations Committee refused to hold hearings on it, effectively derailing it. In the House shortly thereafter, a number of resolutions were presented in support of co-operation with Canada to build the navigation and power facilities. The Public Works Committee, which dealt with all of the resolutions at the same time, was divided on aspects such as whether government or private enterprise should construct the works, whether the federal or state government should develop power, and how the power should be distributed, by a public agency or private power companies. Hearings which lasted most of two months brought out railway and coal interests and representative of eastern and Gulf states. Strong arguments were put forward saying that the project was not needed for defence, but rather the money should be put into the Korean War, that there was sufficient iron ore available, that iron ore could easily be delivered from Labrador to the steel mills, and that, if built, the seaway would be easily attacked and crippled by the enemy in time of war.

After the hearings were over, members of the committee toured the St. Lawrence area, and then voted to table all of the resolutions. The

National St. Lawrence Project, the amalgamation of most anti-seaway forces, with its substantial available funding, had filled the hearings with witnesses and the corridors outside with lobbyists. This activity, and the opposition of most Republicans on the committee, doomed the attempt.[72]

Canada was growing impatient. It was a different Canada than the one which had waited for the United States to act first each time the seaway had been proposed, and with a different leader. It was not just that almost all Canadian opposition to the idea of a seaway had subsided. During the Second World War, Canada had changed from a country which wanted to avoid international commitments, into one in which almost 10 percent of the population served in the war. By the end of the war it had the third largest navy among the Allies in terms of numbers of ships, and the fourth largest air force. A large percentage of the ships and planes were built in Canada. The country emerged from the war with a new sense of confidence. The economy was doing well by the early 1950s, partly based on new industrial activity generated by the war, partly based on American investment encouraged by a continuation of the Defense Production Agreement signed by Roosevelt and King in April of 1941, and partly based on heavy post-war immigration from Europe. The cautious Mackenzie King had retired in 1948 and been replaced by his secretary of state for external affairs, Louis St. Laurent. A Quebec City lawyer who had joined the government at King's request in 1941 to become the leader of the important Quebec wing of the Liberal Party after the death of Ernest Lapointe, St. Laurent was a man of strong opinions and considerable energy. He and his under-secretary, Lester Pearson, had convinced the cautious King to embrace the United Nations when it was formed in 1946, despite King's dislike of foreign commitments. White haired and always impeccably dressed, the 68-year-old (in 1950) St. Laurent cultivated the public image of kindly "Uncle Louis" given to him by the press, but his strong convictions made him a formidable figure in determining government policy.[73]

In January of 1949, St. Laurent had told the House of Commons that, if the 1941 agreement was not approved by Congress, the government would have to seriously consider pursuing power separately. Shortly thereafter, St. Laurent reiterated this point in private discussions with Truman. During the election campaign of 1949, St. Laurent repeatedly told Canadians that, while the government favoured the 1941 scheme, it had advised the Americans that delay would force it to support the agreement made between Ontario and New York for power development alone. In 1950 he requested support for Truman's efforts to get the agreement through Congress at a speech given at St. Lawrence University in Canton, New York, again mentioning that Canada was getting impatient. Immediately after, Lester Pearson, now secretary of state for external affairs, in introducing the Niagara Diversion Treaty for parliamentary approval, stated that this measure was not to be seen as a substitute for the St. Lawrence project, but as a needed complement to it. Just as Truman repeatedly pushed Congress to approve the 1941 agreement, the Canadian government repeatedly warned the Americans that time for action on the seaway had arrived.[74]

In the summer of 1950, St. Laurent had a change of heart. He discussed the issue with his minister of transport, Lionel Chevrier, whose riding embraced Chevrier's home in Cornwall, Ontario, the start of the International Section. St. Laurent suggested that it was time to prepare opinion on both sides of the border for the possibility of an all-Canadian seaway and Chevrier was the man to do it. In September the minister made a speech at Cornwall, underlining the urgency to obtain additional power, and stating clearly that, if Congress did not act on the seaway, Canada would. The reaction was predictable; in Canada, national pride, and in both countries, disbelief. After so many years of letting the United States take the lead, and being a country with a population only one-tenth of that of the United States, it is not surprising that few believed the statement on either side of the border. When asked if he spoke for the government, Chevrier explained that this was his personal opinion, further encouraging the idea that this was not a serious idea. In the following year Chevrier gave more speeches on the same topic, and others in the government echoed the idea. In late 1951 the Canadian cabinet formally adopted the policy, and St. Laurent went to Washington to tell Truman and seek his support. Truman wanted a joint development but agreed to support the Canadian proposal if Congress still refused to approve joint development.[75]

While opinion about the Canadian government's plan continued to be skeptical, the cabinet moved ahead with plans. Two bills were introduced in the Commons in December of 1951. One incorporated an agreement reached with Ontario to allow the province to build the power facilities in the International Section in conjunction with an unnamed American entity, and the second, the St. Lawrence Seaway Authority Act, created a Crown corporation to expropriate land and build the navigation aspects of the project, in concert with the United States, or separately. Chevrier explained the benefits in terms of a large amount of power, cheaper transportation for western Canadian grain, and the development of mines in Quebec and Labrador. The bills were passed unanimously. Chevrier attributed this to the realization on the part of some members from areas such as the Atlantic provinces that would not obtain any obvious benefits, that the seaway would benefit all of Canada, and to a feeling that the United States should be shown that Canada was able to stand on its own.[76]

Truman responded in January of 1952 with three messages to Congress over a period of two weeks. He inserted a substantial warning in his annual Budget Report and a small reminder in his annual Economic Report. Finally, he sent a special message to Congress urging it to pass the 1941 agreement. In the messages, he reiterated past arguments and added a warning about Canada building the seaway. In his Budget Report he stated that the hydroelectric power was enough justification for beginning the project immediately, but that the looming iron ore shortage "makes it a strategic necessity." Canada had announced that it would build the seaway alone, and Truman would support that, but it would mean that Canada controlled the waterway. Truman felt that the project was "so vital [to the interests of the United States] that we should join as a full partner in its construction and operation." In his special message he gave a brief history of the negotiations over the previous 50 years, pointing out that every president and every prime minister since the First World War had supported the concept, that the various public bodies and numerous senators had endorsed the seaway as a national security necessity, to which had recently been added the need for a secure supply of iron ore, and that the seaway was also necessary for peacetime commerce. He stated that the seaway cost would be self-liquidating through tolls, but that Canada could decide the level of tolls, and might even go on charging them after the seaway cost was paid. He acknowledged the opposition of the railroads and port interests, but suggested that they were short-sighted. He indicated that the American government had agreed to support the required application to the International Joint Commission, under the provisions of the Boundary Treaty of 1909, but hoped that Congress would vote for the 1941 agreement immediately so that both countries could participate in the project:

> The project is of great importance to our national security and our economic growth. The materials and manpower to build it are available. The funds invested in it will be repaid with interest. And in return for making a self-liquidating investment, we will gain the inestimable advantage of having an equal voice in the management and control of this key link in our national transportation system. I do not see how anyone can fail to recognize the common sense of participating in this project.... It seems inconceivable to me, now that this project is on the eve of accomplishment, that the Congress should allow any local or special interest to divest our country of its rightful place in the joint development of the St. Lawrence River in the interest of all the people of the United States.[77]

In February of 1952, one year after the head of the Senate Foreign Relations Committee had refused to hold hearings on the resolution to pass the 1941 agreement, and obviously responding to the president's message, the members of the committee revolted against their chairman and insisted on hearings. The same arguments were brought out again. Supporters insisted that for reasons of defence, employment, the maintenance of previous co-operation with Canada, and the fixing of tolls, it was best to have American participation. Opponents suggested that the Canadians might not really be going to build the seaway on their own, but if they did, the United States would have a waterway without cost to them. Canada would not deny use to the Americans, given past practice, and even if the United States participated, there was no guarantee that the Canadians would allow access to portion of the St. Lawrence totally within Canada. They even paid Canada a compliment, pointing out that Canada regularly had budget surpluses, while the United States was the opposite, making it logical that Canada should pay. The committee reported the resolution to the full Senate without a recommendation, given the strong arguments on both sides. The measure was not considered for some time, and then a similar debate to the one in the committee took place, also bringing in some of Truman's arguments. In the end, neither side was persuasive enough, and the matter was referred back to the Foreign Relations Committee for a recommendation. Watching the Senate send back the seaway resolution was Dr. Danielian. With substantial contributions from steel companies, and the support of Ford, General Motors, and the United Auto Workers Union, the Great Lakes–St. Lawrence Association had mounted a vigorous lobbying campaign of the type not seen since the days of Charles Craig. The defeat was devastating for Danielian, who believed that he had influenced enough senators. The association executive then decided that it, like Truman, had to accept "second best" and back the Canadian plan, though Danielian informed the Canadian government that another attempt might well be made in the next Congress to endorse the 1941 agreement, and that the association would back such a move, if the Canadian plan was not well advanced by January of 1953.[78]

By now the summer of 1952 had arrived, and the presidential election campaign, in which Truman had decided not to take part, was beginning. There was no time left for another attempt in Congress by supporters of the seaway. Like his predecessors Roosevelt and Hoover, Truman would not be able to celebrate victory in what he believed should have been solely a matter of common sense. He had done everything he could, year after year, to stress defence, iron ore, and additional power as reasons to build the seaway, but the opposition was still too great, even after the steel companies had begun to switch sides. No president was more persistent and more committed to the cause.[79]

The Truman administration indicated to the International Joint Commission that it supported the Canadian initiative to build the project itself and the IJC gave its approval, under certain conditions. There would be a Joint Board of Engineers to approve the plans for power development, and a Board of Control to maintain lake levels and to protect residents along waterways from water damage. As weeks turned into months, the Canadian government became increasingly frustrated, as power was becoming a critical issue. In November of 1952, Canada sent a note indicating that it felt the 1941 agreement was no longer up for discussion. The same month, the new president, Dwight D. Eisenhower, was elected.[80]

A joke of the period claimed that the (thrice elected) Roosevelt had proved that a man could be president as often as he wanted, that Truman had proved that any man could president, and Eisenhower proved that the country did not need a president. The media loved to show him playing golf, as if it was his favourite pastime. Historians have argued ever since whether or not he cared that much about political issues. It appears, though, that Eisenhower was a president with a philosophy somewhat like that of Calvin Coolidge. He saw the role of Congress as creating legislation, rather than the president taking a leading role. Whenever he felt strongly on an issue, however, he would try to influence Congress. The question at the start of his term was whether the president cared about the seaway issue. As Army Chief of Staff, Eisenhower had endorsed the seaway as a needed defence project. During the election campaign he had endorsed the scheme in public and in private correspondence. It came as a shock then when he became non-committal after the election. Like Roosevelt after his election, Eisenhower wanted to study the political pros and cons of putting the presidential stamp of approval on the concept. Because of the fight in the FPC and the courts, he had the time. In the meantime, supporters of the seaway were not giving up. In December of 1952, Representative George Dondero of Michigan asked the State Department to tell Canada that he would introduce a bill in the House calling for American participation as soon as Congress convened, and Senator Alexander Wiley of Wisconsin indicated shortly thereafter that he would introduce a similar bill in the Senate. In his parting words to Congress on the subject, President Truman said in his Budget Message on January 9, 1953, that the administration had co-operated in arranging for Canada to build the seaway: "I regard these alternative arrangements as much less desirable than the 1941 agreement ..." He felt that, if details could be worked out in Congress for joint construction, "there might still be an opportunity for American participation," and he urged Congress to make these arrangements.[81]

The Canadian government, which had been ready to act since 1950, and had been working on construction plans for some time, was ever more frustrated with the American delays. Public opinion in Canada was in favour of a quick beginning for the project and, with the wait, pressure for an all-Canadian canal system was increasing. Ontario was desperate for more power to meet the needs of its rapidly expanding population and industry. Nothing could be done, though, until the issue of which American entity would build the American half of the power project was settled by the FPC. The Department of External Relation let it be known that Canada would consider American participation once the critical issue of appointing an entity to work with the Ontario Hydro-Electric Power Commission on power development had been settled. Given the possible action by the United States Congress, the cabinet had to discuss a further delay while the American Congress decided if the country would ask to participate in the seaway project. While there was much to recommend that the Canadians tell the United States that it was too late to participate, the need for continued goodwill between the countries dictated that the Canadian government give the Americans a chance to change their minds. The government made it clear, however, that it would not tolerate "any serious delays."[82]

Eisenhower discussed the seaway with his cabinet. He believed firmly that the members should have a strong role in creating the administration's policies. Among the most vocal members on the subject was Secretary of the Treasury George Humphrey, late of the M.A. Hanna Company and Iron Ore Company of Canada. When the various departments were polled as to their opinions of the project, however, Humphrey declared a conflict of interest over his support and refused to comment, but every department, including his, indicated its support, or had done so previously. Opponents of the project, including the Chicago Chamber of Commerce, warned Eisenhower about the high cost of using the proposed seaway, and Eisenhower had always been concerned about the cost of construction. It was not until the Wiley bill had been discussed in sub-committee and the hearings had been adjourned because of the lack of support from the administration that Eisenhower indicated that the United States would participate in the seaway project. He had been advised by the National Security Council, he said at a press conference on April 23, 1953, that the seaway would be useful for defence. While he could not say yet what the extent of American participation would be, he supported the policy of letting the New York Power Authority participate in building the power facilities. In fact, both the NSC and the Permanent Joint Board on Defence had endorsed the seaway project.[83]

He then threw his support behind the Wiley bill in the Senate, which was really just a statement the United States would participate, not a treaty or an agreement. Danielian and Harry C. Brockel, secretary of the Great Lakes–St. Lawrence Association, who, as director of the Milwaukee Port Authority, had joined the Seaway Council through the Great Lakes Harbors Association during the Second World War, worked closely with Senator Wiley in crafting the bill. Not only did it provide for tolls to pay for the cost of the navigation-related construction, but also it omitted any reference to deepening of the channels west of the Welland Canal, thus cutting the cost of the seaway project in order to win over those senators who opposed the project on the basis of cost. The costs were further reduced when Ontario, which was becoming ever more desperate for additional power, offered, with the support of the New York Power Authority, to pay all of the costs common to both power and navigation. While the American government objected, on the basis that such a policy would raise the cost of electricity unfairly, Canada prevailed, and most of the common costs were paid for by the two power bodies. Meanwhile, the Federal Power Commission, which had been reluctant to act, given Truman's opposition to New York control of power generation and then Eisenhower's earlier refusal to commit his administration to the St. Lawrence project, arranged, in May of 1953, for New York to become the American agency to work with the Ontario Hydro-Electric Power Commission. The seaway opponents then appealed to the Power Commission and then to the courts, to stop the project.

While matters dragged on in Congress and the Power Commission, Canadian cabinet ministers gave speeches in the United States urging quick American action. They suggested that the Americans could build their own canals in the International Section later on if they wanted to, but they should not hold up progress on the Canadian canals and the power project. One of those ministers was Lionel Chevrier, who would remain a champion of an all-Canadian set of canals on the St. Lawrence.[84]

The Great Lakes–St. Lawrence Association now had very substantial financial resources to put behind the effort to get the bills through Congress, thanks to its support by steel interests. There was lots of time to use for this purpose since Congress adjourned after the Senate Foreign Relations Committee endorsed the bill. It was not until January of 1954 that it finally came to a vote in the Senate. By that time the association and Eisenhower had been working for some months to convince recalcitrant senators and members of the House, especially of the House Public Works Committee, which had to pass the bill before sending it to the House, to support the bill. Promises were made and arms were twisted in the Senate. Eisenhower appointed a staff member whose job it was to determine what actions would persuade various opposing senators and members of the House to change their votes. The U.S. Administration then followed up on his advice. On January 14, shortly before the vote, Eisenhower's representative wrote to President Eisenhower's special assistant, Sherman Adams, "We are so badly in need of four additional votes that we are about ready to offer arms, legs, 'Passamaquoddies' [development of power in Maine], or whatever else is necessary to get them." Senator Ferguson of Michigan asked Admiral Arthur Radford to endorse the proposed seaway as essential to national security, which he did. As the past commander of Allied forces in Europe, Eisenhower's insistence that the seaway was needed for defence carried considerable weight with some opponents in the Senate. One senator who changed his mind without being offered a trade-off or having his arm twisted was the young John F. Kennedy of Massachusetts, a state, he said, that had not voted for a seaway proposal for 20 years. Kennedy indicated that the "Seaway [would] work an economic hardship on Massachusetts," but that his analysis of trade patterns indicated that neither the port of Boston nor rail lines going out of the city would be appreciably hurt by the waterway. While there would be no appreciable benefit to Massachusetts either, it was time New England "recognize[d] the legitimate needs and aspirations of other sections ..." He believed, he said, that regional self-protection meant that other regions, in turn, opposed projects that would benefit New England.[85]

On January 20, 1954, the Senate passed the bill. Public opinion in the United States began to shift in the aftermath of the vote. The powerful

International Brotherhood of Locomotive Engineers, for instance, dropped its 25-year opposition to the project. General Motors had already abandoned its sometimes neutral, sometimes antagonistic attitude toward the Seaway and had joined Ford, Chrysler, the smaller automotive companies, and the United Autoworkers in using their networks to push the project. In the House, which had never had the opportunity to debate the various previous attempts to build a seaway, the opponents managed to hold up the bill in the House Rules Committee for two months after the Wiley bill passed the Senate. When debate finally took place in the House, the same sectional interests advanced similar arguments to those in the Senate. In an echo of Kennedy's approach, Representative Otto E. Passman from Louisiana, president of the Mississippi Valley Flood Control Association, who had supported Louisiana port interests against the seaway for seven years, announced that he had read the various reports on the St. Lawrence after being challenged by representatives from the Midwest as to his stand, and now supported the bill. Having received large sums of money in the past to deal with flooding, and soon to ask for more, he asked rhetorically how Louisiana could ignore the problems of other parts of the country and expect those parts to vote more aid to the Gulf states. On May 6, the Dondero bill, similar to the Wiley bill in its design, passed the House with a large majority. The following day, in a voice vote, the Senate accepted the slightly different Dondero version. The act also created a new agency, the St. Lawrence Seaway Development Corporation, responsible to the president, to oversee seaway construction on the American side.[86]

There would be a joint seaway after more than 50 years. Logic says that it should have been built much sooner. It had the support of every president since Taft, and of every prime minister since Borden. It made no sense to build canals and clear channels as far as Prescott/Ogdensburg but not to complete the remainder of the waterway. Additional power had been needed in Ontario and in the northeastern states for nearly 20 years. But logic does not always overcome regional and economic forces in a federal state.

There were celebrations across the northern states when the bill passed. Even in places such as New York, Chicago, and Ogdensburg, which had been opposed sometimes or always, there were those who celebrated the victory. The *New York Times*, until recently an opponent, claimed that there would be new opportunities for "every food grower and machine maker between the Alleghenies and the Rocky mountains." In Canada there were celebrations too, although some still felt that Canada should build the seaway itself. The members of the Great Lakes–St. Lawrence Association celebrated, too, in Washington, along with their allies, such as senators Wiley and Aiken, men from the steel companies, from Ford Motors, and from the Army Corps of Engineers, which expected to build the American portion of the seaway. Probably the happiest man there was Julius Barnes, who had worked selflessly for the cause for 40 years.[87] He had always kept a positive attitude toward the cause. As one admirer said, "He was like a round bottom doll. You knock him over and he comes right up." When he received the news that the seaway bill had passed, he claimed that "he was ready to dance."[88] The dream of thousands of people stretching back over 50 years, and the dream of those who lived on the shores of the Great Lakes and along the St. Lawrence, was about to become reality. In June of 1954, the United States Supreme Court rejected the legal challenges to the Power Authority of New York building the American power dam, brought forward by power interests, by Pennsylvania coal interests, by the old anti-seaway alliance represented by the National St. Lawrence Project Conference, and by those who claimed to speak for Lake Ontario shore owners. In August, Canada formally agreed to United States participation.[89]

Canadian acquiescence was not without reservations. Over the previous three years the idea of an all-Canadian canal system in the St. Lawrence had gained momentum in Canada as the United States hesitated. St. Laurent's cabinet had to demonstrate clearly to Canadians that Canada had the primary role in the plan, especially since there would be no credit to Canada for the money spent to enlarge the Welland Canal, as provided for in previous agreements, and since the United States would have an equal share of control in the Seaway, despite paying only about one-third of the cost of the new construction (though shipping to and from American ports was likely to pay the largest portion of the tolls). When negotiations took place, Canada insisted on building a canal on the Canadian side at Iroquois, despite the fact that the Wiley-Dondero Act required all canals to be on the American side, and insisted that Canada maintain the right to build a parallel canal system to the American one west of Cornwall, around the power dam at Barnhart Island, at a later date, thereby creating an all-Canadian system. On the issue of coordinating tolls and regulations the two governments could only agree to consult before taking action. While these negotiations did not remove all sources of possible friction in the future, they paved the way for an immediate start to what now seemed, with hindsight, like a long-delayed essential international project rather than the end of a 140-year struggle over controlling access to the Great Lakes area.[90]

# Building a Dream: Seaway Construction

What followed this long awaited agreement between two friendly but still cautious allies was one of the greatest logistical, engineering, and construction projects of the twentieth century. Oft-quoted statistics cannot convey the scope of the effort. A 100-square-mile lake was created behind the power dam at Barnhart Island, backing up water for 28 miles on the Canadian side and causing the flooding of some 22,000 acres, 225 farms, seven villages, three hamlets, part of an eighth village, 18 cemeteries, 35 miles of the main east–west highway, and 40 miles of main line railway, as well as displacing about 6,500 people in Ontario. Fifteen hundred were moved in Quebec. This did not include over 1,000 summer cottagers. On the American side, although almost as large an area was flooded — some 18,000 acres — the population was sparse and only 1,100 residents had to be moved. Some 225 farms and 500 cottages were affected. Over 210 million cubic yards of earth were moved, more than twice that removed in building the Suez Canal, and between six and seven million cubic yards of concrete were used. Some 69 miles of channels and locks were dug or dredged and some 45 miles of dikes were built to protect the Cornwall and Massena areas from flooding.[1]

This project was managed by a complex array of organizations, all of which had to co-operate, sublimating their egos and their suspicions or, in some cases, meshing their egos. There were the two national governments, although their roles were largely confined to negotiations concerning additional issues. Equally important were the governments of New York and Ontario, which tended to step in if they felt their interests were being harmed by the actions of the national governments. More important were the two organizations set up to build the navigation facilities, the St. Lawrence Seaway Authority and the St. Lawrence Seaway Development Corporation. The latter brought in an additional organization by giving the work on the American canal to the United States Army Corps of Engineers. A good deal of the land acquisition and the work on the power facilities was done by the two power authorities, the Ontario Hydro-Electric Power Commission and the Power Authority of the State of New York. Work on the St. Lawrence was supervised by a Joint Board of Engineers, created by the International Joint Commission for the specific purpose of supervising Seaway construction. The commission also created an International Lake Level Board to deal with the issues related to lake levels emerging from the building of the Seaway, but retained overall authority over boundary issues. Several subsidiary organizations were also involved. That all of these bodies were able to work together on a mammoth project that had to be completed in four years was a testimony to the tact, professionalism, and tolerance of the members, as well as to their belief that the project was extremely necessary.[2]

Lionel Chevrier was seen by those in government in Canada to be the natural choice to run the St. Lawrence Seaway Authority, due to the fact that he had been its most visible champion. Chevrier was reluctant to leave the cabinet, and political life, for what he believed might be a minor post, but he ultimately accepted. Because of his extensive experience in government, having been a member of Parliament since 1935, assistant to the Minister of Munitions and Supply during the Second World War, and Minister of Transport since 1945, he was able to borrow able men with whom he had come in contact to serve in the Seaway Authority. In turn, these individuals made extensive use of the engineering expertise within the Department of Transport.[3] In the United States, the chief promoters of the Seaway had been the members of the Great Lakes–St. Lawrence Association, who were given prime roles with the St. Lawrence Seaway Development Corporation. Lewis Castle, the immediate past president and former Duluth bank manager, became the head of the corporation. The five-person Seaway Advisory Board included John C. Beukema of Muskegon, Michigan, Harry C. Brockel of Milwaukee, and independent supporter Edward J. Noble.

Lewis Castle.

Castle struggled with his new role, which was nothing like making quick decisions on local banking matters. He had to deal not only with the other organizations involved, but also the Washington bureaucracy and with congressmen and lobbyists on both sides of the Seaway debate, who were quick to blame the corporation for any perceived failure. Luckily, much

Lionel Chevrier.

of the corporation's work was taken on by the Army Corps of Engineers.[4]

The role of the Corps was itself a contentious one. Having been responsible for building and maintaining the vast majority of national waterways, including canals, channels, harbours, and flood-control projects built in the previous century, the Corps expected to build and maintain the Seaway, including the power project; however, the Power Authority of the State of New York decided to use private engineers when its role was approved by President Eisenhower in November of 1953. Congress created a public, self-financing agency to build the navigation portions on the American side. Both of these decisions were in keeping with Eisenhower's desire to cut federal government expenses. Not only was this a threat to a possible role for the Corps in the Seaway construction, but it seemed to threaten future use of the Corps by the government in civilian projects. The Corps lobbied hard through the Defense Department and the secretary of defense to ensure a role in this project and, by implication, in future projects. Chief of Engineers, Lieutenant General Samuel D. Sturgis Jr. courted Castle, even before he was appointed as administrator of the Seaway Development Corporation, and the Corps offered advice on costing and technical matters to the new organization. There was some pressure on Castle, though, not to appoint the Corps as construction agent.[5]

The Corps had a good claim to the position. All federal canals in the United States were supervised by the Corps. It had been involved closely with the idea of a seaway since it participated in a study of possible routes to the Atlantic from the Great Lakes in 1899–1900. The original two-person Joint Engineering Board of 1921, on which the American member was from the Corps, concluded that navigation and power were interdependent, and the Corps came to believe that the two were necessary. Though it had to avoid a political stand, the Corps had provided technical expertise to government studies, including the survey authorized by Roosevelt in 1940, had worked closely with Canadian engineers, and had provided advice to the New York Power Authority in its application to the Federal Power Commission in 1952, and in its subsequent defence before the commission and in the courts. When the International Joint Commission, which had representation on it from the Corps, created the St. Lawrence River Joint Board of Engineers and the Joint Board of Control, both also had members from the Corps. It was not until September of 1954, some four months after legislation creating the Seaway Corporation passed, that the Corps was given the design and construction role. Tensions remained between the two organizations, however, and would ultimately turn to hostility. Even in the beginning the Corps was unhappy about having a subordinate role, particularly since it felt that the Seaway Corporation had no experience upon which to draw and that any failures on its part would reflect badly on the Corps.[6]

The largest percentage of the work was given to the two power agencies. Since the Ontario Hydro-Electric Power Commission (HEPCO) had extensive experience in expropriating property, it was given the task of amassing the land in Ontario that would be flooded, as well as building the Canadian half of the power dam, leaving the Seaway Authority to acquire land on which to build the Iroquois lock and control dam, and land in Quebec needed for the Lachine Canal and the seaway channel. The land for the locks and provision for a channel at Beauharnois was already provided for in the original agreement with the Canadian government. On the United States side, the Power Authority of New York State (PASNY) would buy up the land to be flooded and land needed for both the power pool behind the dam and for the canal to bypass it, using the New York Department of Public Works, which had experience similar to that of HEPCO. The Seaway Corporation and the Army Corps of Engineers agreed to use the same body to acquire land for the American channel, and reached an agreement with PASNY that land acquired for the power dam that was needed for the canal would be turned over to the corporation after being acquired by PASNY. This process of acquiring property had to be started quickly, as the completion date for the whole project was set at December 1959. It would continue during construction, with priority given to land that was needed at each stage of the construction. So speedy did the process need to be that, at times, work was begun before arrangements to expropriate a particular property were finalized.[7]

It so happened that both power agencies were led by the right people for the time. HEPCO had always been run by effective civil servants, but the head of the commission in the period leading up to and including the early years of construction was a particularly dynamic individual. Robert H. Saunders is largely forgotten today, except with regard to the dam that bears his name. A lawyer who had experience in banking, Saunders had entered municipal politics in Toronto in 1934, serving as alderman and then controller from 1935 until 1945, after which he was elected as mayor four years in a row. Known as "Grassroots Bob" because of his plain-speaking style and his concentration on issues that would improve the life of the people of Toronto, he pushed for a traffic safety program for school children, Toronto's first subway, and slum clearance. In 1948 he was asked to assume the leadership of HEPCO. Under his leadership, HEPCO carried out the difficult task of converting Ontario from 25 cycle electrical current to the more efficient 60 cycle current. This involved not only installing new equipment, but also replacing all appliances in the province that would not run on 60 cycle, an expensive and complicated process. Almost from the day he took over the agency, he campaigned continuously for St. Lawrence power in both Canada and the United States, because he quickly realized that Ontario was desperately short of power. In a 1949 speech, for instance, he commented that, "I think we all realize that the greatest single need for the future development of this province is the development of the St. Lawrence." In 1950, he made a similar statement in saying, "Let us all realize that the greatest single need in Ontario is the right to harness the falling waters of the St. Lawrence River."[8]

The outspoken Saunders put himself in the centre of the struggle to build the Seaway and the power dam. In speaking to the American Association of Port Authorities in 1953 about the "preposterous" idea that Canada would carry out the work on its own, he said, "I would like you to know that we have borne the cost of two wars. We didn't receive a five cent piece of lend lease [United States aid to Britain in the Second World War], and donated more than $2 billion to our allies. We have paid our way [and] ... we balance our budgets."[9] When confronted in 1951 by an impasse between the federal and Ontario governments over which should pay for part of the construction of the combined power and navigation facilities in the St. Lawrence, Saunders announced that Hydro would pay: "This project cannot be delayed any longer". In frustration with American hesitation to join the project, he said, "The bickering in the United States over this project would be laughable if it were not so tragic. Never in the history of North America have we witnessed such a spectacle. Never were the private interests of a few so allowed to impede the progress and protection of two great countries.... The Canadian Government should say, 'Uncle Sam, we can't afford to wait any longer. Our people must be protected and the industrial progress of our country must not be impeded.'"[10] Even before the Americans approved participation he had HEPCO engineers and planners working on the project.

On the New York side was another dynamic public servant, but one who had much less tolerance for government interference in what he did. Robert Moses could be considered either the New York Adam Beck, with more power, or Beck could be considered the precursor of Moses in the techniques that he employed. After work advising the governor on government reform in the 1920s, Moses had refurbished and massively expanded the park system in the city of New York and in the state, since he worked for both, as well as building bridges and other public structures. He drafted the legislation for his various positions, at one time numbering 12, which gave him considerable independence. Using federal relief funds during the Great Depression, and funds generated by other projects, such as the Triborough Bridge, which could issue bonds as a public authority, he often had more money available for projects than the city for which he worked. With this money, he did what he thought best. His parks often featured elaborate architecture, and the parkways that he built, especially on Long Island, were set in grassland with simple wooden fences and sweeping curves. No roads were allowed to enter at grade, and there were no stoplights or commercial operations to spoil the effect. Landowners who tried to prevent these roads from crossing their land were swept aside or had to engage in expensive litigation. Whenever a mayor or governor tried to limit Moses, he threatened to resign and, until Governor Nelson Rockefeller shocked him by accepting his resignation from all of his state positions in 1962, he generally got his way. He worked at least 15 hours a day, and was always willing to take on another project, such as a world's fair, especially if it would lead to another park. Opposition to his schemes began to emerge in the 1950s, as he became a champion of two urban renewal ideas, the inner-city expressway and slum clearance, both of which destroyed old neighbourhoods in New York and substituted physically divided communities and sterile apartment blocks. When the plan for St. Lawrence power finally was nearing approval in the early 1950s, however, Moses was still riding the wave of popularity, and he happily accepted Governor Dewey's offer to head up PASNY in 1952, believing that he could use the position to create parks on the St. Lawrence, and to bring industry to the underdeveloped St. Lawrence Valley. The Power Authority had become somewhat of a political dumping ground in the period since its early years, having no substantial responsibilities, and Dewey revitalized it with the appointment of some highly qualified individuals, including Moses. Though past retirement age when Seaway construction began, Moses brought the same energy and the same intolerance of the views of others to this new project. Luckily for the power plan, his approach and that of Saunders were compatible.[11]

Saunders' agency, anxious to begin generating power on the St. Lawrence, had 150 men working on the project at the time that Canada and the United States agreed to joint development, working with plans begun 18 months earlier. HEPCO had first begun surveys before the First World War and had amassed a considerable amount of data. On the American side, the Army Corps of Engineers had begun work six months before Congress began discussing participation in January of 1954. Their work was based on a 1942 report, arising out of the Corps' work on the St. Lawrence in 1940. This work had been ordered by Roosevelt to justify building the seaway as a defence measure. This report was revised in 1946, after tests at the Corps' Vicksburg Mississippi Waterways Experimental Station, and further subsurface tests on the St. Lawrence. In January of 1954, still before congressional approval, the Corps began adjusting the 1942 report to separate the power and navigation portions, both of which they had anticipated building in 1942, and to take into account modern technology.[12]

All the construction approved by the various bodies was to be done by private contractors, and the Seaway Authority was the first to post a contract. Lionel Chevrier was appointed president on July 1, 1954. The official opening took place August 10, 1954, at Cornwall and Massena, and the first contract was signed in October, for a portion of the construction of the new canal to bypass the Lachine Rapids. Chevrier had attempted to get Premier Duplessis of Quebec to agree to build a power dam in the Lachine Rapids at the same time as the canal was built, to save money on the Quebec power facilities, but Duplessis was as opposed to any co-operation with federal authorities as ever. Concerned about the short period for construction, Chevrier decided to proceed, ignoring the idea of a power dam in the Lachine Rapids. The Seaway Authority also quickly expropriated land south of the old Galops Canal in order to build a new canal across Iroquois Point. The contract for this construction was posted on December 1. Not only was the Seaway Authority moving quickly to build its share of the Seaway, it was also ensuring that the Americans could not build the canal on the American side that the Wiley-Dondero legislation authorized. The Canadian government had already informed the Americans that it would do this, but needed to be sure that the Americans did not proceed anyway. In February of 1955 the two federal governments, by an exchange of notes, agreed that the Americans would abandon their plan for a canal opposite Iroquois, and the Canadians agreed that they would not build navigation facilities at the power dam "under present conditions."[13] The Canadian government wanted to leave the door open for a Canadian canal to be built around the power dam when traffic increased. Chevrier was particularly adamant on this since the current arrangement would mean that his home city of Cornwall would be bypassed by the new canal. Originally he intended to keep the 14-foot canals operating as well as the new ones, but the high cost of doing so turned Parliament against the scheme. In addition, HEPCO did not want any extra delays and the Americans opposed the idea because they needed the tolls on their canal to pay for their construction. Chevrier's solution was to build a removable section in the dike constructed to the west of Cornwall, wide enough to fit the new lock width, and to dredge west of that to the depth of 27 feet. All that would be necessary would be to widen and deepen the old canal that ran in front of Cornwall up to the removable section of the dike, and to install a lock, to have a 27-foot Canadian canal. The American government consistently opposed the dredging, despite continued Canadian insistence, eventually simply acknowledging that the Canadians were doing it, but warning of possible consequences.[14]

This reluctance on the part of the Seaway Authority to let the Americans control what went on in the International Section spilled over into their relations with the Seaway Corporation, and led to one of the early problems to occur among the various agencies. Early in the process, the two agencies set up regular meetings. At the first two, the corporation executives arrived with the agenda already prepared, without consulting the Canadians. This aroused feelings among the Seaway Authority representatives that Canadians often felt, that the Americans just assumed that they were running things. Chevrier, the consummate politician, refused to create a public fuss and instead phoned Castle and easily straightened out the situation. In fact, Chevrier, the lawyer from a small city near the beginning of the St. Lawrence canals, and Castle, the banker from a small city at the other end of the Great Lakes, became close friends during the process. It was often difficult for the Americans to understand the Canadian point of view, so, as part of his attempt to put this Canadian approach in a broader context, Chevrier invited Castle to meet and talk with the prime minister, Louis St. Laurent. Castle responded in kind, leading to an amusing incident.

Chevrier, in spite of all of his political experience, had a certain naiveté about him in situations that were foreign to him, a fact that he was not afraid to mention in his memoir about the building of the Seaway. In the meeting with Eisenhower, the president asked Chevrier to point out Massena on a globe. While this was being done, Eisenhower turned to Chevrier and jokingly said that it seemed ridiculous, since Americans and Canadians looked, acted, and spoke alike, to remain separate: "Why didn't Canada become the 49th state?" Chevrier was stunned and did not know how to answer, unsure if the president was joking. He decided to reply seriously, and told Eisenhower that no Canadians wanted to join the United States. Perhaps the response that he thought of afterward would have been more in keeping with the humorous intent of the question, to suggest that the United States become the 11th province.[15]

These meetings were part of a much broader process, designed to build the Seaway and the power works as rapidly as possible. Other meetings went on among the various agencies, to try to coordinate a great many different activities, and with governments, municipalities, and public bodies. Even though HEPCO and the Army Corps of Engineers had studies going back several decades, more work was needed. While soil types had been noted in general, tests had to be done on every portion of the lock and the powerhouse areas to discover potential problems. Even then, contractors sometimes discovered costly surprises. HEPCO, the Seaway Authority, and the Seaway Development Corporation all hired outside experts, and the Corps farmed out work to divisions across the country, even though its Buffalo District was in charge of the construction. HEPCO created a large-scale model of the International Section of the St. Lawrence in its Islington Laboratory, west

Hydro testing facility at Islington, Ontario, outside Toronto, *circa* 1958.

of Toronto, and tested the effects of various alterations on such things as the rate of flow in the river. The Corps used its Vicksburg facility to test designs of the channels on either side of and between its two locks, and the University of Minnesota to test the lock designs. The Seaway Authority took over the Department of Transport Hydraulics and Special

Projects facilities in Montreal, and built a large model of the Lachine area to conduct tests. The National Research Council built a model of a Welland Canal lock in Ottawa to learn how to fill and drain locks as fast as possible. The St. Paul District of the Corps did the same work for the American locks as the National Research Council did for the Canadian. The Corps also made use of both the Islington and the Ottawa facilities.[16]

This testing went on as construction was being carried out, as did the expropriation of property. No time could be lost. Neither HEPCO nor PASNY expected significant problems in the acquisition of property. In Canada, the people along the St. Lawrence had known for decades that the Seaway was going to come, and little effort had been put into building up the communities. Nevertheless, when faced with the reality of having to move, many were upset. This area of Ontario saw the earliest large-scale non-native settlement in the 1780s, and many families and buildings traced their origins back for generations. Along old Highway 2, which meandered along or near the shoreline, bracketed in many places by large old trees skirting the turbulent waters of Long Sault, were the villages of Iroquois, Morrisburg, Aultsville, Farran's Point, Dickinson's Landing, Wales, Moulinette, and Mille Roches, and the hamlets of Woodlands, Santa Cruz, and Maple Grove. Originally most of these villages and hamlets served as stopping points for travellers on the St. Lawrence or as lock-side communities. Some acquired mills, as well. As local mills died out in the late nineteenth and early twentieth century in Ontario, and the need for stopping points decreased, what remained along the St. Lawrence were rural communities, largely frozen in an earlier time. Between them and behind them were farms. Many of the farmhouses were old, some dating to the early years of settlement. Everywhere grand old trees, mostly maples and elms, lined farm lanes and village streets. Most people could easily walk to the waterside to swim, or perhaps to spend a lazy hot summer night sitting by the old canal, watching for the passing of a 14-footer. Faced with losing family heritage or familiar surroundings, some did not want to move. The latter situation was particularly true of older people, who did not want to start over in a new setting, and worried about taking on mortgages.[17]

Others were happy to replace aging buildings with new houses, at least until they found out how much they would receive for their

A "14-footer" in the Cornwall Canal by the Long Sault Rapids.

existing property. Hydro was at first rather vague about how it would value properties, believing that its extensive experience was all that was necessary to deal with property owners. As it sent its agents into the valley to inform people that their land would be needed, Saunders announced that the commission would pay market value plus a small percentage for inconvenience, which was later fixed at 15 percent of the value. Since property values were depressed after years of neglect, and there could be no buyers since the land was going to disappear under the power pool, even those who were prepared to move were upset. A few drove the agents off their land, but most resorted to protest meetings.

Public protests initially concerned, but did not move, Saunders, who sent Vice Chairman George H. Challis, a native of Morrisburg, to be berated at a large public meeting for defending HEPCO's approach. But the protests were heard by the politicians, who always kept the need to get elected in mind. Premier Leslie Frost, himself the product of a small-town upbringing and a politician who was keenly aware of rural Ontario, was constantly monitoring HEPCO. Although it had been nominally independent of government since Adam Beck created it, Frost was very aware that it had to be seen as responsible to the people, since the province guaranteed its bonds. He was particularly concerned that the aggressive Saunders might act in a way that seemed insensitive to public wishes. As a result of the protests, Frost created a provincial government office in Morrisburg to assist citizens who had problems with the Hydro methods. The local officials met with the premier in Toronto to air their constituents' concerns, and Frost, with the agreement of HEPCO, also created a review board to which those who felt they were being treated unfairly could apply. The board acted only in an advisory capacity to Hydro, which did not accept every decision.

In most cases the extra money requested was a small amount, perhaps a few thousand dollars. In some cases it was not extra financial compensation that was sought, but the right to keep some portion of the expropriated property that might not be needed for the power pool or the relocation of services. It could be the house, a store, or a portion of the property. Those who did not feel that this process was adequate could appeal to the Ontario Municipal Board, which had the power to order Hydro to comply with its decisions. Some 14 cases went to the OMB, but the cost of hiring a lawyer probably discouraged others. If the board ordered increased compensation it was usually a small increase, some of which would be consumed by the legal fees. It is difficult to determine if others did not seek extra compensation for fear of taking on the large and powerful HEPCO, which had a reputation from previous expropriations of being a tough opponent, or if some felt that having to justify their position in the face of probing questions from members of the Review Board made the effort not worthwhile. Undoubtedly, the tendency in Ontario to respect public institutions also played a part.[18]

Plans developed in the 1940s envisaged new towns being built to house the displaced. When the seaway project was begun in the summer of 1954, Hydro announced that Iroquois would move, that the Morrisburg business district would be flooded and replaced, and that all the other small communities would be replaced by two new towns. The westernmost towns and hamlets would relocate to one, later named

Ingleside, and Moulinette, Mille Roches, and Maple Grove would move to the other, to be called Long Sault. Since there was so much concern, especially among the elderly, that there would not be enough money in their financial settlement to afford one of the new houses, and since some residents did not want a formula modern house to replace the one with character that they already had, early in 1955 Saunders relented. He announced that Hydro would consider moving houses to the new sites, if they were capable of being moved. The houses would be fitted with basements and modern services, given minor repairs, painted, and landscaped. There would still be a 15 percent payment for the inconvenience caused. This move on his part, along with the review procedure, relieved a good deal, though not all, of the frustration and anger among the residents of the villages and hamlets.[19]

The same respect for public institutions could not be said to exist on the other side of the St. Lawrence, where a certain level of skepticism about the decisions of government existed. Unlike on the Canadian side, most residents were surprised when told that their land would be flooded, or needed for the new canal or the control dam. When approached by agents of the Department of Public Works or the Corps of Engineers there seemed to be a greater tendency to accuse them of acting like Russians, in confiscating land. While HEPCO agents did haggle to a certain extent, and raised the amount offered if new information was provided, there was little haggling in New York. People who settled early received less than those who settled later. Although apparently it was possible to appeal to the state government if the Department of Public Works was responsible for the expropriation, few knew this and few did. The only alternative was to go to court, and the courts tended to side with the Power Authority.[20] Moses made the situation worse when he announced that some of the land could be used for parkland. Farmers already upset about losing land to the Seaway were even more upset when they felt their land was being taken under false pretences. Used to confiscating large amounts of land for parks, Moses tended to see those who tried to get more money as speculators, and had no patience with them.[21]

While planning, designing, and expropriations went on in the spring of 1955, construction began on a grand scale. As contracts were let, men and machines poured into the St. Lawrence Valley and the contiguous areas of Quebec. The combined project sucked up much of the available skilled labour in eastern Canada and the northeastern United States. Machine operators, carpenters, masons, and engineers were desperately needed. Even truck drivers were in short supply. Word went out to more distant parts of Canada and the United States and more men flooded in from the Maritime provinces and the Prairies, from the southern states and the West. Anyone who could do rough carpentry or drive a truck, be he farmer or storekeeper, could earn a good salary with steady work. There were jobs for bookkeepers and security guards, men to direct traffic, and men to work on surveying gangs. Students could find summer work, and local residents, used to a very limited economy based largely on tourism on the Canadian side and on Alcoa on the American side, had their choice of jobs. Mohawk steelworkers from the nearby reservations, famous for their fearless work high above cities such as New York, easily found work close to home. Before long, some 22,000 workers toiled on the navigation and power facilities. Even at full employment, the valley could only provide 38 percent of the workers on the Canadian side and 50 percent on the American. One source of workers was hardly exploited. This was the 1950s, and female construction workers, even in non-skilled positions, were a great rarity. However, restaurants, hotels, guest houses, and guest cottages flourished, providing increased employment for girls and women.[22]

The arrival of so many men, a goodly number without families, greatly changed the nature of society along the St. Lawrence. Suddenly everywhere was crowded. Every house within many miles of the river in the International Section that could be rented was, even if it did not have running water or electricity. Trailer parks sprang up in New York State to house the overflow. With these changes, life became more exciting. Incidents of crime increased, though much was of a minor nature often involving drunkenness or rowdiness, but this was still shocking to the small communities. There was a desperate shortage of schools, as many men did bring their families, leading to sub-standard or temporary buildings being used in the tight housing market, and to multiple school shifts. A lack of hospitals caused Hydro to build a temporary one for its workers. It also built some barracks for workers, and generally did more to assist its employees that the Power Authority did. While the American federal government had planned to provide housing, health care, schools, and other facilities in its plans for the 1941 agreement, Moses felt that such things were not necessary, since it was unclear how many workers would be needed. The trailer parks that became a feature of construction in New York State were created because contractors could not keep workers and therefore promised to guarantee rent payments if entrepreneurs would establish parks. The Power Authority did underwrite the cost of 133 houses in Massena, but these were reserved for engineers. The housing shortage caused a swift rise in rents, which the construction workers could handle, but for long-time residents on fixed incomes, hardship resulted. The building of new schools was left up to municipalities, with limited financial resources. Most of the schools that were built were not completed until construction was winding down.[23]

Machinery came in, too. Engineering magazines in the next few years were filled with advertisements for the latest construction machinery, as "used on the St. Lawrence Seaway." The latest earth scrapers, which had wheels taller than the average car, and could be longer than the average house, arrived, as well as bulldozers, power shovels, draglines, cranes, piledrivers, rollers, rock crushers, drills, dredges, haul units (massive earthmovers), and trucks old and new. There was machinery to tear down houses and uproot trees; machines to rip up soil and machines to haul it away; machines to scoop up the river bottom and machines to build cofferdams and cut off the flow of the mighty Long Sault; machines to destroy and machines to create.

Some of the first contracts given out by the Corps were to build construction roads and to relocate power lines, the latter job involving coordination with HEPCO, the Federal Power Commission, and Alcoa, which owned lines bringing power from Canada. Its first construction contract, however, brought in two draglines, a type of power shovel. One of these was among the largest pieces of equipment used on the Seaway. The Badgett Mine Stripping Corporation successfully bid on a contract to dig a long upstream section of the American canal, and to do work on the dikes to be built near Massena. The Badgetts sent two draglines, one a monster 650-ton Bucyrus Erie 450-W with a 165-foot boom, nicknamed "The Gentleman," and the other a much smaller 5-W weighing only 170 tons, with a 135-foot boom. These two machines normally were used in open pit coal mining. Rather than have them dismantled and sent in thousands of pieces on flat cars and then reassembled, which would take a great deal of time, the Badgetts sent the two by barge. They both walked overland on huge pontoon-like feet from Madisonville to the Pond River, some 18 miles, getting stuck in thawing spring mud for two weeks on the way. They then walked onto two barges and travelled by way of the Green and Ohio rivers to the Mississippi and Illinois rivers, coming through the Chicago Sanitary and Ship Canal. It was perhaps ironic that they used an old competitor to reach the St. Lawrence. At Chicago they were modified by the Corps of Engineers for work on the Seaway. Both were loaded on one barge, along with extra buckets, a bulldozer, two jeeps, a boom truck, and spare parts. From there they took Lake Michigan, Lake Huron, Lake St. Clair, Lake Erie, and the Welland to reach Lake Ontario and the St. Lawrence. The greatest challenge was taking the barge through the Galops, Iroquois, and Rapide Plat rapids. Though ships had been traversing these rapids, downriver, for decades, it was quite another task to steer a large, heavily loaded barge through the rough waters. "The Gentleman" had its boom bolted on as well as its large bucket, capable of excavating a house cellar. On the way down the rapids, the tug that was guiding it cut off its power because there was no way to push the barge around in the fast-flowing river. Shortly thereafter, as the barge and tug left the rapids, a 14-footer appeared around a bend. Unable to control the barge, the crew of the tug prepared to jump overboard before the seemingly inevitable collision. At that point, Roger Badgett ordered the bucket on the dragline dropped into the bottom of the river, where it caught and stopped the barge. The canaller slipped by only feet from the tug. A few miles farther on the barge wedged itself between two small islands. Badgett ordered the man at the controls to use the bucket to dig the barge out, which he did in short order. The barge and tug were then able to reach Long Sault Island. The equipment had travelled about 2,000 miles in 68 days.[24]

Other equipment also dwarfed the earth scrapers and earthmovers, which themselves were the size of small houses. Another massive dragline, "The Glutton," was sent by rail from Wyoming in thousands of pieces. It took about a month and a half to reassemble it. Several other draglines were also employed on the project. When it could not

The Gentleman.

get bids on some of the channel dredging, the Corps brought in its own dredge, the *D.D. Gaillard*, and rented another, the *Paraiso*, from the Panama Canal Company, a vessel built by the same firm as "The Gentleman." The two huge craft, relics from an earlier age, had somewhat of the appearance of smoke-breathing dragons as they scooped up large portions of the riverbed in their amply sized jaws, belching black smoke from their stacks. Reputedly, at the peak of construction activity there were nine dredges, 140 shovels and draglines, 80 scrapers, 400 tractors, and 730 trucks at work in the International Section. In portions of the area the whole landscape seemed to be on the move during the day, so many vehicles were at work.[25]

Work was well underway on the Lachine section in 1955. Here the construction was not difficult, as much of the land was shale and easily removed. Though earlier plans had envisioned a canal skirting the southern edge of Montreal, since the original canal was now surrounded and could not be enlarged, the amount of time that it took to approve the Seaway meant that the area where the new canal would go was now also heavily built-up. The canal was therefore shifted to the south shore of the St. Lawrence, which was far less developed. A channel could easily be dug most of the way around the rapids without significantly disturbing industry or housing. Where expropriation was necessary, it was done by the Lands Division of the Department of Transport. One of the biggest problems involved the four bridges crossing the river to Montreal. The fact that they would have to be altered to allow shipping to travel under them was another factor in the decision to build on the south shore, where alterations would not be complicated by the need to work in a heavily populated area. The problem, though, was that the four were owned by different entities, each of which had to be dealt with separately. In addition, attempts to get Premier Maurice Duplessis to assist in altering the bridges by building new road approaches failed, as he refused, as always, to assist a federal government project.

The two bridges that crossed into downtown Montreal were particularly difficult to deal with because the heavy volume of traffic on them meant that they could not be shut down for any length of time. Each bridge had to allow for 120 feet of clearance. Innovative engineering solutions were necessary. The problem of the first bridge, the Jacques Cartier, was solved by the man who had designed it in 1929, who happened to be working as a consultant with the Seaway Authority, and by the company that had built it. The portion of the bridge over the canal was jacked up, while leaving the remainder at the lower, approximately 60-foot, level. This was an extremely delicate operation involving placing four huge jacks, each capable of lifting 500 tons, on each of the piers and jacking slowly, six inches at a time. Specially made blocks fabricated to very strict tolerances were inserted as the bridge rose slowly some 50 feet. One longer span, with its supporting steelwork on top rather than underneath to provide maximum clearance below, was positioned alongside the bridge and, when the existing bridge could no longer stretch to cover the added height, was quickly slid into the place of an existing span. While initially too long, as the bridge continued to rise, it slipped smoothly into place, and the risers used to allow traffic to reach the added span while it sat on top of the roadway were removed. This innovative solution was studied by engineers in other countries, so unique was it.

The next bridge, the Victoria, was also a problem. The Jacques Cartier Bridge was owned by the National Harbours Board, which was willing to work with the Seaway Authority to solve the problem, covering part of the cost. The Victoria Bridge carried both rail and vehicle traffic and was owned by the Canadian National Railways. The bridge, built in 1898, was too low to jack up, and an elevated bridge would have created too steep an angle for trains to use. The CNR president, the strong-willed Donald Gordon, insisted that traffic could not be interrupted by a lift span, and that the company would not pay any of the cost of solving the problem. The matter went all the way to the federal cabinet before Chevrier and Gordon reached an agreement. Again the solution was unique. The Seaway Authority and CNR engineers designed a long, almost semi-circular second approach to the bridge that started well back on the roadway and rose to meet the bridge in mid-river. A lock was built under the two approaches, with one gate under each one and a lift span put in each approach. When the lift span was installed in one approach, traffic could use the other. Once in full operation, when a ship approached one gate, the lift span there was raised and traffic was diverted onto the other approach. When the ship reached the second gate, the first bridge was lowered and traffic routed to that approach. This solution was another engineering triumph.

The third bridge, the Honoré Mercier Bridge, carried substantial traffic, which was expected to increase, and had very heavy and complicated concrete approach ramps. The only solution that could be found was to build a whole new span high above the Seaway and to replace the approaches, which were blown up in one great explosion. To prevent an interruption of traffic during construction, a huge earthen ramp was built which cut over to the remaining portion of the bridge at the river's edge. Instead of $2 million to build a lift span, it cost $12 million to solve the problem. The fourth bridge was a rail bridge, and like the three others upriver at Beauharnois, carried only a limited amount of traffic, making lift spans practical. Although the Seaway Authority had, by its mandate, only the responsibility to provide lift spans in all the bridges, the outcry from drivers in the Montreal area, the Quebec government, and the CNR would have been politically damaging to both the Authority and to the federal government.[26]

Northway-Photomap Inc./AO C30 ES-18-949.

The Victoria Bridge, 1963.

The other problem that the Authority encountered in the Montreal area was a political and public relations one. Toward the western end of the 16-mile canal, the channel would cut through the village-reservation of Caughnawaga (now Kahnawake). Originally a native mission established by the Jesuits when what is now Quebec was controlled by France, the area had been recognized as native land by the British government. The new Seaway channel would cut right through the outer edge of the reservation, requiring 1,260 acres. The Seaway Authority offered the same terms as it offered non-natives along the canal right-of-way, current value plus 10 percent. The offer divided the Mohawk community. Those who needed money or believed it was wrong to rock the boat were willing to settle, whereas the band leadership and those who did not want to move under any circumstances opposed any settlement. A vote of residents overwhelmingly endorsed the latter position. It is easy to see why there was vigorous opposition. The community was a small one, without any ability to add more land; it would lose a portion of its waterfront; and the majority felt that the Canadian government had no right to interfere in any way with native land, granted by the British government. The chief and the band council took the issue to the courts, to the press, to the British government, and ultimately to the United Nations and to the World Court. Their argument was that treaties between the British government and the Iroquois Confederacy, of which the Mohawks were a member, and later British policies, precluded expropriation. When this argument failed, they insisted that they be given fair compensation. In truth, the British government, which was suppose to have protected them in the past, had expropriated some of the reserve in the 1850s. The opposition in Parliament took up their cause, though, and insisted that the channel should be moved out into the river, where it would not require Mohawk land. Chevrier rejected this because of the added expense, since the Seaway Authority had a limited budget.[27]

To Chevrier, the matter was a result of a misunderstanding of what the Authority intended to do, and the desire of some "to make money out of the seaway." Sometimes he felt that the Mohawks were "just having a lot of fun at the expense of the seaway." At one point he made a requested friendly visit to the village, only to find that the press had been invited, a surprise which he took as an attempt to embarrass the Authority. After explaining the Authority's policy regarding the land, Chevrier was invited to smoke a pipe of peace with the leading figures. Again, as with Eisenhower, he showed his lack of worldliness by smoking the pipe upside down. His intentions were good, but he had no comprehension of why the majority opposed the expropriations. Eventually, a policy of winning over some individuals by giving cash advances on their property, providing benefits to the community as a whole (such as filling in a swampy area, building playgrounds, and providing water and sewage systems), increasing the amount paid to those who held out, and expropriating the land of those who could not be persuaded, brought the matter to a close. Some 177 families were bought out in the community, but a substantial number bought back their buildings at auction and moved them. However, one woman who refused to move saw her house bulldozed while she hung laundry. Another older couple had their well run dry as the channel was dug on either side of their house, which they refused to leave until paid a substantial amount of money. The husband

The government elevator at Prescott.

Looking at the Fourth Welland Canal at the twinned flight locks, Locks 4, 5 and 6, facing toward Lake Ontario, July 1963. The channel from Lake Ontario is relatively straight compared to the curved channel of the first three Welland canals, used to ascend the escarpment.

Iroquois before the flood.

Construction on Iroquois Point, with the old canal in the foreground, January 1957. The control dam is half finished and the new canal is in its preliminary stage of construction.

The dredge *Paraiso*.

A ship in one of the 14-foot canals, 1955.

The Long Sault Rapids, drained, 1957. Note the half-finished Long Sault Control Dam (middle right) and towers to build the stone cofferdam (on the left).

The Barnhart Dam completed, most of the cofferdam removed, and the area flooded. Notice that Barnhart Island is much smaller now; the massive 162-foot-high, 3,300-foot-long dam looks much smaller now than it did before the water was allowed into the construction site.

Road to nowhere. Old Highway 2 emerges from Lake St. Lawrence on the Long Sault Parkway.

The Soulanges Canal Lock 3, facing east, 2008; compare this to the view in chapter 2.

A "salty" in the Iroquois Lock: the Iroquois Control Dam can be seen behind it.

A ship and a tug–barge combination meet in the Wiley-Dondero Channel, viewed from the Eisenhower Lock.

held out on the advice of the Ministry of Citizenship and Immigration, which dealt with native affairs, that the original offer was inadequate. The resistance of this man, Louis Diabo, created international publicity, and this publicity probably earned him the $70,000 that he received and goaded the Authority into doing more for the community. The needs of the many outweighed the concerns of a few, at a time when the public had little understanding of the native peoples' point of view.[28]

The other section of the Seaway within Quebec for which the Seaway Authority was responsible was the Soulanges section, in 1954 served by the Soulanges Canal on the north shore. The Authority dredged a new channel across Lake St. Louis to the Beauharnois powerhouse on the south shore. The arrangement made in 1929 allowed the Canadian government to build locks beside the power channel and to use it to move between Lake St. Louis and Lake St. Francis. This channel was dug in the early 1930s through farmland, some 3,300 feet wide and 16 miles long, to provide a sufficient head of water for the powerhouse. The company also was required to dig and dredge a navigation channel 600 feet wide and 27 feet deep within the power channel. In doing all of this work, the company removed more earth than was dug out of the Panama Canal.

Adding the locks at the eastern end of the channel seemed a relatively easy task. Quebec had been building a four-lane highway past the powerhouse when the Seaway was approved, and had immediately stopped construction. Premier Duplessis, who had previously refused any co-operation in the Montreal area, surprised the Seaway Authority by offering $300,000 to help with a tunnel under the locks. In building the two locks, the Authority's contractors found the work not as easy as expected. Instead of digging through easily removed soil, the ground was found to contain a large quantity of sandstone, which wore down construction machinery. It was necessary to resort to dynamite to complete the work.[29]

Chevrier maintained that the most difficult work that the Authority did was in the Lachine section of the Seaway, but the International Section had its share. For some of the contractors, the Corps, and the Seaway Corporation, this part of the Seaway was a nightmare. Aside from the canal and control dam at Iroquois to control the level of Lake Ontario, the construction involved another dam on the American side at Long Sault Island, the American canal to bypass the power dam, the dam itself, and all of the dikes around Cornwall and Massena. Work had not even begun when problems began to arise. Probably the most serious was the change in the date when the powerhouse and the new canals had to begin operations. The Corps of Engineers' original planning was for the canals to be ready for the 1959 navigation season, but when the four organizations responsible for the building were in place, it was told that the canals had to be ready on September 1, 1958. In November 1954, when planning was well underway, and the Seaway Authority was issuing its first contract, the two power agencies announced that their mandate required them to begin generating power by July 1, 1958. The two agencies were, of course, under considerable pressure to begin generating needed power. This decision meant that the power pool had to be raised in time to begin generation, and as the pool rose, it would flood the old canals. The new canals would have to be operating at the same level, 14 feet, by the time the waters rose. This caused consternation in the Corps, which had been calculating how to squeeze the construction schedule to finish by September 1. The only way to achieve the July date would be to pour concrete during the winter of 1956, which would raise the cost and, in the minds of Corps' engineers, jeopardize quality. The Corps and the Seaway Corporation told PASNY that it would have to pay the extra. Moses refused and the Corps looked for an alternative way to save time. The only solution that it could see was to cut out the contingency time built into the construction schedule. Every engineer knows that there will be delays in a project, caused by strikes, unforeseen problems, and material shortages, so it was with serious misgivings that the Corps accepted this.[30]

The Hydro-Electric Power Commission of Ontario received a shock in 1955. Flying from Windsor to London, Ontario, Robert Saunders' plane crashed on its way into the latter city, and he died from his injuries. While HEPCO had sufficient depth in its management structure to survive this, and the basic planning had been completed, Saunders' energy was missed. He had been the driving force behind the push for urgent action on St. Lawrence power, and the person who had Hydro personnel working on the project before it was approved. Shortly after he was appointed in 1948, Saunders is supposed to have flown over the Long Sault Rapids and to have vowed that he would never give a speech without mentioning the project. By all appearances, he kept his word.

Saunders learned before his death that his name would be on the power dam, but he did not live to see his dream completed.[31]

The two American bodies, the Seaway Corporation and the Corps of Engineers were being harassed from both sides. Opponents were watching for any hint of fiscal incompetence or unfair subsidizing of commercial transportation by water. Supporters, it seems, wanted to tell the agencies how to build the Seaway. N.R. Danielian had taken over the positions of president from Lewis Castle and also became treasurer of the Great Lakes–St. Lawrence Association in 1952. He had begun publishing *The Heartland*, an influential business publication, and hosting a series of well-regarded development conferences, under the title The Heartland Conference. With his increasing prestige and less fettered by his council since becoming president, Danielian had begun to go his own way. He began working, for instance, with some who had opposed the seaway concept, for his methods involved much wheeling and dealing and political manipulation. This technique alienated long-time supporters of the seaway concept and gave Danielian even more power in the organization. Beukema was squeezed out by the new president, and Brockel quit near the end of construction over Danielian's methods. Danielian tried to tell the Seaway Corporation and the Corps of Engineers how to manage the project. He put forward his own list of candidates for the Board of Advisors, tried to tell the Corps that its Buffalo District should not have control of the construction, insisted on being informed of all developments, and tried to influence other decisions. The Corps found him offensive and tried to keep him at bay, using seaway proponents Castle and Congressman Dondero to try to hold him in check. In spite of this, Danielian continued to be an influential irritation for the life of the project. Unfortunately for the Corps, Lieutenant General Samuel D. Sturgis Jr., Chief of Engineers, called Danielian a "damn fool" for his meddling, and perpetuated a confrontational situation.[32]

One final issue that caused problems at the start of construction for those in charge of the navigation work was the size of the locks. Shipping interests and the United States Department of the Navy pushed for locks larger than those already approved, which were 800 feet long, 80 feet wide, and 30 feet deep. They pressed for locks that were larger in all dimensions. Castle put this to the Canadians along with the opinion

Artist's conception of what the International Section would look like after construction.

that larger locks would allow more of the world's shipping in and would eliminate the need to rebuild the locks later. Canadian officials replied that they were only authorized to spend enough money to build locks to the original size, and that larger locks would drive up the cost beyond what was authorized. What Castle's real opinion of larger locks was is unclear, as the Seaway Corporation, backed by the Corps of Engineers, also rejected the idea of larger locks in discussions with potential users, arguing that there were too few larger ships to justify the expense. Whether this position was the result of discussions with the Canadians or whether it was an independent conclusion is difficult to determine.[33]

The contractors working on the various aspects of the project were unaware of the problems besetting the agencies that hired them, and were too busy with their own problems to care. There were literally hundreds of contracts, big and small. Firms from all over Canada and the United States were involved, as well as firms from several European countries. To facilitate construction, the two countries agreed to let workers from each country work in the other, and agreed to let all materials used in construction, and construction machinery, come in duty free. Since there was a good deal of prestige to be had from working on the power and navigation aspects, as well as on the associated work such as building roads, moving buildings, and clearing areas to be flooded, firms tended to put in bids as low as they thought practical in order to secure a contract. Some large firms submitted joint bids in order to reduce the risk for each individual company. When it came to construction, bids were made on the basis of assessments of soil conditions by the Corps of Engineers, HEPCO, or the Canadian Ministry of Transport.[34]

By the spring of 1955, Iroquois Point, south of the old canal, was being reworked by heavy machinery. It would contain the new Canadian lock and, just south of that, the control dam. From 1906 to 1953, the level of Lake Ontario was maintained by a natural stone barrier put in the river near Prescott. Unjustified claims by waterfront owners on Lake Ontario in the early 1950s that this barrier, known as The Gut, was causing high water and erosion, led to its removal in 1953. The dam was to replace it. The Long Sault Dam on the American side, farther downstream at the north end of Barnhart Island, close to Long Sault Island, would control the flow past the powerhouse in the South Channel of the river. Both were constructed by creating a cofferdam around half of the site, building that half, and then letting water through the completed portion while the other half was built. These cofferdams were very difficult to construct because of the force of the water flowing through the two branches of the river. Long, thin interlocking flat steel pilings were driven into the riverbed by piledrivers, creating almost semi-circular pods, which were then filled with rock brought in by dump truck. In the South Channel the increased flow of water as the width of the channel decreased during construction of the cofferdam started washing away the pilings before they could be driven into the riverbed. Large slabs of concrete had to be dropped by crane in front of the pilings to break the force of the water, and moved along as work progressed. The second half of the Long Sault Control Dam could not be built until the flow of water through the Long Sault Rapids was stopped, because the dam would stretch across a portion of that mighty torrent. In the meantime, the water from the now closed South Channel backed up through a deep cut made through Long Sault Island into the North Channel.[35]

While all of this was being done, another, longer cofferdam was being constructed in the same manner across the North Channel, from Barnhart Island to the Canadian shore, where the river was narrow and the banks were high. The Americans built a pontoon bridge and pulled it out from the mainland until it reached Barnhart Island. The Canadians built two tunnels under the still-operating Cornwall Canal to get to the worksite. When the cofferdam was finished, it stretched for about 4,200 feet, more than four-fifths of a mile, and closed the North Channel. About two and a half miles west, where the North Channel was very narrow, a second cofferdam was built to isolate the site of the power dam between the two. Then the water was pumped out. Volunteers rescued the game fish that were isolated, and dumped them into the Cornwall Canal. Coarse fish, of which there was almost 15,000 pounds, were dressed and sold.[36]

Once the first half of the Long Sault Dam was complete, a more difficult task connected with the building of the dams was attempted. The North Channel was sealed off a second time, this time by a stone cofferdam just west of the Long Sault Rapids. Because of the fast-moving water and the hard riverbed at that point, a steel cofferdam was not possible. A tower was erected on the Canadian shore and another on Long Sault Island. Between them, heavy wires were stretched and a large scoop-shaped, flat-bottomed

*Ontario Power Generation/SLU Collection 40, Mabee Series, Box 52.*

Working to close the stone cofferdam at Long Sault.

bucket capable of holding 25 tons of rock was attached. This then moved back and forth across the river, depositing an equal layer of stone from one side to the other, with the idea that eventually the deposited rock would rise to the level of the water and cut off the flow. When this process took longer than anticipated, the contactor decided to have trucks dump more stone, working from the Ontario shore into the channel. The problem with this was that it constricted the flow of the river and forced the same amount of water through an ever smaller space. The consequence of this was that truckloads of large stones were washed away as fast as they were dumped in the river. At one point, 30 feet of cofferdam disappeared down the river. This continued for some time until engineers had the idea to throw a six-legged steel "hexapedian," much like the obstacles used on Normandy beaches in the Second World War to impale landing craft, into the gap in the cofferdam. Tethered by a cable to the shore, the first one washed away, but the second caught and formed a base upon which rock could be poured. Slowly the final gap was closed.

Once the cofferdam was closed, four months after its completion had been expected, it diverted the entire flow of the North Channel through the cut in Long Sault Island into the South Channel, through the completed first half of the Long Sault Dam, and around Barnhart Island. During the entire process the engineers were constantly measuring water levels and adjusting the gates on the half-completed control dams, and the flow of water through Long Sault Island. This policy was necessary to keep water levels in the Cornwall Canal and the Alcoa power canal steady to protect operations. As the water drained from the channel, it was then possible to build the second half of the Long Sault Dam, which would sit where a portion of the rapids used to run.

Once the mighty Long Sault Rapids were drained, they became for one last time a tourist attraction. People wandered through the desolate landscape of water-smoothed rocks, holes worn in the rock riverbed by centuries of swirling waters, and stacked stones that had thrown up white foam to terrify passengers on the steamers that used to make regular runs through the rapids. Some came to search for "treasure," anything interesting that might have fallen off a vessel or been knocked off by a calamitous collision with a boulder. The most that could usually be found was a piece of rudder or an anchor. One young man got lucky, however, and found a few cannonballs that, some speculated, might have come from the fighting on the St. Lawrence during the War of 1812. Newspapers took photographs so they could tantalize their reader with the secrets of the great Long Sault.[37]

The cofferdams were tough work. Pushing one of the great rivers of the world back and forth across its channels and then drying up a huge swath of the riverbed was not a task that had been done before by the engineers and construction companies working on the St. Lawrence. In fact, few construction people in the world had this type of experience, and engineers from around the world came to study the St. Lawrence. The construction superintendent at the Long Sault Dam said that it was the most difficult job that he had ever attempted. When the cofferdams were completed, the construction problems were just beginning. To win contracts, firms cut prices to the bone. Any unexpected problem would quickly lead to losses. The Hydro-Electric Power Commission and the Corps of Engineers were aware of unusual soil conditions before work began, but they failed to realize how unusual these soils were and did not know how extensive the deposits were. Extensive soil testing led to the Iroquois Dam and the power dam being relocated to provide better foundation rock under them, and the Corps included information on soil issues in their contract tenders, but the tests missed some pockets of the two problem soils, and these soils proved to be more of an issue than originally they were thought to be. Marine clay was a soft, easily worked material until it became wet. At that point it became a sticky, glutinous mass which was impossible to remove with scrapers, bogged down equipment, and would not flow out of dump trucks. Glacial till, on the other hand, when dry was almost impossible to excavate. Harder than concrete, it quickly destroyed equipment used to dig or scrape it.[38] Daniel J. McConville, who worked with a small, family-owned construction company, McConville Inc., on various Seaway contracts, either as a subcontractor for large firms or as the prime contractor on small contracts, described the effects of glacial till this way:

> The abrasiveness of the hard-packed till was unbelievable. In the excavation we'd been doing before the Seaway, a set of removable teeth on a shovel dipper would last six months or more. Working in glacial till, we found we had to install a new set every shift. The friction of the glaciated material made dipper teeth and scrapers' cutting edges hot enough to burn a bare hand. The pre-Seaway 5,000 hour life of a set of tractor crawlers was reduced by two-thirds.... The prospect of tough excavation didn't faze another pair of brothers, Jack and Jim Maser. They emerged from the Pennsylvania coalfields to take on the glacial till at Robinson Bay, site of the Eisenhower Lock [the Robinson Bay Lock was renamed the Eisenhower in 1956], with a fleet of rubber-tired scrapers. By October 1955, having moved close to a million cubic yards of the stuff (half the amount called for in the contract), the Masers gave up and went home. "They couldn't make enough to pay for their cutting edges," said one of the project engineers, referring to

the replaceable hardened steel blades attached to the leading edges of the scraper bowls.[39]

Contractors quickly learned that road-building equipment was too light for the work, and relied more on mining equipment. Draglines and power shovels, the latter soon to be replaced in this type of construction by front-end loaders, were the most efficient way of dealing with the two problem soils. Even this heavier equipment was not always up to the task. The Dutcher Corporation used shovels, draglines, and scrapers at the site of the Grasse River Lock (renamed the Snell Lock in 1958), but the marine clay defeated them and the firm went bankrupt. At the Iroquois Lock the contractor took to dynamiting the glacial till before excavating, a method sometimes used at other sites. In some of the construction, contractors ran into glacial till with pockets of marine clay, the worst of conditions, since each had to be treated differently.[40]

Aside from soil conditions, weather was a factor, particularly for firms used to working in warmer parts of the United States. The experience of one firm was described this way:

> The first construction job, which began just north of Massena in September 1954, didn't bankrupt the contractor, for the Dravo Corporation had deep pockets. But it humbled the Pittsburg firm, a successful lock and dam builder with long experience on the inland waterways.... Before winter was over, the Dravo project [to cut the channel through Long Sault Island, and construct the cofferdam to allow the Long Sault Dam to be built] was hampered by overnight temperatures close to minus 40 degrees Fahrenheit. That kind of cold changes all the rules of equipment operation. Engines must be left running for days and nights on end, whether working or not. Dravo learned quickly that restarting every piece of equipment on a sub-freezing Monday morning could use up most of a ten-hour shift.
>
> As temperatures plummeted, equipment costs zoomed upward. The crawler pads of shovels and

bulldozers and other parts subject to stress cracked and crumbled. Drive chains flew apart, cables snapped, and fuel lines iced up. Material excavated from below the frost quickly froze in the trucks' dump bodies and could not be ejected. And anything metal, especially cast metal, was liable to crystallize and break into pieces.[41]

Perhaps that was one of the reasons why the Canadians, used to working in winter conditions, chose to pour concrete at the site of the power dam year-round, while the Americans rarely did winter concrete work anywhere, and only when time constraints forced them to do so. Both countries' workers did, however, work night and day during the construction season, turning the Barnhart site at night into what looked like the set of a science fiction movie, with its many lights illuminating a giant concrete structure that seemed beyond the scale of human use.[42]

Because of the situation where contractors walked away from their worksite, or went bankrupt, and the numerous complaints from other contractors that they had not been given full information about conditions, the five bodies, and especially the Seaway Corporation and the Corps of Engineers, felt it necessary to reopen contracts and to pay more. If it was necessary to replace a company that could not complete a contract, it usually cost two or three times as much. At the Eisenhower Lock, the Masers were replaced by another firm, at a higher price, and that firm was replaced by another at a still higher price. To ensure that firms would not launch a suit after an area had been flooded, claiming that soil conditions warranted a larger payment, constant tests were made of conditions in areas where excavation was taking place, these in addition to the ongoing tests which led to numerous changes in design, of locks, of dikes, of channels, all of which ate up valuable time.[43]

By the end of 1956, even getting bids on dredging in the South Channel, below Cornwall, became a problem. Other work in the Great Lakes was available to dredging companies, labour was scarce and therefore expensive, and infighting among unions also worried companies. No doubt the knowledge that contracts were being reopened also was a factor in the firms' decision to bid high. The Seaway Corporation, under increasing pressure from critics because of escalating

*Ontario Power Generation/SLU Collection 40, Mabee Series, Box 52.*

The Barnhart cofferdam with the powerhouse under construction. On the right can be seen the Cornwall Canal, partially filled in, and a diversion canal which includes the framework for a lock in the possible future Canadian 27-foot canal.

costs, then pressured the Corps to hire workers and do the work itself. Reluctantly, since the Corps was not allowed to pay the higher salaries of union workers at a time of labour shortages, the Corps agreed. The Corps brought in its own dredge, the *Gaillard*, hired and trained workers, and did the work so efficiently that the Seaway Corporation asked the Corps to continue dredging from 14 feet up to the 27-foot level. The Corps then rented the dredge *Paraiso* from the Panama Canal Company and completed the dredging, much to the annoyance of the dredging companies, which felt the government was undercutting them.[44]

Every delay, every failed contractor, every time-wasting dispute among the various agencies, threatened the completion date of July 1, 1958. The Corps constantly felt that the corporation did not understand construction and threw up impediments to the process. Wherever possible, the Corps helped contractors and suppliers obtain needed materials, and tried to speed up deliveries. During a steel strike in 1956,

*Ontario Power Generation/SLU, Collection 40, Mabee Series, Box 52.*

Work on the Barnhart powerhouse went on 24 hours a day.

the Corps negotiated with steel companies to give priority, once the strike was over, to shipments for a company that built needed equipment for locks. During a strike among concrete manufacturers in 1957, the Corps arranged to buy concrete in Canada for American construction companies, by requesting a government exemption to purchasing laws.[45]

While contractors and the agencies which issued contracts had problems, so did the men who did the work. Construction is a dangerous task at the best of times, but when working on high cofferdams and dams, and working over fast-flowing water in many instances, conditions became even more dangerous. It did not help either that many of the people working in construction had not done this type of work before. In some situations, equipment was lost to the river, but in others men were killed or maimed. An engineer examining a dike in the Lachine section, which was being pressured by a buildup of ice, was drowned when the dike broke. A boy fell off a tug near the Barnhart cofferdam and was swept to his death. Two Mohawk workers lost their lives in accidents near Massena. Two men working on winching the pontoon bridge out to Barnhart Island were seriously injured, one losing a leg, when a cable snapped back. Numerous others suffered major or minor injuries, although the accident rate was remarkably low for a project of this size. According to figures supplied by the Seaway Corporation, the accident rate was considerably higher on the Canadian side than on the American, but still only 55 hours lost per million hours worked. Work, though, was difficult, with mud, marine clay, bone-jarring work on scrapers, unyielding glacial till, long exhausting hours, bitterly cold winters and, often, the threat of falling from high places or into deadly waters.[46]

As thousands of men and hundreds of machines carved out canal channels, dried the riverbed, built new roads, and began to slice off the tops of islands in preparation for flooding, the five bodies responsible were increasingly at odds. The two power agencies seemed to get along, but several issues created animosity among the partners. Undoubtedly the pressure to complete the work on time and within budget added to the stress.

In 1956, the Seaway Authority and the Seaway Corporation were about to begin dredging the channel south of Cornwall, leading to the American canal. This dredging would not only allow ships to use it but also would lower the level of the water downriver from the power dam, thereby increasing the difference in height between the water above and below the dam, allowing more power to be generated using this extra amount of water. The American government and the Seaway Corporation insisted that the two hydro agencies pay the cost, since they were responsible for any joint power–navigation costs. Both refused, and continued to refuse for well over a year. Robert Moses was particularly incensed at this attempt to get his money. To him, having to deal with other agencies was an imposition. Already, during the planning stages of the seaway, he had denounced the American members of the St. Lawrence Joint Board of Engineers for repeatedly asking him for more information on plans and schedules, accusing them of trying to run the power and navigation projects and calling them "bureaucrats who operate with an astounding and high handed attitude," an accusation often leveled at Moses. When PASNY engineers were slow in designing dikes, the Corps did the work itself, only to be told when the PASNY engineers finished their designs that the Power Authority insisted that its designs be used. When it came to the dredging issue, Moses accused the Corps and the corporation of mismanaging the project, suggesting that the corporation was trying to keep escalating costs down by having the power agencies do the work, and that the Corps had miscalculated the costs, forcing the corporation to this position. He railed about being unfairly saddled with costs and predicted that the dispute might delay the project up to two years. Worried about any delay in bringing the generators online, HEPCO finally agreed to pay $12 million, and PASNY agreed to cover half of that. The Canadian government, which felt that the power agencies should only pay a fraction, since only a portion of the dredging would benefit the generation of power, pressed the Seaway Authority to compromise. The two Seaway agencies each paid the same amount, about $12 million, and Castle, who came up with the compromise amount, agreed to pay any extra costs.[47]

While this dispute was dragging on, another arose. The Roosevelt Bridge, a low-level bridge carrying the New York Central rail line as well as road traffic onto Cornwall Island, had to be replaced because it crossed the shipping channel. Robert Moses had made arrangements to reroute traffic from Cornwall Island by a circuitous route across the shipping channel farther west, at the Snell Lock, so that he could also bring Canadian vehicles into the new park he was building along the St. Lawrence in the expropriated lands. Planning was well underway by the two Seaway agencies and the two hydro agencies, as well as local officials, when the two Seaway agencies decided to try to persuade the railway company to abandon its line to Ottawa, allowing the bridge to be built on approximately the same line as the original low-level bridges, as a high-level road bridge, and saving millions in construction costs over the circuitous route. The New York Central at first refused, but, after receiving a financial offer from the Reynolds Corporation to locate on lands which would form part of the relocated railway right-of-way in New York State, the railroad company changed its mind, provided that it also received financial compensation for abandoning the Canadian section. This change was eagerly accepted by the Canadian government, which had been quite concerned about the inconvenience the new low-level bridge would cause to those it termed "Canadian Indians" on the St. Regis Reserve on the south shore. They would have to travel many miles farther by way of the new low-level bridge to reach the stores, schools, and hospital in Cornwall. Robert Moses, on the other hand, was furious at having his park plans thwarted. He would be left with a lovely highway to nowhere, as he had already completed the road to the original site of the bridge. He again claimed that the change in plans would delay the project a year. Castle insisted this would not happen since "ships don't run on bridges," and explained at length why this was the best plan. Moses replied with his usual tact, "Our relations are not improved by long-winded self-serving explanations from you." The bridge was designed and built quickly, a model of Canadian–American co-operation, as the Canadians built the substructure and Americans the superstructure, with each being encouraged by the two Seaway authorities and the Corps to hire subcontractors from the others' country when working there, to avoid labour troubles.[48]

Further friction developed at the same time as the other disputes when the Canadian cabinet insisted, against the wishes of the American government, that Canada would dredge the North Channel to 27 feet so that an all-Canadian canal would be possible when traffic warranted it. This added to the costs for which the Seaway Authority was responsible, but the move was cheered by those who still harboured dreams of showing the Americans that Canada could go it alone. Costs were, in fact, becoming a problem for both the Seaway Authority and the Seaway Corporation. The expense of dredging the North Channel was only one of numerous issues. Unexpectedly difficult work in deepening the Welland Canal from 25 to 27 feet due to rock formations, the need to pay a portion of the cost of dredging in the South Channel, the problems caused by glacial till and marine clay, the shortening of the time to build the Seaway, inflationary pressures, and poor cost estimates all contributed. Chevrier received criticism from the opposition in Parliament when he asked for an increase in the amount of debt that the Authority could take on from $300 million to $335 million but, with the Liberal Party still firmly in control, the criticism was only a minor embarrassment.[49]

This criticism was not nearly as strong as that received by Castle when he had to go to Congress, where enemies and late converts to the seaway cause were sure to jump on the failure to stay within budget, as were Democrats who saw the issue as a way to attack the administration. Originally the Corps of Engineers had estimated American costs at $67 million, but Congress had authorized $105 million. After compromising on the costs of the dredging in the South Channel, Castle went to Congress asking for an increase to $140 million. He blamed the added cost on the failure of the Corps to include numerous items in the original estimates, and by doing this he caused an open split between the two bodies, each of which had always been suspicious of the competence of the other. During House Public Works Committee hearings and later at a Senate hearing, N.R. Danielian testified that the fault was Castle's. One senator suggested that Danielian had failed to point out to Castle, his former boss, that the estimates were wrong. Danielian denied knowing they were wrong, and blamed the problem on Castle's incompetence, particularly on Castle's agreement to pay a large part of the cost of dredging below the power dam, instead of insisting that the power authorities pay for the work, and on making many changes in plans. He suggested that the added cost would result in tolls so high that shippers, which he also represented as spokesperson for the Users' Committee on St. Lawrence Seaway Tolls, would be discouraged from using it.[50]

In criticizing Castle, Danielian had broken with the former president of his organization, as he was doing with other senior members. In the wake of Danielian's denunciation, Harry C. Brockel, director of the Port of Milwaukee, member of the Seaway Advisory Committee, and member of the Great Lakes–St. Lawrence Association executive, wrote a letter to the vice-president of the Cleveland Chamber of Commerce. In it he defended Castle and the Seaway, suggested that people should not lose faith in the Seaway, and warned that the waterway was under attack by anonymous letters coming out of Washington, probably created by steel interests. Danielian then wrote a letter to the mayor of Milwaukee, repeating his charges, and attacking Brockel, who worked for the city, for defending Castle. In the midst of this dispute, Castle prepared a series of notes to use in an attack on Danielian, but most were never used. In the notes he accused Danielian of intentionally misrepresenting the facts to Congress, of undermining the Development Corporation with the Canadians, a charge that Castle also made publically, and of other unethical activities. He suggested that Danielian stayed in the Seaway Association just to collect his salary, and called him "arrogant, pedantic, and greedy." Danielian would continue to lead the Great Lakes–St.

Lawrence Association until 1965, but the organization became fractured as a result of his policies and lost its collective influence, which passed to the highly visible Danielian. Increasingly he devoted his time to the International Economic Policy Association, an organization founded by him in 1957 that became quite influential. In spite of this, his high profile on Seaway matters prompted President John F. Kennedy to appoint him to the St. Lawrence Seaway Advisory Board in 1961. While Danielian kept his reputation as a highly knowledgeable Seaway authority, Castle, on the other hand, was being attacked by those on both sides of the issue.[51]

His actions in blaming the Corps escalated into a battle in 1957 over whether it would assume its normal role of maintaining the Seaway once it was built, or whether the Seaway Corporation would do so. Castle argued, in presentations to the Bureau of the Budget, that the corporation could do the job more economically. While the belief that the Corps had handled the original estimates poorly no doubt played a role, the fact that the Corps made derogatory statements about the corporation to the bureau was seen as an attempt to undermine the corporation rather than legitimate criticism, and the Corps was deprived of an ongoing role. In June of 1958, the Seaway Corporation was transferred from the Department of Defense to the Department of Commerce, at the request of the corporation, which believed this would promote use of the seaway. With this transfer, the Corps lost its biggest ally in dealing with the corporation.[52]

When Lionel Chevrier decided to relinquish his post at the head of the Seaway Authority in 1957 and to return to the House of Commons, only to see his party defeated in the election that year, he was asked what the hardest aspect of his job had been. He replied that it was dealing with the Americans. Had the same question been asked of the leadership of the Corps of Engineers, the reply quite possibly would have been that it had been dealing with the Seaway Corporation. Had Castle been asked, he could well have said that his biggest problem was dealing with his critics, inside and outside Congress. Had Robert Moses been asked, he no doubt would have replied sarcastically that it was dealing with all the shortsighted people in all the agencies that he dealt with who interfered with his plans and wasted his time.[53]

Although deprived of an ongoing role, the Corps continued its work on the Seaway through 1958 and into 1959. In finishing the South Channel, it encountered an issue similar to that faced by the Seaway Authority at Caughnawaga. The final portion of the channel would cut off a small section of the St. Regis/Akwesasne Reserve, and would involve dredging through waters that joined parts of the reservation in Canada and the United States. Though somewhat bigger than Caughnawaga, with the largest portion in New York, and portions in Quebec and Ontario, including Cornwall Island, the same basic issue applied as in the other Mohawk community; the residents did not want to lose their land. Though only a few homes had to be moved as a result of the Seaway construction and of the rerouting of Highway 37, some 86 acres would be lost from the tip of the reservation, known as Raquette Point. Two other issues complicated negotiations. The people of St. Regis laid claim to Barnhart Island as a part of their traditional lands, a claim which Robert Moses dismissed with disdain. In addition, some 130 acres of Cornwall Island were taken by the Canadian government for approaches to the new high-level bridge, causing additional resentment. The people of St. Regis initiated an unsuccessful New York court case in 1956 to try to get compensation for the loss of Barnhart Island.

The Corps could not expropriate native land in New York courts and was concerned that federal courts might not be as sympathetic. On the other hand, it worried about bad publicity if it took a hard-nosed approach to negotiations. Begun in late 1955, these talks dragged on until January of 1957 before a settlement was reached, one which did not satisfy all factions within the St. Regis community nor within the Corps. This settlement was reached only days before the bids were opened for work in the area.[54]

The Corps of Engineers were responsible for dredging in the Thousand Islands section, in co-operation with the Canadians. Most of the channel was in American waters, but in the Canadian section the Corps did hydrographic surveys for the Canadians to assist in Canadian dredging. Work could not be totally separated and American equipment worked in Canadian waters and vice versa. Workers from each country sometimes served on vessels from the other.

Despite tensions at the higher levels, international co-operation generally worked very well during the whole period of construction. The building of the high-level bridge at Cornwall was a good example, but there were many more. Americans built the Iroquois Dam and Canadians worked on the cut across the American Long Sault Island. Construction vehicles from each country used the most direct route to where they were going, regardless of the international boundary. The Corps did test boring in the Canadian North Channel, bringing equipment that the Canadian government excluded from paying duties. Dredging by both countries went on in the International Section until a depth of 29 feet was reached, to guarantee 27 feet of water. This was achieved by the official opening day of July 1, 1959. Aside from some later studies on the feasibility of keeping the Seaway open in winter, and a small amount of maintenance work, largely dredging, this marked the end of Corps involvement in the Seaway.[55]

However, it did not mark the end of the involvement of the Corps in the broader seaway concept. Supporters had left the deepening and improving of the channels west of the Welland out of the Wiley-Dondero bills to keep the apparent cost of the Seaway lower. In 1955 the Corps recommended to Congress, through the Secretary of the Army, that the channels through the Upper Lakes be deepened to provide 27 feet and that a channel be cut through Canadian territory in the St. Clair River, if Canada agreed to allow it. When presented to the House and the Senate, the proposal generated almost no negative comments in committee, in a two-day hearing in a House Public Works Subcommittee and a Senate Public Works Subcommittee. The measure then passed both chambers unanimously. With the Seaway approved and the request by Castle for more money yet to come, opponents of the Seaway chose not to fight what they saw as a losing battle against an expanded seaway system that would at last give the Upper Lakes area what supporters of the deep waterway idea had wanted for almost 60 years. The Corps continued this work until the task was in large part completed in 1962.[56]

Tolls were another issue that caused problems for both Canadians and Americans during construction. In 1955, both Seaway agencies established committees to recommend levels of tolls. Once public discussions began, it became apparent that a substantial number of

Canadians were opposed to tolls, which had not existed since 1903, and even more were opposed to tolls on the Welland, since it had been completed in 1932, long before the Seaway, and was wholly in Canadian territory. In the United States, many of the old foes of the Seaway reappeared, the railways and the ports on the Atlantic and Gulf coasts, arguing that no tolls or low tolls would give the St. Lawrence an unfair advantage. Unless the tolls were high, they also argued, the Seaway would not be able to pay off capital and interest, operating and maintenance costs in 50 years, as required by law. Low toll forces, which included shippers and ship owners and representatives from the Midwest, argued that low tolls were necessary to encourage use, which would increase the collection of toll revenue. N.R. Danielian, speaking for the Great Lakes–St. Lawrence Association and for the Users' Committee on St. Lawrence Seaway Tolls (an alliance of industry, shipping interests, and farm organizations), argued that it was unrealistic to expect reasonable levels of tolls to pay off all the costs in 50 years. It would be better, he argued, to allow a longer cost-recovery period and write off a portion as a defence cost. Faced with these divergent opinions, the committees came up with mid-range tolls that most users could accept and most neutral observers thought could pay off the debt. Both governments accepted these recommendations early in 1959, with the understanding that the rates would be reviewed in five years.[57]

Of the many thousands working on the power and navigation projects, hundreds were employed by HEPCO to move the people from the communities along the water. Neither the Power Authority nor the Seaway Authority actually moved buildings. They just paid the owners and let them move the buildings if they wanted to do so. HEPCO had not envisaged the extent of the task when Saunders first responded to demands to move a few buildings. Eventually, moving buildings became a part of the policy to deal with relocations. Some of the finest examples of early Ontario architecture were moved to a new living museum, Upper Canada Village, a representation of life in the early nineteenth century located adjacent to the relocated memorial to the Battle of Crysler's Farm and a collection of relocated tombstones from area graveyards. This, along with a golf course and a small fly-in airfield for visitors, became the centrepiece of a large expanse of parkland along the St. Lawrence, created out of expropriated land not used for communities. Another feature of this parkland was the creation of a camping and picnicking area by joining the tops of hills left exposed when the land was flooded, called the Long Sault Parkway. This parkland rivalled that created by Robert Moses on the opposite shore. Here there would be camping and nature preserves as on the Canadian shore, but the centrepiece of his park was the combination of the dam and the Eisenhower Lock, with their visitor centres. Of course, being a creation of Moses, the centre at the dam was more elaborate than the one at the lock.

Specially built equipment from New Jersey was brought in for some of the moving. Houses were lifted off their foundations and gently transported to their new sites. For the benefit of television, a small house was picked up with all furniture, dishes, etc. in their usual places, transported to its new site, lowered onto its basement, and the services connected, all within an hour, and with no damage to the contents. While not all moves went that smoothly, the vast majority did no damage, and if they did, HEPCO made it right. Neighbours could stay together in the new location if they so desired, and HEPCO would store perennials over the winter and plant them in the spring. As well as gardens, houses received a new lawn and, of course, a basement and services. About 550 homes were saved in this way. Communities were given new churches, schools, shopping centres, paved roads, and sidewalks. Farmers were assisted in finding new farms. HEPCO even provided temporary housing for those whose new home was not ready when they had to move. In New York and Quebec, the displaced were on their own in dealing with all of these things. While some buildings in Ontario were not moved because of their state of disrepair, others were rejected because they were on rural roads that could not handle the large house-moving rigs. Some fine examples of nineteenth century brick buildings had to be abandoned because the brick was only a facing, not a structural element, and the structures could not have survived the move. Others were too large to move. There also existed a large number of cottages on Sheek Island, between Barnhart and the Canadian mainland. Though these were on land leased from the government, and no compensation was necessary under terms of the lease, the cottagers made a very public fuss and won

Moving houses.

a promise of new locations on new islands that would be created after the flooding. Some chose to slide their cottages across the ice during the winter of 1957, with consequent damage, but others had theirs moved. An archaeological dig on the island in the two years prior to the inundation revealed what appeared to be a very early native settlement, but the area was flooded before the dig was finished.[58]

Cemeteries had to be moved, as well. Families were asked if they wanted graves moved. If they did not, the graves were covered with stones to stabilize them, and the headstones were moved. Some 6,000 headstones were moved, but the number of graves moved is not clear. It was definitely a small number. One estimate from a HEPCO property official who worked in the area was 20 percent. In each case where a disinterment took place, a clergyman was in attendance. Headstones were relocated to existing cemeteries, a new union cemetery, or to the Crysler Battlefield Memorial Park. On the opposite side of the river, the Power Authority moved all graves, as well as the headstones.[59]

Once the houses and other buildings had been moved, any buildings that were left were auctioned off, and could be stripped of any useful material, a sad ending for a number of fine buildings. However, some small buildings survived because of this policy, as people bought them as sheds, chicken coops, etc., and moved them out of the flood zone. They were later reunited in the Lost Villages Museum, in Ault Park near Cornwall, a replacement for the old Ault Park on Sheik Island.[60] The remaining buildings in Aultsville, some already stripped, including a brick church and a large two-storey fraternal hall, were turned over to the National Research Council to use for fire tests to develop fire safety standards. Several buildings were rigged with extensive monitoring equipment and burned. The scientists set fire to different types of buildings, frame and brick, large and small, to determine the differences in the rates that fires spread. One of the conclusions reached was that smoke would render people unconscious long before the fire reached them. This research was reputedly one of the reasons for the development of smoke detectors rather than heat detectors to warn residents of fires. It was definitely used to revise the fire code.[61]

While houses were being moved, the destruction began. Telephone and hydro poles were cut down to make room for houses to be moved. Buildings remaining after the auctions were burned as training exercises by volunteer firefighters, or were bulldozed. The large Provincial Paper Mill at Mille Roche was blown up, and the hydro plant there, one of the earliest in Ontario, was destroyed to ground level, leaving the intakes in the river and some of the below-ground workings for divers to explore in later years. A similar fate befell the small powerhouse at Iroquois. Fences were torn down in large numbers, and anything else above ground. Cellars, wells, and cisterns were filled in. Old Iroquois and the business district of Morrisburg looked like deserts when the bulldozers had finished. The final indignity came when crews ranged the countryside, cutting down every tree. Nothing could remain that might interfere with navigation. Those residents who chose to watch saw trees, some more than 100 years old, reduced to stumps. These guardians of farm lanes vanished as the leafy canopy over the curving shore hugging Highway 2 was reduced to logs and sawdust. The logs, like the tombstones, were transported out of the area to be

*Ontario Power Generation/SLU, Collection 40, Mabee Series, Box 52.*

New Iroquois. The new towns of Ingleside and Long Sault were very similar.

flooded. Even walkways that used to lead fathers coming home from work and children coming home from school to welcoming doors disappeared. To long-time residents the landscape became desolate and featureless.[62]

North of the area to be flooded, the new communities emerged. Highway 2 was rerouted to be as straight as possible, for the old highway was romantic but dangerous. From Iroquois to Morrisburg the new road followed the old Canadian National right-of-way, with the railway being moved farther north. HEPCO had designed the new communities on the latest planning principles. Main streets lined with stores and apartments above were out. Instead, each community would have plazas along Highway 2, and the community would be behind. Streets would not be built on a grid pattern as in older villages. Instead, streets would loop around, and were designed so that churches and schools were easily reachable from any part of the community. Iroquois, the first to move, hired their own planner, who came up with a location on the water, not far east. HEPCO felt the site was not suitable, especially since it contained deposits of marine clay, and outwitted the townspeople by arranging with the one industry in the village, Caldwell Linen Mills, to move north of the existing village, where HEPCO wanted to place the new Iroquois. About one-third of Morrisburg was to move, essentially the business district. Local officials were reluctant to let HEPCO dictate what their new section would look like. In 1955 they heard that Massena handled planning issues differently and sent the village and township planning board to find out how things were done. Upstate New York had a tradition of citizen participation in government that predated the founding of the republic. The same tradition had greeted PASNY's expropriation procedures with accusations of Russian dictatorial tactics. The Morrisburg Planning Board then called together representatives of all community organizations and began a lengthy and difficult process of defining what they wanted and deciding if Hydro was offering it. Ultimately the decision was that Hydro was doing most of the right things, but citizen participation gave the people a strong sense of ownership of their new community. The other two "new towns" encompassing the villages and hamlets between Morrisburg and Cornwall accepted the HEPCO plans, having little knowledge of planning themselves.

South of the St. Lawrence, there was little need for planning. Most of the land consisted of farms and cottages. The village of Waddington, the one village partially affected by the flooding, saw land between it and the river disappear, which included a plant for processing local milk. It was not rebuilt because many of the farmers in the area lost part or all of their farms, lessening the need for local processing. The inhabitants were offered the choice of where the river road, which had to be relocated, would go. They chose to route it through town, in the hopes of boosting tourism. For most of the displaced inhabitants in New York, though, it was a case of living with a smaller farm, or having to find a new one, or finding a new cottage to buy. Many would lose their cherished view of the river.[63]

The general consensus on the Canadian side was that living conditions were better in the new towns. While there was some grumbling about the years needed to replace trees, about increased taxes on new stores, about the odd way the streets were laid out, about problems caused by having a house moved, most people seemed to feel their physical surroundings had improved. HEPCO had done far more than required to make people happy, far more than the other Seaway entities had done for the people that they displaced. But physical surroundings are not everything. It is impossible to put a value on a way of life. There would be no more sun-dappled walks by the Long Sault Rapids, no more trips to the favourite fishing spot or swimming hole, no more kicking a can down a dusty back street, or strolling down the farm lane in the moonlight, the trees on either side creating strange, twisted shapes on the ground. There was something sterile about the new plazas, especially compared to the variety of architecture and the feeling of age on the old main streets. It was the older residents who felt this the most, but as the years went by, memories became more vivid for the younger, and nostalgia for a rose-coloured past increased. It was not unusual for residents who could do so to go down to the water's edge years later, to look at the stumps of trees sticking out of the water on what had been their property, and remember what used to be. One of the consequences of the nostalgia was the creation in 1977 of The Lost Villages Historical Society and later a Lost Villages Museum near Cornwall, to collect buildings and information about the area's past for future generations.[64]

Despite strikes, companies abandoning their contracts, time-consuming disputes among the five Seaway agencies, changes in design, labour and material shortages, and lack of bids on some of the contracts, the power dam and the canals were ready enough to provide power, and navigation to 14 feet, by the specified date, July 1, 1958. Most of the cofferdam below the power dam had been removed and 30 tons of dynamite set in the stone cofferdam blocking the St. Lawrence. A large crowd gathered to see what many believed would be a wall of water surge down the valley to the dam. When the detonation took place at 8:00 a.m., there was an initial surge, but the area to be covered was so vast that, almost immediately, the flow became a series of small creeks and larger rivulets, moving slowly toward the dam. By the afternoon, water was backing up and beginning to swallow the past. The first to go were the Cornwall Canal and Mille Roches, soon to be 50 feet below the surface of the new Lake St. Lawrence. As water washed over the embankment of the canal, 100 years of transportation history disappeared. Over the next four days the water rose and backed up along its path. As it rose, it submerged the grave of Sir James Whitney, the premier of Ontario who had fought Alcoa's plans to dam the St. Lawrence, seemingly so long ago. As it rose farther, it lapped over the lower portion of Crysler's farm, symbolically inundating the battlefield where American, British, and Canadian forces fought for control of the St. Lawrence in 1813. In four days the sites of all the villages east of Morrisburg were gone, along with one-third of Morrisburg and the Farran's Point and Rapide Plat canals. Old Highway 2 and the old CNR right-of-way were underwater, except for a few high points where the highway and the right-of-way poked out of the river for a short distance, looking like the survivors of some great natural catastrophe. By the fourth day, both the Canadian and American shorelines looked nothing like they had only days before, and the islands between had changed dramatically. Some had disappeared altogether and others were only a shadow of their former selves. Lake St. Lawrence now lay across half of Barnhart and most of Sheek Island. On the fifth day, Prime Minister John Diefenbaker, whose Conservative party had replaced Louis St. Laurent's Liberals in the election of 1957, threw a switch in the powerhouse to begin sending power from one generator out to Ontario. The first American generator began operating on July 17. The remaining 15 Canadian generators were brought online over the next year and a half. It would be mid-December of 1959 before the final generator began operating, but the deadline had been met.[65]

Only two former presidents were alive to enjoy the moment, but it was fitting that they were two who had been among the most tireless promoters of the project, Herbert Hoover, attracted to the movement 40 years before by Julius Barnes, and Harry S. Truman. Neither man would have been entirely happy with the power portion of the Seaway, as Hoover wanted power developed by private interests under federal jurisdiction and Truman wanted it developed by the federal government, but both had essentially capitulated on their point before leaving office. Overall, it gave both men what they believed was necessary for the country. In fact, a large percentage of the new power that went to public use in New York and Vermont, states where it was distributed, was handled by private companies like Niagara Mohawk. Of the power generated by the American half of the dam, a surprising 57 percent went to three industries. Despite attempts by federal, state, and local officials to attract new industries to the depressed economy of the St. Lawrence Valley, only two were enticed, Reynolds Aluminum and a General Motors fabricating plant to use the Reynolds product. The new power did not prove a boon to the local economy, as many had hoped, but it did keep hydro rates steady at a time of increased demand for power in the two states.[66]

It was a time of celebration and of sadness for some of those who had laboured over the previous years to see the power and navigation projects developed. Interviewed in Massena, E.B. Crosby, the leading figure in the movement in Upper New York State, said that he did not want credit, for he saw the cost of the Seaway as well as the potential benefits. Too many old friends were hurt by it, including the employees at the Alcoa powerhouse, which would have to close as a result of the building of the Wiley-Dondero Canal, and the old farmers along the St. Lawrence who lost their property. In Duluth, Julius Barnes, that grand old man of the deep waterway movement, who had pursued the dream for almost half a century, read on April 19, 1959, of ships piling up at Montreal, waiting to enter the Seaway when the first official season opened. Life had not been easy for him in recent years, but he remained completely optimistic about the future. His wife and her two sisters had died within the last 18 months and he was at odds with his sons, who possibly felt he had wasted too much of his own money on public causes. He and a friend calculated that he had spent over $4 million on promoting the seaway concept and on public buildings for Duluth. Barnes, like others in the movement, had broken with Danielian over the latter's policies, leaving Barnes out of the official activities of the Great Lakes–St. Lawrence Association, though he continued to promote the Seaway on his own. Castle, friends with Barnes since their days in Duluth, had invited him to the opening of the Eisenhower Lock in 1958, but Barnes felt he was too old to travel, and his memory was beginning to fail him. He had been honoured at the opening of the new Duluth cargo terminal and had a school named after him in the previous year, but he was largely

*George Starkey, Duluth Herald Tribune.*

The official opening of the Seaway at Duluth, July 1959.

forgotten outside of Duluth. Yet, in spite of his ups and downs, Barnes must have been proud to know that ocean-going ships would at last be able to reach his beloved city. A life-long believer in health culture, he had his usual breakfast of oatmeal while reading the paper and then decided to go up to his room in the hotel where he had lived since his wife's death. There had been a storm on Lake Superior the previous night and he was tired, so he went for a nap, from which he did not wake. After his decades-long wait, he was not there to celebrate the arrival of the first ocean ship, the *Ramon de Larrinago* when it docked on May 3, or for the official opening later in the summer.[67]

Neither were other native sons, S.A. "Deepwater" Thompson, Charles P. Craig, and Frank Flowers (from Superior) there to celebrate, as they were long gone from the scene. Nor were many of the men from other parts of the Midwest who had promoted the seaway concept over the previous 60 years: John Lind, Charles Townsend, Horace Gardner, Henry Allen, William George Bruce, and many others, from places like Muskegon, Milwaukee, Chicago, and from small towns and cities across

*Duncan Cameron/LAC PA-121475.*

The official opening of the St. Lawrence Seaway by Queen Elizabeth II and President Dwight D. Eisenhower.

the Midwest. Most were now just names, who used to be people, who shared a dream. Without pressure from the Americans in the previous 50 years, resulting mostly from pressure from the Midwest, it is questionable whether the Canadians would have decided to build the Seaway on their own. Without the constant effort to promote a seaway in Congress by these men, over a period of 60 years, it is questionable whether the Canadian decision to build the Seaway would have prompted the United States to participate.

This dream formally became a reality on June 26, 1959. By the beginning of the shipping season in April, the first ships could use the full 27-foot depth all the way through from Montreal to the Lake Erie end of the Welland Canal. In June the Royal Yacht *Britannia* sailed up to the St. Lambert Lock, the beginning of the Seaway, and Queen Elizabeth for Canada and President Eisenhower for the United States formally opened the system. With them were the Canadian prime minister and cabinet, members of Parliament, congressmen, and thousands of others, including representatives of foreign shipping lines which would use the system. The Queen then travelled on to the American locks where the next day a second ceremony was held, with Vice-President Richard Nixon substituting for the president. The dream of men going back as far as Jacques Cartier, and later encompassing both Canadians and Americans, to be able to extract the riches of the interior of North America through the St. Lawrence was about to be achieved.[68]

# Reassessing the Dream: The Seaway in Operation

The whole of the Great Lakes seemed to vibrate with excitement in the years before the Seaway was finished and during the first full year of operation. It seemed that the old motto of deep waterway supporters, "Every Lakeport a Seaport," was about to come true. Everywhere people were dreaming and planning. *Newsweek* reported in 1955:

> The St. Lawrence Seaway will bring the Seagoing world to the shores of Lake Ontario and the lakeside cities, in a rosy glow, are getting ready to receive it. Toronto harbor added a second freight terminal only last month and three more are planned. The Hamilton Harbor Commission is rushing multimillion dollar improvements to be ready for the opening of the seaway. New foreign shipping lines, anxious to stake out early claims, are already coming in.[1]

In 1958, the *Toronto Telegram* noted that the Toronto Harbour Commission general manager predicted that overseas trade in and out of Toronto would be three times what it had been prior to the opening of the Seaway.[2] The *Minneapolis Star* reported in 1955 that:

> Ray C. Fischer, the Minneapolis freight forwarder, this year opened an office in Milwaukee to service accounts with Lakes shipping. He believes the Lakes potential

is tremendous, particularly after the new seaway is in operation. He estimates savings to shippers at 10 and even 20 per cent, depending on the commodity handled — some move at higher freight rates than others."[3]

Buffalo, western entrance to the Erie Canal, railway shipping point serving New York City, and competitor with the St. Lawrence for close to a century and a half, had dreams of profiting from the Seaway as well. *Newsweek* reported in 1955 of Buffalo: "It is the largest milling centre in the world, the nation's sixth largest steel centre and the biggest inland port; it is second only to Chicago as a railroad hub. Nine of the nation's 12 largest manufacturing companies (excluding oil companies) have plants in the city ..." In contrast to the previous year, when only 27 foreign ships put in to Buffalo, the city believed that it would have access to 80 percent of the world's shipping, to bring it raw materials and to take away manufactured goods. Local businessmen saw huge opportunities for replacing New York as a trucking distribution centre, using the recently completed New York State Thruway. Due to the fact that Buffalo was halfway between Labrador ore and the Mesabi Range, and the Seaway could also bring ore from Liberia and South America, steel production was likely to increase, and spinoff industries with it. Since the city had a large grain-storage capacity, left over from its days as the American transshipment point for grain coming down the Great Lakes, it assumed that it would also be a grain distribution centre. It saw the Seaway as bringing in the petrochemical industry and hoped that the city could also sell goods manufactured in Buffalo to the world. Every aspect of the city's economy was going to grow, in the minds of its business people. As the chairman of National Gypsum put it, "Smart men will see the potential here and will move in and 10 years from now Buffalo will enter a period of great growth. I don't know anything that can stop it." The only actions necessary to make this happen, *Newsweek* reported, would be to spend $26.9 million to build new piers, extend old ones, and construct storage facilities. The city would also have to find $50 million to deepen the harbour to 27 feet.[4]

Perhaps the most enthusiastic view of the future was in *The Chicago American* in 1957:

No geographic change in all of history has offered the golden promise of the $300,000,000 St. Lawrence Seaway project, now thrusting its eager fingers deep into the nation's heartland.... Chicago, as befitting its world status, marches in the vanguard. Its mighty Lake Calumet port is a reality.

Opening this spring, it will accommodate a dozen ocean leviathans at one time. In 1959 the great Seaway will be ready. Three years later the Calumet–Sag Channel, after its own face-lifting, adds a vital link.

The vast, combined waterway will do more than boost Chicago's people and prosperity manyfold. It will multiply the entire Midwest economy. Add Chicago's new status as hub of the inland waterway network to its present status as hub of the nation's rail, air and motor carrier networks. Combine this unmatched distribution system with the heartland's rich market and productivity in commerce, industry, agriculture. Stir in the plans abuilding to insure a flow of ore, grain and other cargoes, using the new seaway to its capacity of 33,000,000 tons a year. Put them together and the Midwest's pictured destiny is no idle dream. Eight states along the new frontier which is America's Fourth Seacoast teem with virile preparations.... Illinois looks beyond Chicago to new major ports like Joliet, Peoria, 13 principal centers on its waterway. Uncle Sam invests $160,000,000. Indiana, with only 42 miles of shoreline, boasts four harbors, plans a fifth, envisions a navigable St. Joseph River from the lake to Elkhart. Michigan's 23,000,000-tons-a-year port at Detroit, supported by those at Muskegon, Grand Rapids and elsewhere, expands apace to meet the challenge with an ambitious $70,000,000 development program under consideration. A new industrial giant stirs amid Iowa's cornfields; and Kentucky sees commercial access to another part of the world through its Louisville port. Milwaukee paces

Wisconsin with $10,000,000 invested in its magnificent harbor, $9,000,000 still to be spent. Goal: 1,000,000 tons annually in a decade. Proud of St. Louis and Kansas City, its queen river ports, Missouri readies for a new traffic surge with the opening of the seaway and Cal–Sag Channel. And Minnesota, Star of the North, pushes $25,000,000 improvements in the Duluth–Superior harbor, farthest west of America's Fourth Seacoast.[5]

Aside from its almost lurid description of preparations in the Midwest, the article suggests that Chicago will now reverse its old idea of sending trade down the Mississippi to New Orleans, and will draw trade north from the Mississippi Valley, to be shipped out via the Seaway.

Even ports that would not logically benefit from the Seaway did not want to be left behind. Kingston, Ontario, which had at times acted as an alternative to Prescott for the transshipment of grain to the 14-footers, hoped for some spill-over from the vast amount of traffic expected to use the Seaway. Oswego, which had made its money from being the northern end of the Lake Ontario branch of the Erie Canal, believed that it could attract more business for its grain elevator, and more shipping business from industries in the area, and hoped for a new steel mill, a brewery, and a petrochemical plant. It hired a port director and set aside $11 million to deepen the harbour and build a new breakwater. It believed that it could capitalize on its position as the easternmost port on the Great Lakes. Ports from Quebec City to the far end of Lake Superior all wanted and expected to be able to capitalize on the coming of the Seaway. Everywhere there were dreams of riches to come.[6]

The reality of the first year in operation was far from this expectation. The officers of ocean-going ships did not know the system, there were too few pilots, and the channels were different from what they had been, leaving even veteran pilots confused. The result was that ships moved very slowly through the locks and narrow channels that were still being dredged on the Upper Lakes. The greatest delay was at the Welland Canal, where the multiple single locks, inexperienced ship crews, and lack of necessary equipment on some ships caused long delays. From information available at the time, one observer commented:

Accidents were frequent. Ships scraped their sides on the concrete walls, ran into gate fenders, smashed navigation lights, wandered off course, and hung on the rocks. When a fuse blew out in a Beauharnois Canal lift bridge as it was going up, an oil tanker approaching it too fast tried to stop suddenly, but swung sideways and stuck in the mud, blocking the channel for 15 hours. In a fog, the radar-less Liberian freighter *Monrovia* crashed into a Canadian ship in Lake Huron and sank. During the first few weeks of the Seaway's operation, about one-third of the world's major marine casualties were on the St. Lawrence system.[7]

Though dozens of ports from the lower St. Lawrence to Duluth were either making improvements or planning them, many had not been finished. In some cities the harbours were not deep enough for ocean-going vessels. Reportedly, only Detroit, Toronto, Hamilton, and Windsor harbours had a depth of 27 feet. In others, such as Detroit, there were not enough docking facilities, and ships backed up in the river wasting valuable time waiting to unload. Only Chicago, Milwaukee, Toronto, and Hamilton could handle multiple ships at the same time. Some faced the same problem as Duluth–Superior, which had built a huge general cargo terminal that stood largely empty for the first years, while grain ships backed up at the elevators in Superior. The chutes to fill them were designed for lakers, the decks of which were not as high above the water as were those of ships designed for the world's oceans. Sea-going ships had to fill their ballast tanks to sink lower in the water, and gradually empty them as their holds were filled, wasting time and money.[8]

Despite the difficulties, the first year was a modest success. A four-month steel strike hurt ore shipments from the Mesabi Range and from Labrador, but tonnage through the Welland rose by 29 percent and through the St. Lawrence by 75 percent. Overseas trade with Toronto, Milwaukee, Muskegon, and Cleveland was three times higher than it had been in 1958. Toledo and Chicago saw an increase of 400 percent. Hamilton trade increased by 700 percent, Buffalo's by 800 percent, and Rochester's by 1,000 percent. Kenosha, from which cars and machinery were shipped, saw its international trade jump to 23 times what it had been, and Duluth–Superior to 78 times. Toronto reported that 800 foreign ships visited, from countries around the world. Grain shipments from Chicago were 21 times what they had been the year before, and Duluth-Superior shipments were 110 times as great.[9]

Near the end of the shipping season, Castle announced that total tonnage would be about 20, 000,000 tons (around 18,144,000 tonnes), about 20 percent below the previous year's estimate. This allowed the Seaway's opponents, the railways and east coast ports, to demand an immediate increase in tolls to make up for the revenue shortfall. This was a demand that they would continue to make, as they argued that original estimates of traffic were inflated to make the Seaway seem viable. Castle was able to point out that the tolls agreement signed in March allowed for a review in five years, not before. He was confident that, by then, the system would be viable. In fact, early in 1960 he predicted a usage of 50,000,000 tons (around 45,360,000 tonnes) per year by 1968.[10]

Although there is some variation in usage data among different sources, the Seaway achieved this goal. The figures compiled by the two Seaway agencies show a total tonnage for 1968, in the new metric measurement, of over 60 million tonnes (almost 66.5 million tons). By 1979, the total had risen to over 74 million tonnes (just over 80 million tons). The general trend had been upwards each year, except for 1969, and for a sudden drop in 1974, the year after the oil crisis. In order to stimulate additional traffic, steps had been taken to expand the capacity of the Great Lakes canal system and to mitigate problems encountered by ships using the system. At the Soo, which was not part of the Seaway, but was seen as part of the Seaway system, a new Poe Lock was constructed to handle ships of an ever-increasing size, being 1,200 feet long, 110 feet wide, and 32 feet deep. A new traffic control system was developed to increase the speed with which ships could pass through the Seaway portion of the Great Lakes. By 1964, transit time had dropped from 46 hours to 22 hours, a significant saving of time. The Welland, officially part of the Seaway, with its eight locks was the slowest portion of the entire system from Montreal to Lake Superior. In 1973 a bypass was opened to take ships around the city of Welland which, with numerous lift bridges and a narrow, winding channel, significantly slowed traffic. Though captains still fretted about the amount of time it took to get through what was called "the ditch," the most frustrating portion could now be avoided. The future outlook for the Seaway looked rosy indeed in 1979, especially given the generally upward trend. The twentieth anniversary of the opening was a time to celebrate the success of the venture.

After 1979, however, the general trend was down, except for a slight increase in 1984 over the previous year. By 1993 the total was about 41 million tonnes (about 44 million tons). Between that year and 2006, the total fluctuated between 40 and 51 million tonnes, with the high point of usage being 1998 and the low point 2003. In other words, there were years when total tonnage was just over half that in the peak year of 1979. Something had gone seriously wrong.[11]

This drastic drop in use was the result of numerous factors, some of which might have been predicted, but several of which were the result of rapidly changing world conditions. In 1962, tolls on the Welland, unpopular in Canada, were suspended, and a modest flat-rate fee for using the locks was substituted in 1967. Since revenues were not covering interest on the debt in either country, and Canada's cumulative debt was rising faster, given that it had paid about 70 percent of the original cost, the Canadian government proposed an increase in tolls in 1976, including tolls on the Welland. After negotiations with the United States, which resulted in lesser increases than Canada proposed for grain and for general cargo (usually considered as manufactured goods), which both countries wanted to encourage, new tolls were approved in 1978, to be phased in over three years. The new tolls effectively doubled what had been paid previously and clearly had an immediate effect on usage, given the rapid decline. While shipments of grains out of the St. Lawrence, the largest proportion of which was wheat, with corn, barley, and other grains, plus soybeans making up the remainder, continued to increase during the 1970s, a significant proportion of the harvest went out through the Mississippi. In fact, traffic on the Mississippi increased by 500 percent from the 1950s to the 1970s, as areas south of the Great Lakes chose to send grain by that route. Other bulk cargoes also were sent by the river, which had no tolls. In earlier years, Chicago had tried unsuccessfully to send the trade of the Great Lakes down the Chicago Ship Canal and the Mississippi. Now it tried unsuccessfully to lure the trade of the Mississippi Valley up through Chicago and onto the Seaway.

Some grain also went by rail, as American railways offered better mileage rates to the Atlantic coast than to the Great Lakes, using so-called unit trains, trains devoted to one type of cargo, in order to take business away from the Seaway. By 1976, unit trains had won back 16 percent of the American grain trade for Atlantic ports, from a low of 6 percent in 1971. The Seaway carried only 11 percent in 1975. The majority went out by the Mississippi. Canadian railways were regulated and long-distance rates held down to benefit areas like the Maritime provinces, making unit trains an affordable alternative to water transportation. When operating subsidies were eliminated by 1996, Canadian railways were put on the same unregulated footing as American ones, able to work out private contracts with individual customers. Interestingly, the railways then saw their competitor not as the Seaway, but as the trucking industry.[1] The American Interstate Highway system, like the Seaway, was a product of the Eisenhower years. The Canadian Trans-Canada system followed soon after. Both allowed long-distance trucking on a scale not envisaged when the Seaway was being contemplated. By the 1990s, a great deal of general cargo, as well as grain, was transported by truck.

By 1970 most shipping on the Great Lakes was carried in Canadian vessels, as Canada provided subsidies on new ships and the United States did not. Much of the older lake fleet had to be replaced because of age and size. So did the sturdy workhorse 14-footers, which rapidly became obsolete, being too small to operate economically in the larger canals. The latter were scrapped, or sold off to become coastal vessels in the United States or the Caribbean.[13] Until 1970, most new American lake vessels were built for steel companies, to transport iron ore on the Upper Lakes. In the late 1960s a number of industry lobby groups, primarily port representatives, but also including shipping, warehousing, freight forwarding, banking, and labour interests, feeling that the Seaway Authority was not doing enough to stimulate use of the system, lobbied government extensively for changes. In fact, the opponents of the Seaway had made sure that legislation authorizing the creation of the Seaway Corporation prevented it from advertising or promoting usage. Lewis Castle, with his conservative background in banking, saw his role only as providing efficient and cost-effective leadership. He was succeeded by his deputy, who had the same philosophy. It was not until 1969 that a new administrator was willing to challenge the ban on advertising, by claiming that he was merely explaining the Seaway to the public. This head of the corporation, David W. Berlin, also put his organization behind the lobbying for improvements in treatment of the Great Lakes as a transportation corridor. The result was the Merchant Marine Act of 1970, which not only reclassified the Great Lakes ports as seaports, making ships built for the Great Lakes eligible for subsidies, but also cancelled interest payments on the Seaway debt.[14]

Most ships built under The Merchant Marine Act were large bulk carriers for use on the Upper Lakes. Few built for use on the Seaway even though a large percentage of American military goods and foreign food aid had to be carried on American ships and much of these materials originated at the time around the Great Lakes. In fact, foreign trade dropped off generally in the 1970s and 80s. General cargo, which was seen when the Seaway opened as the future growth area, began to decline in the late 1960s. This was largely the result of containerization, which began about the time the Seaway was finished. Mixed goods packed in containers and transported on ever-larger ships to container ports, could then be transported overland on unit trains and transferred to trucks for the final short leg of the journey. Montreal was, at first, a major container port and a few other ports could handle a modest volume of containers, but the majority of container ships quickly became too large for the Seaway. Oil tankers also grew beyond the capacity of the locks, but this became largely irrelevant after 1976 when the Sarnia–Montreal pipeline opened, bringing western oil east. As with earlier canals, the designers of the Seaway built for the present, using the Welland, designed before the First World War, as the model. Estimates vary, but something like 80 to 85 percent of all ocean-going ships could enter the seaway in 1959. In 2009, no more than 25 percent and perhaps as little as 10 to 15 percent of ships can enter.[15]

These developments have left the Great Lakes largely to bulk cargoes, which used to use the 14-foot canals. The major element in the trade is grain, with iron ore second, and coal, used in steel mills and power stations, making up the third largest segment. Cement, stone, chemicals, sugar, salt, and other building materials comprise most of the remainder. American grain going out by the Seaway is largely loaded in foreign ships on the Great Lakes for transportation overseas, with the rest sent down the Seaway in Canadian ships. Canadian grain is largely transported to the Lower St. Lawrence, where it is dropped off to be sent overseas by large (foreign) ocean-going ships. Until fairly recently, cargoes of iron ore were picked up in exchange, for the return voyage. While it was anticipated in the early 1950s that ore from the Mesabi Range would soon run out, a new process allowed the use of low-grade ore and significantly prolonged the life of the range. This development has meant that a significant proportion of the ore only travels from Lake Superior to Lakes Michigan, Huron, and Erie, not entering the Seaway. Much that is transported from Labrador and from the Upper Lakes is now semi-processed into pellets, which concentrate the ore and therefore produce less tonnage for shippers. The decline in the North American steel industry since the 1980s, in the face of lower-cost foreign alternatives, the use of less steel in automotive products, and the shrinkage of the North American automotive industry in the face of foreign competition, have also led to a decline in the need for iron ore.[16]

Shipments of grain have not only been hurt by competition from the Mississippi, but also from changes in trade patterns. Both countries began selling substantial quantities of wheat to the Soviet Union after the Seaway opened. Some went out through west coast ports, but much used the Seaway. The American trade embargo against the Soviet Union in the mid-1980s, after the Russian invasion of Afghanistan, and the collapse of the Russian economy after the disintegration of the Soviet Union at the beginning of the 1990s, destroyed much of this market. The development of the European Common Market, with its heavy subsidies to its farmers, has led to a decline in that market for North American grain. New markets opened up in Asia, especially in China, but this has led to an increase in the use of west coast ports to serve this market. It was reported in 1994 that grain tonnage on the Seaway was half of what it had been 10 years earlier. In several years in the 1990s and the early years of the 21st century, iron ore carried on the Seaway exceeded the amount of grain. It is not unusual now for iron ore to be brought from Labrador without a corresponding cargo of grain to fill the holds of downbound ships. With this overall decline in the use of the Seaway, there has been little incentive to renew the merchant fleet that serves the Seaway. By the early 1990s, half of the Canadian ships that had worked the Seaway in the 1960s had been retired, and most of the rest were well along in their lifespan.[17] Since a good deal of trade on the Great Lakes is between the two countries, recent years have seen the increased use of tug–barge combinations, but this is not suitable for large quantities of bulk goods.

In 1977 the Canadian government converted the Seaway debt into government equity in the Seaway. Congress wrote off the American Seaway debt in 1983. These actions relieved the two Seaway organizations of major burdens, but did not solve the financial problems. Congressional supporters of the seaway concept had been so anxious to overcome opposition in the late 1940s that they proposed the idea of tolls without considering all costs. When Canada and the United States worked out the tolls originally they did not take into account possible changes in the rate of inflation, possible fluctuations in traffic, and the true cost of maintaining the system. Both the rate of inflation and the cost of maintaining the seaway proved to be much higher than was expected. In the 1970s, for instance, the Eisenhower Lock was discovered to be suffering from premature aging. Thus, even with both the interest and the debt written off, the Seaway still had trouble paying the bills. The national governments have had to step in, in both countries. In the 1980s, after a lock wall collapsed in the Welland, Canada spent $175 million to refurbish the Welland and has since committed more to refurbishing the Canadian portion of the Seaway. The government of the United States is currently spending tens of millions in a 10-year renewal and modernization program.[18]

The problem was seen in government circles and in the two Seaway agencies as one of how to boost traffic and therefore revenues. In the mid-1960s, while tonnage was still increasing but was still below expectations, Congress, at the urging of members from the Midwest, authorized a study by the Army Corps of Engineers of the feasibility of extending the navigation season on the Seaway and the Great Lakes. Initially a four-year study beginning in 1965, it was extended until 1976, and a demonstration program was added in 1970. Other federal agencies also co-operated in the study. The demonstration program brought the issue of winter navigation into public view, however, and the nascent environmental movement became alarmed. Led by the Save the River Committee, centred in the Thousand Islands area of New York, but including Canadians and some supporters from outside the area, environmental groups suggested that winter navigation would destroy the river. Atlantic ports and the railways attacked the idea of extending the season, as would be expected, and the power agencies worried that disturbing the ice cover in the St. Lawrence would inhibit their ability to generate power in the winter, a process which depended on a stable cover. The Canadian government was comfortable with extending the season by a few weeks but not with a prolonged extension, and insisted on a cost–benefit analysis of keeping the waterways open. In the United States, the General Accounting Office and the comptroller general both questioned the conclusions of the Corps that the demonstration project was a success. The Corps tried to show that the concept was practical and affordable, but ultimately could not prevail, as the Save the River Committee won the support of New York's governor and its influential senator, Patrick Moynihan, and an environmental assessment was demanded. The program was abandoned in 1977.[19]

A parallel study by the Buffalo District of the Corps in the early 1970s recommended a canal on the American side at Niagara to relieve congestion on the Welland, and a second study by the Corps recommended parallel locks in the St. Lawrence, which would be longer and wider, and would be able to accommodate more of the world's shipping. Congress even toyed briefly in the mid-70s with the idea of an enlarged New York State Barge Canal. In Canada at the same time, the Seaway Authority, while building the Welland bypass, expropriated land near the Welland Canal so that a parallel system could be built when needed. In both countries these plans generated little enthusiasm in government because of the huge cost associated with the projects at a time when North American economies were suffering from both large-scale inflation and a low rate of growth.[20] In environmentalist eyes, each succeeding Corps study of the Great Lakes was suspected of secretly examining winter navigation, or larger locks. A 2002 study did, once again, suggest that larger locks were the answer to the problem of decreased traffic, and once again environmentalists, who seem to have even more public support than in the 1970s, attacked the study as leading to further degradation of the environment.[21]

Faced with the need to generate more revenue, the two agencies have tried various options. During the 1980s and 90s, representatives went to Europe to look for business, tolls were raised at various times, and considerable progress was made in cutting costs. In the 1990s, incentives were offered for firms which significantly increased the amount of cargo that they took through the Seaway, and for those which brought new business to the waterway. In 1998 a new round of toll increases by Canada on the Canadian locks was accompanied by a move on the part of the Canadian government to free itself from the possibility of having to cover future deficits. Canadian operations were turned over to a not-for-profit corporation, the St. Lawrence Seaway Management Corporation, which was expected to pay for operations, including routine maintenance, while the government would continue to own the infrastructure and cover repairs.[22] This body, which included representatives of users groups, together with the American Seaway Development Corporation, devised a new marketing plan which was put in place in 2004. The Seaway was renamed Highway $H_2O$ or $HwyH_2O$, and was marketed in Europe as a cost-effective and environmentally friendly alternative to congested east coast ports combined with costly, polluting road or rail transport. Shipping companies and port authorities were offered the opportunity to become partners in the campaign. In addition, toll reductions for a three-year period were offered for substantial quantities of goods which were new to the Seaway. Some of the new shipping business was from Europe and some was short sea shipping, that is, business on the Seaway and within the Great Lakes. Short sea shipping is defined as adding a water leg to shipping that would usually travel entirely by land. In total, more than 500,000 tonnes (551,150 tons) of new cargo was enticed into the system, helping to make 2006 the best year since 1999 at just over 47 million tonnes (52.8 million tons). This gave the two bodies hope that they could increase the use of the Seaway, which was running at less than half capacity.[23] In 2008, the incentive program brought 1.63 million tonnes (1.8 million tons) of new cargo.[24]

However, in 2007 the Seaway experienced a dropping off in total cargo carried to 43 million tonnes (47.3 million tons) and in 2008 tonnage dropped to less than 41 million tonnes (45.2 million tons). A portion of this decline could be attributed to the major recession of 2008.[25] The early months of 2009, when the economic downturn was seriously affecting world economies, saw a 40 percent drop in cargo carried when compared to 2008. This was largely the result of steel plants in the northern United States and in Canada being shut down or operating at very much reduced capacity. The president of the Seaway Management Corporation explained that "iron ore is down over 60 percent, coal almost 50 percent, the imported steel that goes to the United States down 30 percent, and no steel slabs at all were imported this year.... European utilities have had strong demand for low-sulphur coal from the Powder River Basin in Wyoming and Montana through the Seaway, and that is down." The good news was that grain shipments were up, but the clear implication was that, no matter how hard the Seaway agencies worked to improve business, the Seaway could not isolate itself from the world economy.[26] Its level of success would have to be measured over a number of years, not in claims of turning things around over one or two years.

To further increase the use of the Seaway, various technological innovations were introduced or have been the subject of trial usage. In 2003, satellite-guided navigation was introduced. A hands-free vessel mooring system for locks has been tested in the Welland Canal and is likely to be introduced soon. Testing has also taken place of a system to allow crew members on the bridge of a ship to see their approach to a lock, as viewed from the lock itself, to make entering locks easier, and of a 3-D system which displays a model of the channel bottom, to maximize the use of channel depth. All of these are designed to speed up passage through the Seaway, thus saving ship owners money.[1]

The emphasis in the $H_2O$ campaign on the environmental benefits of using the Seaway rather than road and rail is both a function of the increased sensitivity toward environmental issues and a reaction to attacks made on the Seaway, the power dam, and the studies by the Army Corps of Engineers. Ecological concerns have been a public concern since at least 1980. In 1985, the Canadian government declared a portion of the International Section an [environmental] Area of Concern, but nongovernmental organizations in Ontario, New York, and Quebec were already raising issues. The situation was a complicated one because it linked direct effects of the Seaway construction and operation with indirect results and, to a certain extent, with pre-existing pollution. In a 1996 report, Environment Canada detailed many of the concerns of environmental groups: the sealing off of Lake St. Francis by the Moses–Saunders Dam and the dredging of the channel through the lake, resulting in the destruction of floodplain wetlands, the elimination of spawning routes for various types of fish, leading to the disappearance of some species from Lake St. Francis, the intrusion of non-native varieties of plants, and pollution from older factories in Cornwall and newer ones in Massena. The report noted that the people of Akwesasne/St. Regis had seen their fishery altered, their shoreline eroded, some of their island land seized, and their winter travel made difficult by the late and early operations of the Seaway. Fluoride pollution from the Reynolds plant that had moved into the Massena area as a result of the building of the power dam had destroyed a flourishing native dairy industry on Cornwall Island, and heavy metals and chlorine compounds, some of which came from old Cornwall factories, had contaminated fish stocks which were used as food. Aside from building an eel ladder in the dam, which partly corrected the inability of the American eels to reach their spawning grounds, and the introduction of pollution control at the Reynolds plant, which reduced but did not eliminate emissions, little had been done up to the time the report was issued. The Cornwall industries had closed after the Seaway was built, but the metals and chemical compounds remained in the river.[28] To address problems such as these on the Great Lakes, Canada, the United States, provincial, and state governments have set up Areas of Concern, and are creating Remedial Action Plans to deal with all aspects of improving water quality. A similar program is being undertaken by Quebec riverside communities. As noted above, the stretch of river from the eastern end of Lake St. Francis through Cornwall to the Moses–Saunders Dam is one of these areas.[29]

Environmental groups have seized on the effects of the dam and on the issue of invasive species, which has been much in the news since the arrival of the zebra mussel, as central to a campaign to return water levels to where they were previously and to put restrictions on the Seaway. They have used the invasive species issue in arguments to stop the enlargement of the canals and the deepening of channels, which they insist will only bring more unwanted species to the Great Lakes, as well as dredge up harmful sediments which will have to be disposed of in a safe manner.

Winter navigation they see as disrupting the natural pattern of the river, threatening the ecosystem. In opposing expansion of the Seaway and winter use, they have had a formidable ally in the people of Akwesasne/ St. Regis. An increasing public awareness of previous mistreatment of native peoples meant that it was more difficult to brush aside their concerns, which happened to correspond to a majority of the concerns of environmentalists. The inhabitants of both Khanawake and Akwesasne were upset by the industry attracted to their areas by the Seaway, industry that brought pollution, which, in turn, made it difficult to continue their way of life. They also resented the loss of land, for which, in the case of the people of St. Regis/Akwesasne, they had never been compensated. The use of icebreakers to extend the shipping season and the threat of dredging and of the shore damage done by larger ships in a larger canal caused the people of Akwesasne/St. Regis to take a very public stand. In 2004, they took the United States Department of Transportation, which had taken over responsibility for the Seaway Corporation from the Department of Commerce, and the Seaway Corporation, to court over the decision to use icebreakers to open the season early in 2004. They reached an agreement in 2006 with the two, and with Transport Canada, that they would be consulted about the opening date and provided data used to determine the date. A joint study would determine the effect of icebreaking on native land.[30]

Faced with a public campaign that highlighted a current public concern, the environment, one that included native groups, which had some public sympathy because of past mistreatment and threats to their way of life, both Seaway bodies and the two national governments have tried to allay fears about the future direction of the Seaway. The two governments brought in legislation which forces foreign shipping to exchange the water in ballast tanks while at sea or, for ships without ballast tanks, flushing their holding tanks, thereby killing foreign organisms. Discussion is underway as to the possibility of forcing vessels to run an electric charge through the tanks as a further guarantee that any invasive species are eliminated.

In 2003, the two Seaway bodies, the two national transportation departments, Environment Canada, the United States Fish and Wildlife Service, and the United States Army Corps of Engineers undertook a study of the future of the Seaway and of the entire Great Lakes transportation system up to 2050. This was the first time that agencies responsible for the environment were included in such a study, a clear reflection of the changing times and of the growing influence of the environmental movement. The $20 million study acknowledged that the Seaway must be maintained and grow without unduly damaging the environment. It also explained that many of the environmental issues affecting the Seaway are the result of factors other than navigation and that, in consequence, measures to protect the environment must be done in concert with other sectors of the economy. Recommendations dealt with invasive species, the effects of dredging, of ship wake, of exhaust emissions, and of declining water levels, and the need for the development of mitigation strategies. On the other hand, the study emphasized the reduction in polluting emissions resulting from the use of ships rather than trucks or trains to carry larger quantities of cargo, and the relatively few polluting accidents in the system. It suggested applying wake-reduction strategies used on the Seaway to the remainder of the Great Lakes system and suggested monitoring and the development of management strategies for most environmental issues. Though it acknowledged the possible detrimental effects of icebreaking on shorelines, on animals which use the ice cover to migrate, and on aquatic vegetation and organisms, it provided no recommendations as to how to deal with these issues.[31]

In reply to the 2007 report, 43 environmental, sports fishing, recreational boating, labour, and native groups, plus shoreline residents, from both the United States and Canada, criticized the study as inadequate. They expressed pleasure that the report did not discuss expansion and did deal with the environment, but insisted that both governments must clearly disavow enlargement of the system as an option. In dealing with environmental issues, they were highly critical of the scope of the discussion, pointing out that some of the same groups had repeatedly raised the same issues in submissions to the study. Specifically, the groups faulted the report for its failure to measure the cost of environmental damage, and economic and social costs, against the benefits derived from the Seaway and, in addition, to consider the lesser cost associated with transshipping international cargoes to avoid invasive species. They further criticized the study for its declaration that the environmental impact of navigation is minimal, and that adequate policies are in place to keep it that way. The arrival of invasive species after 1959, the detrimental effects of dredging on the Upper Lakes, which has resulted in lower water levels, and the failure to recognize that current regulations regarding ballast water only minimize, but do not eliminate the threat of further alien invaders, are all mentioned as serious omissions. Finally, the response points out that the costs of increased short sea shipping, which the groups feel would be a good way to handle international products, are not spelled out, and there is no evidence that container traffic will increase, as the report predicts. In fact, the evidence is the opposite.[32] The simplified meaning of all of this criticism is that the Seaway will continue to feel the effects of public criticism by environmental organizations that have a substantial degree of public attention. Placing the Seaway in the public eye in this manner will necessarily reduce its flexibility in adapting to changes in the international economy and ultimately will force the system to build environmental controls into the cost of running what has been, until relatively recently, essentially a transportation business. Already, several states have imposed their own ballast-water regulations, as they do not feel that federal regulations have been strict enough.

Other pressures will also have to be dealt with in the coming years. Currently, the Great Lakes are experiencing a period of low water levels. Should this prove to be a long-term problem, as some scientists believe, the effect of global warming, this will be an additional challenge for the Seaway and for the Great Lakes system generally. Even a few inches of loss in water levels in the canals and channels can represents a loss of hundreds of tonnes of cargo for ships, a situation which erodes the cost advantage of water transportation.

Facing the challenges of a low volume of traffic, and very little in the way of foreign ships, environmental challenges, and the serious possibility of reduced tonnages as a result of declining water levels, the future of the Seaway is somewhat uncertain. A Canadian parliamentary committee pondered the issue in 1994 of whether the Seaway had outlived its usefulness and should be shut down. The 2007 report on the future of the Seaway looked at ways that Seaway traffic could be rejuvenated. It suggested that a period of slow growth was possible, under certain conditions, in the short to medium term. The solution, the authors of the study claim, is in short sea shipping, of two types. Currently, the vast majority of shipping on the Great Lakes is between ports on the Seaway system. Since road and rail corridors along the border are becoming congested, as are border crossings, there is an opportunity, they believe, to substitute water transportation to a limited extent. Semi-finished products, normally shipped by truck, could be sent in vessels that could carry truck bodies, so-called Roll on-Roll off (Ro-Ro) transports. Containerized materials, on the other hand, could be handled in vessels that were loaded and unloaded by crane (Load on-Load off, or Lo-Lo). The study recognizes that only some ports could currently handle either type of shipping, since such ports would need specialized equipment, space, and easily available forms of land transportation in and out of the area. The development of ports and of arterial roadway or rail connections would be necessary to make this idea work on a larger scale. The second use of short sea shipping would involve bringing containerized cargo, that elusive foreign general cargo, to the Great Lakes from Atlantic ports, particularly Halifax, and through Montreal. Again the authors see congestion as providing the impetus for a shift to short sea shipping, in this case congestion in the ports and on the land transportation routes to these ports. Currently, a large portion of trade is coming from Asia, and west coast ports are becoming congested. Some goods are now shipped through the Panama Canal to the North American east coast ports. It is conceivable, the authors feel, that, at least until the Panama Canal is enlarged in 2015, large container ships will come from Asia through the Suez Canal, perhaps dropping some cargo off in Europe, and then proceed to one of the closest North American ports set up to handle container ships. There are a limited number of such ports, and Halifax is one of them. With road and rail routes from Halifax to the centre of the continent becoming ever more congested, this is another opportunity for goods to be sent by water.

The study acknowledges that trade patterns may not be the same in future, but in terms of what exists today, the report does hold out the possibility of increasing use of the Seaway. This increased use would occur in such a way that it would not involve the possibility of bringing more invasive species from other countries into the Great Lakes, since all short sea shipping would originate in North America. Aside from a passing mention in a different context, the study does not mention another factor which is very likely to influence cargo transportation in the next 40 years — oil — not the existence of it, but rather the lack of it. It is almost inevitable that the price of fuel will rise precipitously within a relatively short number of years. While rail transportation will still remain competitive, only goods which can sell with a high markup, or which are perishable, are likely to travel any distance by truck. Price-conscious shippers are likely to be more receptive to slower but less expensive transportation. The study acknowledges that money will have to be spent on Great Lakes ports and on land transportation routes to reach them, and suggests that there may have to be some financial incentives to do the work. It does not address the issue of persuading companies to build new ships for the Seaway. The report suggests that medium to large Seaway-sized vessels capable of handling truck bodies or containers are the ships of the future, but does not suggest how to get companies to build them at a time when Seaway traffic is stagnant.[33] For short runs, tug–barge combinations, which are inexpensive, easy to build, and produce fewer emissions, may be an easy solution, but their speed and seaworthiness precludes their use on long routes and in early and late parts of the shipping season. It will take a leap of faith and perhaps government incentives to build a new fleet to take advantage of the possibilities mentioned in the report.

Celebrations of the 50th anniversary of the opening of the Seaway have been considerably more subdued that those accompanying the opening. There have been no royalty, no president, vice-president, or prime minister involved. Festivities have tended to be fairly localized, and have tended to focus on the great achievement of building the Seaway and the Moses–Saunders Dam. If the success of the Seaway has been mentioned, it has been in terms of the total amount of cargo carried over the 50 years, and of the 50 years of operation of the power dam, rather than in terms of the current state of the waterway. This perception of the present operation of the Seaway is somewhat unfair. Traffic is not enough to generate the level of revenue that the two controlling bodies would like, especially international traffic, and the waterway faces environmental and maintenance challenges, but these latter issues can be overcome. Much of the disappointment in the Seaway stems from unfulfilled expectations.

The majority of studies done of relative transportation costs have shown that, in all categories, the Seaway has saved shippers money over the pre-Seaway days, and over competing modes of transportation.[34] These benefits, though, have not been shared equally. Some ports seem happy with the effects of the waterway, but others express varying degrees of unhappiness. Duluth–Superior, for example, while the volume of general cargo has perhaps not reached what was hoped, has acquired the less expensive way of transporting grain to the Atlantic that it had wanted for so long. Toledo sees itself as a port with a future of growth, including in international trade. Chicago, though it has a large and successful harbour, wonders what has happened to international trade, and worries about the loss of business to other ports. The cargo terminals that used to line the harbour at Toronto are now replaced by condominiums, and the grain elevators sit abandoned or have been demolished. The remnants of the port, pushed to one side of the harbour except for a sugar warehouse, include a small container terminal. On the other hand, Hamilton, with its steel mills, has been able to take advantage of lower transportation rates for iron ore and coal. Montreal has lost its place as the main transshipment point for grain and now has a smaller share of container traffic, as large container ships tend to drop their cargo at Atlantic ports to save valuable travelling time but, since container traffic is growing, the city has actually increased its tonnage of containers. Small ports like Oswego, which are not transportation hubs, have not generated the business that they hoped the Seaway would bring. Perhaps the most unhappy of ports is Buffalo, which saw such a glorious future ahead for it in 1955. Once the successful rival of Montreal in the transshipment of grain, using both the New York Barge Canal and the railways, the amount of grain handled in the port plummeted from 59 million bushels in 1956–57 to 802,000 in 1968–69. As in Montreal, the Seaway has made the need for transshipment at Buffalo unnecessary. In the winter, grain can be stored in the West for shipment the next year or transported from the Midwest by train at special rates. The city's industrial sector, which was supposed to bring more ship traffic to Buffalo, has declined dramatically, its steel mill idled. Today, some 25 to 30 ships dock each year in the port.[35]

Had the Seaway been built in the 1930s, when it seemed for a while that it would be, there would not have been the same unrealistic level of expectation that built up over the more than 20 years that a public battle went on over whether it would be built. In a sense, it was the supporters of the seaway concept who built up this expectation in their attempts to win support for the project. They reinforced the idea of the golden dream that had lured humans since the days of Jacques Cartier, a dream that was not realistic. Some ports on the Great Lakes received gold and diamonds, as did the people of Ontario from the power dam, though not as much as the latter had hoped for, while others, like Cartier, received iron pyrites and quartz. Building the Seaway in the 1930s would also have allowed it to operate for 40 years before levels of use dropped, and the situation is more likely to have been seen by the public as a stage in the life of what had been a successful system, rather than the possible failure of a young transportation network which was supposed to bring wealth to everyone around the Great Lakes.

Perhaps it is time to rethink the 1950s concept of the Seaway as a self-supporting system, and to return to the pre-Seaway idea of canals held in both the United States and Canada, that canals provide a service essential to the economic life of the country and, as such, should be used without charge. The American canal at the Soo is run in this manner, unimpeded use of the Mississippi is maintained by the American government at great expense, and the United States stopped charging tolls for the use of their locks on the Seaway more than 20 years ago. There is even some discussion of dropping the port charge that the American government has used instead to obtain revenue from the Seaway system. A Seaway without tolls would not guarantee more traffic, nor would it automatically help those ports which have not benefited from its construction, but it would be one incentive for more ships to use the system. While this history of the Seaway cannot end with the optimism of works done shortly after it opened, or near its 20th anniversary, it can end with a sense of curiosity and excitement about what the 75th anniversary will bring.

# EPILOGUE

## A Trip Through History:
## The Canals Today

Learning about history is often about reading books and studying documents, but sometimes we are able to see and touch history. Much of the physical aspect of the story of the St. Lawrence Seaway and its rivals is still intact and can be visited. People who wish to visit the waterway, and its extended system, will most likely visit three popular sites, including the Eisenhower Lock and the Welland Canal, which have viewing platforms specifically for that purpose. The third, the St. Marys Canal and locks at the Soo, can also be visited and on Engineers Day (the last Friday of June) visitors are allowed past the security fence that is now a feature of all locks on the system, and can walk right up to the canal. The locks at Montreal can be visited, though because of their location in an industrial area, they are not the most picturesque. The Beauharnois powerhouse and the power channel are impressive for their size, but the locks there are not really accessible to the public. The Iroquois Lock, although fenced off as are the others, has a large parking lot on a hill overlooking the lock and the control dam beyond from which an excellent view of the comings and goings of ships can be had.

Anyone wishing to put themselves closer to the history depicted in this story of the five-century struggle to access the Great Lakes can easily do so. While the Welland and the Beauharnois are really part of the history, given that both date from the 1930s, it is possible to go back much farther in time. In Montreal it is possible to walk or ride beside the original Lachine Canal, built in 1824 and ultimately deepened to 14 feet in the late 19th century. Long-neglected after the Seaway was built, and quickly becoming a dirty gash across a decaying remnant of an earlier vibrant industrial area, it was turned over to the Quebec government, which eventually turned it into an urban park surrounded by most of the original industrial buildings. Some of these retain their industrial use and some have been adapted to contemporary uses, as offices or living spaces. Going west into Lake St. Louis, the mouth of the Ottawa River is on the right. While the Ottawa River canals have largely been flooded by later works, taking the journey to Ottawa allows access to the Rideau Canal, which has remained largely as it was when it was built, and which provides a tranquil way to reach Kingston. On the other side of Lake St. Louis, several of the original engineer canals from the 1780s still survive. La Faucille would be hard to identify, except for the sign pointing to it, as it is essentially a wide ditch filled with weeds and small trees. The best preserved of these early canals can be found at the other end of this formerly wild stretch of the St. Lawrence, at Coteau-du-Lac, where Parks Canada has excavated and partially restored the canal there. The mighty St. Lawrence, which made this series of canals necessary, has been tamed at this point by the diversion of around 85 percent of the water into the Beauharnois channel on the South Shore. What remains is punctuated by various dams, both above and below the waterline. Not far north of these remnants of early canals, and running parallel to them, is the Soulanges Canal, in use as one of the 14-foot canals from 1900 to 1959. Although not the beautifully maintained waterway shown in old photographs, it is remarkably intact for a canal that has been abandoned for 50 years. Those lock gates made of wood have deteriorated to some degree, and Lock One seems to have disappeared, but most aspects of the canal are still intact. The Canadian federal government has turned this canal over to the Province of Quebec, as it did the Lachine Canal, and there are plans to refurbish it for the use of pleasure boats, with a hotel and marina added.

On the South Shore of the St. Lawrence, where the Beauharnois Canal and power dam are now located, the old Beauharnois Canal, in use from the 1840s to the early years of the 20th century, used to exist. It has been filled in, except for a few hundred feet from the western entrance into downtown Valleyfield-de-Salleberry. Part of it is used to moor pleasure boats. Although the canal has been filled in, it is possible to take the highway which runs from Valleyfield up to and under the locks on the new Beauharnois Canal and, on the way, to drive through what would have been the outlet point for the power station at Saint-Timothée, While the station now sits high and dry, it originally generated power on a section of abandoned Beauharnois Canal, from 1911 to 1951. It is a strange sensation to drive below the power station and the dam, in the place where torrents of water used to pour out. To the west, the Cornwall Canal is mostly under Lake St. Lawrence now, but the remains of locks and a portion of the canal can be seen on the waterfront of the city. While it is possible to walk to it, the best vantage point is on the international bridge crossing from Cornwall Island. If the canal is followed, it leads to the framework for a new lock in the dike east of the city, placed there at Lionel Chevrier's insistence so that an all-Canadian seaway could be constructed.

West of the dike, most Williamsburg canals are gone, but bits of roadway and the old railway right-of-way can be seen poking out of the water at the Long Sault Parkway. The Galops Canal, however, has survived almost intact. At the east end, at the town of Iroquois, one can still visit the entrance to the canal, although the gates are gone and the higher level of the water in the river has submerged the stone-lined approach. The view from the canal has been altered by the building of the Iroquois Lock and Control Dam, which are directly in front and south of the entrance to the old canal. At the east end of town, a road cuts across the old canal to allow vehicles to reach the new lock, where the parking lot allows visitors to look down on ships traversing it. Surprisingly, most of the area of land which used to contain old Iroquois has not been flooded, but instead forms a large open field. Farther west, where a swing bridge used to allow access to Cardinal, the canal at that point has been filled in to create a roadway into the town, but the deep cut, lined with huge cut-stone blocks laid down by factious Canadian and Italian labourers over a century ago, is still impressive. At the west end of town, another road leads to the western entrance to the Galops Canal, and, at the same point, to the entrance to the only surviving section of 9-foot canal of the pre-1850 period. This canal used to skirt Cardinal on the river side of the village. Now it only runs for perhaps 300 feet, at which point it is blocked by a building. Beyond that, it disappears under the St. Lawrence.

Farther up the St. Lawrence, at Prescott, where lakers used to transfer cargoes of grain to 14-footers, also called "canallers," the large grain elevator built by the government still stands, a reminder of what transportation on the river was like prior to 1959. Across the St. Lawrence, Oswego gives access to the Lake Ontario entrance to the New York Barge Canal, a remnant of the pre–First World War era. It is possible to go farther back in time, however, by visiting some of the remnants of the earlier Erie Canal. While portions of the Erie, either Clinton's Ditch, or the later (1862) enlarged version are scattered across the area where the old canal ran, the best places to get a sense of what it was like are at Camillus Erie Canal Park, where a demonstration stretch of the canal operates, at Old Erie Canal State Park, where it is possible to walk a long stretch of the old canal, only a small portion of which has water in it, or at Schoharie Crossing State Park where a smaller section can be walked.

In the Niagara Peninsula, aside from the 1932 canal, it is possible to see remnants of the earlier canals. Some small portions of the filled-in First Welland poke out of the ground in St. Catharines, and small portions of the Third Welland still are navigable, while some others portions are largely intact, though overgrown and containing little water. Several of the step locks from the Second Canal, essentially a deeper stone version of the First Welland, still exist in a park in Thorold, with water rushing through them, but without lock gates. Portions of the entrance locks to the First and Second Canals, at Port Dalhousie (St. Catharines), still exist, though both lead into an embankment. Here and there throughout the region are other bits of earlier versions, though no attempt has been made to preserve and present these, as has been done to parts of the Erie. Those people with a bent for exploration, and advice from knowledgeable locals, can get a real sense of looking at the past that historical theme parks such as the Camillus Erie Canal Park, which recreate history, cannot convey. Each of these two ways to look at history has its own merits.

Farther west, at Chicago, it is possible to walk the abandoned section of the old Illinois and Michigan Canal, the original attempt to connect Chicago to the Mississippi, now maintained as a park. The last canal on the Great Lakes that provides a sense of the earlier history is the Canadian one at Sault Ste. Marie. While the locks on the American side have been altered at various times, the Canadian canal, and the surrounding buildings, are much as they were when built in the 1890s. In 1987, a portion of the canal wall collapsed and, since a very small percentage of vessels used the Canadian canal by that time, it was going to be abandoned. A public outcry, particularly from pleasure boaters and those who wished to see history preserved, resulted in a smaller modern lock being constructed inside the old one, which is designated as a national historic site. Although the appearance of the old canal has been slightly altered by the construction of the new lock, it is still possible to picture what existed in the 1890s and early 1900s in viewing what is in place today.

The historical tour described here is one that can be taken in the summer of 2009. In five or 10 years it may be different, as physical remains of the past are not static things. Visiting a part or parts of the past history of the struggle to dominate trade in the Great Lakes, whether as they look now, or may look in the future, cannot help but create a stronger appreciation of the great achievement of human persistence, planning, energy, and ingenuity that is the Seaway. Perhaps a young girl or boy will stand beside one of these reminders of our past and be inspired to write a book to mark the 100th anniversary of the building of the St. Lawrence Seaway.

# NOTES

**Chapter 1: The Age of the Innovators: The Early Canals, to 1848**

1.  Marcel Trudel, *The Beginnings of New France, 1524–1663* (Toronto, 1973), 12–19.
2.  *Ibid.*, 19–25.
3.  *Ibid.*, 35–52.
4.  *Ibid.*, 71–72, 78–79.
5.  W.J. Eccles, *Canada Under Louis XIV, 1663–1701* (Toronto, 1964), 208.
6.  *Ibid.*, 164–65.
7.  *Ibid.*, 208–09.
8.  Parks Canada, Coteau-du-Lac National Historic Site of Canada, accessed at *www.pc.gc.ca/lhn-nhs/qc/coteaudulac/natcul/natcul1d_e.asp*, July 13, 2008; James Gilmore, "The St. Lawrence River Canals Vessel," Society of Naval Architects and Marine Engineers, Transactions 1957, 111–61, reproduced in sections at *www.hhpl.on.ca/GreatLakes/Documents/Gilmore/default.asp*, July 13, 2008; see "The Canals," 1–2.
9.  *Ibid.*, George Heriot, *Travels Through the Canadas, Containing a Description of the Picturesque Scenery on Some of the Rivers and Lakes, with an Account of the Productions, Commerce and Inhabitants of Those Provinces* (London, 1807), Vol. 1., 117–22; author's observations at the site of the canals.
10. Heriot, Vol. 1, 123–25.
11. G.P. de T. Glazebrook, *A History of Transportation in Canada* (Toronto, 1964), Vol. 1, 65 (originally published Toronto, 1938); Heriot, *op. cit.*, 234–35, 239–40.
12. William Catermole, *Emigration* (London, 1831), 84.
13. Glazebrook, *op. cit.*, 65.
14. Like bateaux, Durham boats varied in size, but drew the same amount of water under the keel if not overloaded.
15. John M. Duncan, *Travels Through Part of the United States and Canada in 1818 and 1819* (Glasgow, 1823), Vol. 2, 118–21.
16. Robert F. Legget, *The Seaway* (Toronto and Vancouver, 1979), 13; Parks Canada, *op. cit.*; John P. Heisler, *The Canals of Canada* (Ottawa, 1973), 41.
17. Legget, *op. cit.*, 21.

18. George Heriot, *op. cit.*, Vol. 1, 199; International Joint Commission, *St. Lawrence Waterway: Message from the President of the United States Transmitting a Letter from the Secretary of State Submitting the Report of the International Joint Commission Concerning the Improvement of the St. Lawrence River Between Montreal and Lake Ontario for Navigation and Power*, 67th Congress, Second Session, Senate Document No. 114 (Washington, 1922), 17–20.

19. Arthur M. Lower, *Great Britain's Woodyard* (Montreal and London, 1973), 202–04.

20. Ronald E. Shaw, *Erie Water West: A History of the Erie Canal, 1792–1854* (Lexington, KY, *circa* 1966; reprinted American Council of Learned Societies, 1990, as an e-book), 10–11, 13; "Erie Canal Chronology and Bibliography," accessed at *www.history.rochester.edu/canal/chron.htm*, November 15, 2008.

21. Carleton Mabee, *The Seaway Story* (New York, 1961), 11–12.

22. Shaw, *op. cit.*, 14–16.

23. *Ibid.*, 16–21.

24. *Ibid.*, 23–34, 41–42.

25. *Ibid.*, 36.

26. *Ibid.*, 38–40; "The Erie Canal and De Witt Clinton," 1, accessed at *xroads.virginia.edu/~HYPER/DETOC/TRANSPORT/ERIE.HTML*, July 30, 2008.

27. Shaw, *op. cit.*, 51, 53, 56–58.

28. Shaw, *op. cit.*, 61–62, 75–79; "The Erie Canal and De Witt Clinton," 2; "Erie Canal Chronology," accessed at *www.history.rochester.edu/canal/chron.htm*, November 15, 2008.

29. Shaw, *op. cit.*, 92–98, 121, 125.

30. *Ibid.*, 126–28, 130–31, 140–63.

31. *Ibid.*, 104–07, 165–66, 172–78; "The Erie Canal and De Witt Clinton," 2.

32. Shaw, *op. cit.*, 184.

33. *Ibid.*, 255–56, 260–63, 273–76.

34. Heisler, *op. cit.*, 39.

35. Shaw, *op. cit.*, 239–40.

36. William Dunlop, "Recollections of the American War," *The Literary Garland*, Montreal, June to November 1847 (reprinted Toronto, 1967), 24.

37. Robert Legget, *Ottawa River Canals and the Defence of British North America* (Toronto, Buffalo, and London, 1988), 15.

38. Dunlop, *op. cit.*, 24.

39. Quoted in Heisler, *op. cit.*, 38.

40. J. Mackay Hitsman, *The Incredible War of 1812* (Toronto, 1965), 29, 33, 41–42; George F.G. Stanley, *The War of 1812: Land Operations* (Ottawa, 1983), 45–47, 139, 245–46, 253; M. Smith, *A Geographical View of the Province of Upper Canada, and Promiscuous Remarks Upon the Government* (Hartford, 1813), quoted in Gerald Craig, *Early Travellers in the Canadas* (Toronto, 1955), 38.

41. Hitsman, *op. cit.*, 164–70; Stanley, *op. cit.*, 243–65.

42. Heisler, *op. cit.*, 24–27; Robert Legget, *Ottawa River Canals*, 34–36, 38; Robert Legget, *Rideau Waterway* (Toronto, 1955, revised 1972), 26.

43. Legget, *Ottawa River Canals*, 40–48; Heisler, *op. cit.*, 25.

44. Legget, *Ottawa River Canals*, 50–88; Heisler, *op. cit.*, 26–27; Robert Legget, *Rideau Waterway*, 31.

45. Heisler, *op. cit.*, 29–30; Legget, *Rideau Waterway*, 34–35.

46. Legget, *Rideau Waterway*, 55, 58–62; Robert W. Passfield, *Building the Rideau Canal: A Pictorial History* (Don Mills, ON, 1982), 21–29.

47. Legget, *Rideau Waterway*, 41–42, 44–48, 51–54, 74; Passfield, *op. cit.*, 160.

48. Legget, *Rideau Waterway*, 62–67, 114–19, 177–82; Passfield, *op. cit.*, 30–35, 64, 158, 159; Heisler, *op. cit.*, 64–65.

49. Canal Commission, *Letter to the Hon. The Secretary of State from the Canal Commissioners Respecting the Improvement of Inland Navigation of the Dominion of Canada* (Ottawa, February 24, 1871), 21–23 (The Commission used Canadian and American documents to construct a history of canal construction in Canada, to assess the current situation, and to make recommendations as to future construction); Legget, *Ottawa River Canals*, 114–44, 173; Passfield, *op. cit.*, 34.

50. Heisler, *op. cit.*, 25–26, 41, 61–62; William R. Willoughby, *The St. Lawrence Waterway* (Madison, WI, 1961), 11–12.

51. Legget, *Rideau Waterway*, 86–89; Legget, *Ottawa River Canals*, 240–41; Heisler, *op. cit.*, 99.

52. Heisler, *op. cit.*, 30–32, 42, 54–55; Mabee, *op. cit.*, 15–17, 22; J.J. Talman, "William Hamilton Merritt," in *Dictionary of Canadian Biography*, Vol. 12 (Toronto and Quebec, 1990), 545–48; Hugh G.J. Aitken, *The Welland Canal: A Study in Canadian Enterprise* (Cambridge, MA, 1954), 28–34, 38–42.

53. Heisler, *op. cit.*, 32, 36, 87–88; Mabee, *op. cit.*, 17–18; Aitken, *op. cit.*, 47–53.

54. Canal Commission, *Letter to the Hon. The Secretary of State ...*, 17–18, 68; Talman, *op. cit.*, 546; Aitken, *op. cit.*, 57–64.

55. Canal Commission, *Letter to the Hon. The Secretary of State ...*, 18; Talman, *op. cit.*, 546; Aitken, *The Welland Canal*, 68–72, 77–109.

56. G.M. Craig, *Upper Canada: The Formative Years, 1784–1841* (London and New York, 1963), 158–60; Heisler, *op. cit.*, 73–74; Hugh G.J. Aitken, "The Family Compact and the Welland Canal Company," *Canadian Journal of Economics and Political Science*, Vol. 18 (1952), 63–76; "Third Report of the Select Committee Appointed to Examine and Enquire into the Management of the Welland Canal," in *Journals of the House of Assembly of Upper Canada, 1836–37*, appendix 5, Vol. 2.

57. Aitken, *The Welland Canal*, appendix, 142.

58. *Ibid.*, 70.

59. Mabee, *op. cit.*, 22–23; Talman, *op. cit.*, 547.

60. Heisler, *op. cit.*, 43–44, 74–75.

61. Craig, *op. cit.*, 20–63; Gerald Craig, ed., *Lord Durham's Report* (Toronto, 1963), i–ix.

62. Craig, *Upper Canada*, 270–73.

63. J.M.S. Careless, *The Union of the Canadas: The Growth of Canadian Institutions* (Toronto, 1967), 49–50.

64. Canal Commission, *Letter to the Hon. The Secretary of State ...*, 2, 12–15, 19; Careless, *op. cit.*, 104–05; Talman, *op. cit.*, 548.

65. Heisler, *op. cit.*, 110; Careless, *op. cit.*, 105, 122.

66. *Canadian Agriculturalist* (Toronto), September 1, 1849.

## Chapter 2: The Age of the Engineers: The Later Canals, to 1932

1. Careless, *op. cit.*, 16, 77–78, 111; J.C. Dent, *The Last Forty Years: Canada Since the Union of 1841* (Toronto, 1881; abridged edition, Donald Swainson, ed., Toronto, 1972), 191–92, 210–11.

2. Dent, *op. cit.*, 194–213; Careless, *op. cit.*, 122–29; Gilbert N. Tucker, *The Canadian Commercial Revolution, 1845–51* (New Haven, CT, 1936; republished Toronto, 1964), 129–40; *Gazette* (Montreal), October 11, 1849.

3. Careless, *op. cit.*, 129–30; Dent, *op. cit.*, 213–14; Tucker, *op. cit.*, 136–40, 146.

4. Careless, *op. cit.*, 132–39; Shaw, *op. cit.*, 415; Tucker, *op. cit.*, 159–63.

5. Canal Commissioners, *Letter to the Hon. The Secretary of State …*, 36, 39–41; Heisler, *op. cit.*, 115.

6. Shaw, *op. cit.*, 306–07, 396.

7. Tucker, *op. cit.*, 154; Heisler, *op. cit.*, 115; Careless, *op. cit.*, 135; Mary Quayle Innis, *An Economic History of Canada* (Toronto, 1954), 192.

8. Canal Commission, *Letter to the Hon. The Secretary of State …*, 19; Heisler, *op. cit.*, 94, 97, 116; Careless, *op. cit.*, 135; Innis, *op. cit.*, 193.

9. Canal Commission, *Letter to the Hon. The Secretary of State …*, 72; Careless, *op. cit.*, 135; Innis, *op. cit.*, 191.

10. Canal Commission, *Letter to the Hon. The Secretary of State …*, 24–26; Heisler, *op. cit.*, 100, 104, 107–08.

11. Canal Commission, *Letter to the Hon. The Secretary of State …*, 2; International Joint Commission, *St. Lawrence Waterway: Message from the President …*, 49, 110–17, 156; "The Soo Locks," accessed at *www.geo.msu.edu/geogmich/SooLock.html*, September 16, 2008, 6.

12. Willoughby, *op. cit.*, 32.

13. International Joint Commission, *St. Lawrence Waterway: Message from the President …*, 25; "The Soo Locks," 5–6; "The History of the Soo Locks," accessed at *huron.lre. usace.army.mil/SOO/lockhist.html*, September 16, 2008; J.B. Mansfield, ed., *History of the Great Lakes*, transcribed by Walter Lewis and Brendon Baillod (Chicago, 1899), Vol. 1, chapter 19, accessed at *www.maritimehistoryofthegreatlakes.ca/ Documents/HGL/default.asp?ID=c006*, November 6, 2009; Grace Lee Nute, *Lake Superior* (Indianapolis and New York, 1944), 235; Frederick Dunbar Welles and George S. May, *Michigan: A History of the Wolverine State* (third revised edition, Grand Rapids, MI, 1995), 260–61.

14. Willoughby, *op. cit.*, 33–36.

15. Shaw, *op. cit.*, 307–96.

16. Heisler, *op. cit.*, 94, 118–19.

17. The Maritime colonies of Nova Scotia, New Brunswick, and Prince Edward Island were not prepared for discussions of a union broader than one of Maritime union when they met with the Canadian delegates in 1864. The plan for Confederation was in large measure one proposed by the Canadians, and accepted by the Maritime delegates, even after it was presented in more detail at a later meeting.

18. Shaw, *op. cit.*, 394.

19. Quoted in Heisler, *op. cit.*, 114.

20. "The Erie Canal and De Witt Clinton," 3; Canal Commissioners, *Letter to the Hon. The Secretary of State ...*, 41; Heisler, *op. cit.*, 114–15.

21. Roberta M. Styran and Robert R. Taylor, *The "Great Swivel Link": Canada's Welland Canal* (Toronto, 2001), cxii–cxiii; Michelle Greenwald, Alan Levitt, and Elaine Peebles, *The Welland Canals: Historical Resource Analysis and Preservation Alternatives* (Toronto, 1979), 19; Heisler, *op. cit.*, 117–19.

22. Canal Commission, *Letter to the Hon. The Secretary of State ...*, 84–87.

23. Donald Creighton, *The Road to Confederation* (Toronto, 1964), 30, 194–95, 212–14; P.B. Waite, *The Life and Times of Confederation, 1864–1867* (Toronto, 1962), 31–32.

24. Willoughby, *op. cit.*, 36–39; Libby Hill, *The Chicago River: A Natural and Unnatural History* (Chicago, 2000), 106; Illinois State Museum, *Harvesting the River*, accessed at *www.museum.state.il.us/RiverWeb/harvesting/transportation/boats/timeline.html*, October 19, 2008; International Joint Commission, *St. Lawrence Waterway: Message from the President ...*, 38.

25. Willoughby, *op. cit.*, 39, 45–46.

26. Canal Commission, *Letter to the Hon. The Secretary of State ...*, 37.

27. C.P. Stacey, *Canada and the Age of Conflict: A History of Canadian External Relations, Vol. 1: 1867–1921* (Toronto, Buffalo, and London, 1977), 20–23; Willoughby, *op. cit.*, 46.

28. Stacey, *op. cit.*, 23–28; Willoughby, *op. cit.*, 46–47; Donald Creighton, *John A. Macdonald: The Old Chieftain* (Toronto, 1955), 98–99; relevant portions of the treaty are reproduced in Don Courtney Piper, *The International Law of the Great Lakes: A Study of Canadian–United States Co-operation* (Durham, NC, 1967), appendix B.

29. All of the canals were enlarged except for the St. Ours, on the Richelieu, International Joint Commission, *St. Lawrence Waterway: Message from the President ...*, 33; *Letter to the Hon. The Secretary of State ...*, 5, 57–90; Heisler, *op. cit.*, 122.

30. Donald G. Creighton, *John A. Macdonald: The Old Chieftain* (Toronto, 1955), 131–77.

31. P.B. Waite, *Canada 1874–1896: Arduous Destiny* (Toronto and Montreal, 1971), 15; Willoughby, *op. cit.*, 47; Styran and Taylor, *op. cit.*, lii–liii; Petition of Mariners and Vessel Owners of the Inland Waters and Great Lakes of North America, April 16, 1874, Library and Archives Canada, RG11, v. 162, quoted Styran and Taylor, *op. cit.*, 65–66; John L. McWirter to Frederic Braun, June 27, 1872, LAC, RG11, Vol. 158, No. 24159, quoted Styran and Taylor, *op. cit.*, 98–99.

32. Willoughby, *op. cit.*, 48; P.B. Waite, *Canada 1874–1896*, 57.

33. Willoughby, *op. cit.*, 48; Heisler, *op. cit.*, 129; Styran and Taylor, *op. cit.*, lii–liii.

34. Canada, *Sessional Papers*, 1893, No. 9, lxxv–lxxx; Canada, *Annual Report of the Department of Railways and Canals, 1898–99* (Ottawa, 1900), 6–9; Canada, *Annual Report of the Department of Railways and Canals, 1902–03* (Ottawa, 1904), 7, 149, 164–65.

35. Samuel Power to Thomas A. Begly, August 25, 1843, LAC, RG 43 Vol. 2097, Letterbook 1842–43, No. 2671, quoted in Styran and Taylor, *op. cit.*, 376–77; David Thorburn to D. Daly, January 10, 1844, LAC, RG 11, Vol. 68-5, 34–43, quoted in Styran and Taylor, *op. cit.*, 378–81; "Welland Canal Riots," *Thorold Post*, June 23, 1876, quoted in Styran and Taylor, *op. cit.*, 396–97; Styran and Taylor, *op. cit.*, cv–cvi; Legget, *Rideau Waterway*, 158; Elinor Kyte Senior, *From Royal Township to*

*Industrial City: Cornwall, 1784–1984* (Belleville, 1983), 125–29; Cardinal Historical Society historical plaque. Additional information about Irish canal workers in the 1840s can be found in Ruth Elizabeth Bleasdale, *Irish Labourers on the Cornwall, Welland, and Williamsburg Canals in the 1840s*, MA thesis, University of Western Ontario, 1975.

36. Heisler, *op. cit.*, 136.
37. Canada, *Sessional Papers*, 1893, No. 9, xciv–xcv; Canal Commissioners, *Letter to the Hon. The Secretary of State …*, 12–13; *Annual Report of the Department of Railways and Canals, 1891–92* (Ottawa, 1893), xcv; AO, F1198, Frederick Innes Ker Fonds, Box 4, Folder 4.8, Letter R.A.C. Henry, Deputy Minister of Railways and Canals, Ottawa, March 4, 1929, to Ker, General Manager, *Hamilton Spectator*.
38. International Joint Commission, *St. Lawrence Waterway: Message from the President …*, 25–26, 28; Willoughby, *op. cit.*, 55–57.
39. Canada, *Sessional Papers*, 1893, No. 9, lxxiv; Canal Commission, *Letter to the Hon. The Secretary of State …*, 37; Canada, *Annual Report of the Department of Railways and Canals, 1898–99*, 11; Willoughby, 53–54. Dimensions are different in different sources. The depth of 17 feet would be at the high water level. At the lowest, depth would be about 13 feet. Grace Lee Nute, *op. cit.*, 6, gives the low water depth at 11.4 feet. See note 41.
40. Willoughby, *op. cit.*, 49–51.
41. International Joint Commission, *St. Lawrence Waterway: Message from the President …*, 25. Different government reports provide different depths for all of the St. Marys River locks. The reason is that there was a significant rise and fall in the river level. The difference between the mean level and the lowest level was four feet. Thus, measurement of the depth depended on when the measurement was taken. In addition, the level of Lake Huron dropped by one and a half feet after 1900 due to dredging and to the Chicago Diversion lowering the levels in the locks. The size of the Poe Lock is particularly difficult to determine, as several different measurements are given in various reliable sources. Most sources suggest that the Poe was 800 by 100 feet, but provide varying depths. The original plan was for it to be 800 by 100 feet, but it is not clear, even from United States government sources, if it was built to this size. The alternative measurements quoted for the Poe are 704 feet long by 95 feet wide. What is clear is that, by 1900, ships drawing more than 18 feet, the depth of the Canadian channel, used the Poe Lock. The American channel remained a few inches deeper until the Canadians deepened theirs a few years later.
42. Noble E. Whitford, *History of the Barge Canal of New York State: Supplement to the Annual Report of the State Engineer and Surveyor for the Year Ended June 30, 1921* (Albany, NY, 1921). Transcription 1999, accessed November 15, 2008, at *www.history. rochester.edu/canal/bib/whitford/1921/contents.html*, chapter 1 (the transcription is not paginated, but most chapters are the equivalent of only a few pages long).
43. *Ibid.*, chapter 2; Mabee, *op. cit.*, 47.
44. Whitford, *op. cit.*, chapters 1 and 2.
45. *Ibid.*, chapters 3 and 4.
46. *Ibid.*, chapters 5–7.
47. *Ibid.*, chapter 18.

48. International Joint Commission, *St. Lawrence Waterway: Message from the President* ..., 38–40; Hill, *op. cit.*, 105–06; Peter Annin, *The Great Lakes Water Wars* (Chicago, 2006), 86–91. An urban legend, still found in some internet sources, claims that thousands died in an epidemic brought on by the flood of sewage reaching the lake in 1885. However, it was the *fear* of disease, especially after several serious outbreaks of cholera in the 1840s, rather than an epidemic in the year after the 1885 storm that prompted the decision to build the new canal.

49. Annin, *op. cit.*, 92–101; Whitford, *op. cit.*, chapter 10; Willoughby, *op. cit.*, 75, 77, 101.

50. Legget, *The Seaway*, 47; Willoughby, *op. cit.*, 71–72.

51. There was a serious shortage of boxcars to carry grain in both countries in 1906–07, resulting in large losses for farmers. The problems continued, reaching crisis proportions in the United States in 1917, when industrial production also was threatened by car shortages. International Joint Commission, *St. Lawrence Waterway: Message from the President*, 68; Willoughby, *op. cit.*, 68, 71, 73, 77, 85.

52. Canal Commission, *Letter to the Hon. The Secretary of State* ..., 7; Legget, *The Seaway*, 56.

53. Styran and Taylor, *op. cit.*, liii, lxxxviii–ix; Frank E. Sterns, "New Features in Design of the Welland Canal, " LAC, RG43, Vol. 2166, File 780, Pt. 2, quoted in *ibid.*, 246–48; P.J. Cowan on the Ship Canal (from *Engineering*, April 5, 1929), quoted in *ibid.*, 248–49; Jewett to Grant, June 11, 1920, LAC, RG43, Vol. 2164, File 713.3, Pt. 1, quoted in *ibid.*, 239; "Huge Shovels Arrive Here," Welland *Tribune*, December 24, 1925, quoted in *ibid.*, 243; LAC, R5500-0-6-E, Andrew Audubon Merilees Fonds, Items 65526A46, 65682B20, 65902G4; LAC, R5500-7-9-E, Views of Canada and the United States, *circa* 1858–1934, Series B 11, Item 6590; LAC, R9726-0-4-E, John Boyd Fonds, Item 13414.

54. International Joint Commission, *St. Lawrence Waterway Message from the President* ..., 25, 44; Willoughby, *op. cit.*, 71, 74.

**Chapter 3: Whose Dream? Negotiating the Building of the Seaway**

1. The literature given out by the St. Lawrence Seaway Development Corporation as late as 2009 acknowledges that the United States on several occasions refused to take part in building the Seaway, but says nothing about Canada's reluctance.

2. Mabee, *op. cit.*, 46–47; Willoughby, *op. cit.*, 59; O.A. Cooke, "Frederick Charles Denison," in *Dictionary of Canadian Biography*, Vol. 15 (Toronto and Quebec, 2000), 243–46.

3. *New York Times*, New York, July 2, 1893, September 23, 1895, June 14, 1898, February 24, 1900; Manitoba Historical Society, "James Fisher," accessed at *www.mhs.mb.ca/ docs/people/fisher_j.shtml*, January 11, 2008; Oliver A. Howland to Sir Edmund Barton, January 27, 1903, National Library of Australia, *Papers of Sir Edmund Barton*, MS51, Series 1, Correspondence 1827–1921, Correspondence 1903, Item 1071a-6a, accessed at *nla.gov.au/nla.ms-ms51-1-1071a*; Michigan Family History Network, "James S. Dunham," accessed at *www.mfhn.com/forum/topic.asp?TOPIC_ ID=16*, January 11, 2009; Mabee, *op. cit.*, 47–48; Willoughby, *op. cit.*, 59–60.

4. *New York Times*, September 23, 1895; Willoughby, *op. cit.*, 60–61; Mabee, *op. cit.*, 48.

5. *New York Times*, September 23, 1895.

6.  Willoughby, *op. cit.*, 64–66.

7.  Lewis L. Gould, *The Presidency of Theodore Roosevelt* (Lawrence, KS, 1991), 81–86; Frederick W. Marks, *Velvet on Iron: The Diplomacy of Theodore Roosevelt* (Lincoln, NE, 1979), 61–64, 105–11. In 1902, that year's River and Harbor Act called for a six-person International Waterways Commission to study diversion of water from the Great Lakes, power generation at Sault Ste. Marie and Niagara, and issues of maritime regulation, fishing, shore erosion, and navigation in channels on the Great Lakes system. Canada agreed but did not appoint members until 1905, and the commission took almost six years to do its work. By 1913, when it reported, the American Senate had passed Senator Townsend's resolution calling for a co-operative development of navigation facilities (note 14); see Senate of Canada, *Proceedings of the Special Committee Appointed to Inquire into the Development and Improvement of the St. Lawrence River*, Ottawa, 1928, vii–viii.

8.  Willoughby, *op. cit.*, 66.

9.  *Ibid.*, 78; Mabee, *op. cit.*, 50–51.

10. Letters, J. Wesley Allison, Morrisburg, December 26, 1907, A.A. Logan, Morrisburg, December 31, 1907, Irwin Hilliard, Morrisburg, February 3, 1910, J.G. Harkness, Cornwall, February 11, 1910, to Premier Sir James Whitney, in AO, F5-1, *Correspondence of James Whitney*, Box 273269, and copies of letters, Morrisburg Board of Trade to Toronto Board of Trade, December 21 and 24, 1907, in same; Willoughby, *op. cit.*, 78–79; Mabee, *op. cit.*, 51–53.

11. Letter, R.L. Baden, House of Commons, February 6, 1911, to J.P. Whitney, enclosing telegram from J. Wesley Allison, Washington, February 4, 1911, and telegram, J.P. Whitney, to J. Wesley Allison, February 7, 1911, in AO, F5-1, *Correspondence of James Whitney*, Box 273269; Willoughby, *op. cit.*, 54.

12. "Treaty Between Great Britain and the United States of America Relating to Boundary Waters and Questions Arising Along the Boundary Between Canada and the United States, and the Establishment of an International Joint Commission, Signed at Washington, January 11, 1909," reproduced in R.R. Baxter, ed., *Documents on the St. Lawrence Seaway* (London and New York, 1960), 7–9.

13. "Charles Elroy Townsend (1856–1924)" in *Biographical Directory of the United States Congress 1774–Present*, accessed at *bioguide.congress.gov/scripts/biodisplay.pl?index=T000330*, December 10, 2008; H.V. Nelles, "Sir Adam Beck," and Andrew Thomson, "Elias Weber Bingeman Snider," in *Dictionary of Canadian Biography*, Vol. 15 (Toronto and Quebec City, 2000), 55–68 and 960–61; H.C. Gardner, "The Great Lakes–St. Lawrence Tidewater Project," in *The Ohio State Engineer*, 1920, accessed at *kb.osu.edu/dspace/bitstream/1811/34082/1/os_ENG_v04_i03_009.pdf*, February 3, 2009; William Velores Uttley, *A History of Kitchener, Ontario* (1937; reprinted Waterloo, 1975), 334–43, 370–74, 388–90.

14. Robert Craig Brown, *Robert Laird Borden: A Biography* (Toronto, 1975), 223–26; Willoughby, *op. cit.*, 80–83; Mabee, *op. cit.*, 57–60.

15. *Massena Observer*, Massena, NY, September 5, 1918.

16. Mabee, *op. cit.*, 60–61; Willoughby, *op. cit.*, 88–89; the description of Craig is from SLU, Collection 40, The St. Lawrence Collection, Mabee Series, Box 52, Item 3, Interview with John C. Beukema, Muskegon, MI, October 5, 1959.

17. Mabee, *op. cit.*, 62–64; Nelles, *op. cit.*, 962; Jamie Benidickson, "Francis Henry Keefer," in *Dictionary of Canadian Biography*, Vol. 15 (Toronto and Quebec City, 2000), 529–31; AO, F1198, Frederick Innes Ker Fonds, Box 4, Folder 4.10, Letter Ker to John R. Dunbar, Esq., Chairman, Ontario Provincial Division, Engineering Institute of Canada, c/o Canadian Westinghouse Company, Hamilton, Ontario, March 15, 1949, indicates that Ker and Beck were both opposed to the Canadian Association because it supported the Tidewater Association's downloading of navigation costs on the power development.

18. International Joint Commission, *St. Lawrence Waterway: Message from the President* ..., 53–91, 96–98, 120, 136–37, 139–42; for opinions on Canadian views, see AO, F1198, Frederick Innes Ker Fonds, Box 4, Folder 4.8, F.I. Ker to P.S. Fisher, Esq., c/o Wm. Southam and Sons, Ltd., 1070 Bleury Street, Montreal, P.Q., July 28, 1927; Folder 4.8, Same to The Hon. J.L. Perron, K.C., Montreal Trust Building, Place d'Armes Square, Montreal, P.Q., July 26, 1927; Folder 4.8, F.N. Southam, Montreal, to F.I. Ker, October 12, 1927; Folder 4.9, editorial from the *Ottawa Citizen*, September 19, 1932; Folder 4.9, Charles Bishop, Press Galley, House of Commons, Canada, Ottawa, April 8, 1932, to Ker, Managing Director, *The Spectator*, Hamilton; for a discussion of the concerns of Maritime provinces, see Ernest R. Forbes, *The Maritime Rights Movement, 1919–1927: A Study in Canadian Regionalism* (Kingston and Montreal, 1979), and for Maritime opposition, see AO, F1198, Ker Fonds, Box 4, Folder 4.9, F.P. Healey, Managing Secretary, Hamilton Chamber of Commerce to F.I. Ker, May 7, 1932.

19. Most of these arguments can be found in Hon. James P. Goodrich of Indiana, "Lakes–St. Lawrence Seaway, from the Viewpoint of National Welfare; Address to the Ohio Bankers Association," Toledo, OH, June 22, 1923, accessed at *www.archive.org/stream/lakesstlawrences00gooduoft/lakestlawrences00gooduoft_djvu.txt*, February 3, 2009. Goodrich was the former governor of Indiana, and in 1923 was a member of the Indiana Deep Waterways Commission, on the executive of the Great Lakes–St. Lawrence Tidewater Association, and was appointed by President Calvin Coolidge as a member of the International St. Lawrence Waterways Commission (see *Governors of Indiana*, published by the Board of Public Printing, 1930, accessed at *www.countyhistory.com/doc.gov/032.htm*, January 3, 2010); for another version of the pro-seaway arguments, see Charles P. Craig, "From the Great Lakes to the Atlantic," *Saturday Evening Post*, January 26, 1920; OA, F8, *Howard Ferguson Papers*, Canadian Deep Waterways Association, March 1927, to Ferguson, enclosing pamphlet by Frank A. Keefer; Tom Ireland, *Great Lakes–St. Lawrence Deep Waterway to the Sea* (New York, 1934) is a good example of a work which details the various arguments, pro and con, though clearly arguing for the seaway; one large section of the holdings of the Archives of the Owen D. Young Library of St. Lawrence University consists of the papers of Lewis K. Sillcox, president of New York Air Brake, who worked closely with the railway industry and collected numerous pro- and anti-seaway documents, including his own writings in opposition to the project. He claimed to have invented the term *Iceway*, which was used extensively against the seaway proponents. Frederick Innes Ker pointed out in 1926 that the S.S. *Lemoyne*, the largest ship on the Great Lakes, could carry 525,000 bushels of wheat,

even though she could not be loaded to her 29-foot depth — the equivalent of 50 square miles of prairie. Since she could not get through the Welland, her cargo had to be transshipped to eight smaller ships to get the cargo to Montreal. It was cheaper to ship to New York by rail. In 1925 almost half of the wheat went by rail from Buffalo; see AO, F1198, Frederick Innes Ker Fonds, Box 4, Folder 4.5, Supplement to *McGill News*, December 1926; The various arguments, pro and con, can be found also in testimony at IJC hearings on the St. Lawrence in 1921, International Joint Commission, *St. Lawrence Waterway Message from the President*, 53–154. Among those who testified was Julius Barnes, who claimed that the canals were needed to relieve railway congestion, and that the New York Barge Canal could not handle the existing demand for grain transportation.

20. Mabee, *op. cit.*, 62–63; "Julius Howland Barnes," in John H. Ingham, *Biographical Dictionary of American Business Leaders: A–G* (Westport, CT, and London, UK, 1983); *New York Times*, January 30, July 2, 1919.

21. International Joint Commission, *St. Lawrence Waterway: Message from the President* ..., 176–80; the IJC noted that, despite 40,000 miles of track in the American Midwest, the system would not be able to handle future grain production, and that the grain-growing capacity of the Canadian prairies "is hardly more than touched," 50.

22. The motives behind King's rather abrupt refusal to consider the American offer are a matter of conjecture, as King left no record of the cabinet discussions, or his own feelings. The governor general informed the British ambassador that the reluctance was based on financial considerations, but most historians believe that concern over Quebec's reaction played a large part in his slowness to act right through to 1930. See, for example, C.P. Stacey, *Canada and the Age of Conflict, Volume 2: 1921–1948* (Toronto, Buffalo, London, 1981), 110. King's fear of doing anything that might alienate Quebec support can be seen at a later stage in the negotiation in LAC, *Mackenzie King Diaries*, December 3, 1929; King's reluctance to act in the face of Quebec opposition was well known, and can be seen in AO, F1198, Frederick Innes Ker Fonds, Box 4, Folder 4.8, Ker to P.S. Fisher, Esq. c/o Wm. Southam and Sons, Ltd., 1070 Bleury Street, Montreal, P.Q., July 28, 1927, and Folder 4.9, Charles Bishop, Press Gallery, House of Commons, Ottawa, April 8, 1938, to Ker.

23. Peter Oliver, *G. Howard Ferguson: Ontario Tory* (Toronto and Buffalo, 1977), 174–78; power shortages, especially in eastern Ontario are discussed in AO, F1198, Frederick Innes Ker Fonds, Box 4, Folder 4.5, Supplement to the *McGill News*, December 1926, by F.I. Ker; AO, F8, *Howard Ferguson Papers*, Adam Beck, Chairman of the Hydro-Electric Power Commission to Ferguson, June 9, 1924, *Howard Ferguson Papers*; Copy of an Order in Council, June 17, 1924, with accompanying information. The expanded Joint Engineering Board reported late in 1926, largely endorsing the conclusions of the earlier Joint Board, but with the Canadians now favouring a two-stage (two power dams) rather than one plus a control dam upriver, which the Americans wanted. King asked that the appendices, plans, and plates be included, and, when this was done, that the whole report be printed, putting off the final report until the end of 1927. He then asked a National Advisory Committee that he had earlier appointed to report its opinion, which it did in January of 1928. Only then did he have to explain to the United States government that internal

dissention made it difficult for Canada to act, since his government had to deal with both Ontario and Quebec; Senate of Canada, *Proceedings of the Special Committee Appointed to Inquire into the Development and Improvement of the St. Lawrence River*, Ottawa, 1928, xiv–xv, xv.

24. Oliver, *op. cit.*, 180–82, 252, 284–86; Bernard L. Vigod, *Quebec Before Duplessis: The Political Career of Louis-Alexandre Taschereau* (Kingston and Montreal, 1986), 78, 123–25; AO, F8, *Howard Ferguson Papers*, letter O.E. Flemming, Windsor, December 17, 1927, to Ferguson, includes Great Lakes Tidewater Commission of Michigan and Greater Muskegon Chamber of Commerce, press release, January 28, 1927; *Howard Ferguson Papers, La Presse*, Montreal, editorial, June 9, 1927; *Ferguson Papers*, Report on the St. Lawrence Waterway Project by Henry Holgate, C.E., and J.A. Jamieson, C.E., to the Montreal Board of Trade, August 8, 1929.

25. Oliver, *op. cit.*, 184–85, 304–05, 353–555, 363–64; Vigod, *op. cit.*, 125, 147–51; AO, F8, *Howard Ferguson Papers*, Factum, Attorney General of the Province of Ontario, enclosed with letter, Howard Ferguson to Strachan Johnston, September 15, 1928; Telegram, Howard Ferguson to Premier Taschereau, November 7, 1929; Draft letter, King to unknown recipient, February 4, 1930; Letter, Howard Ferguson to L.A. Taschereau, June 7, 1929, enclosing 1) undated copy of speech [likely late May], 2) Letter, Howard Ferguson, February 4, 1930, 3) Letter, William Lyon Mackenzie King to Ferguson, February 15, 1930, 4) same to same, February 15, 1930, Ferguson to King, February 24, 1930, 5) Telegram, King to Ferguson, February 25, 1930, 6) Letter, King to Ferguson, March 8, 1930, 7) Letter, Ferguson to King, April 28, 1930, 8) Letter, King to Ferguson, May 6, 1930; *Ferguson Papers*, Telegrams, King to Ferguson, February 25, 1930, and Ferguson to King, February 27, 1930; *Ferguson Papers*, Frederick A. Gaby, Chief Engineer, HEPC of Ontario to Ferguson, March 6, 1930; Willoughby, *op. cit.*, 127–29.

26. The Engineering Board had recommended either a less expensive north shore canal, plus power generation in the river, or a south shore canal, if power was not needed for more than 11 years. The IJC had chosen the south shore route as there was no expectation of a need for power for quite some years; see *St. Lawrence Waterway Report of the United States and Canadian Government Engineers on the Improvement of the St. Lawrence River from Montreal to Lake Ontario Made to the International Joint Commission*, Supplementary to Senate Document No. 114, 67th Congress (Washington, 1922), 4–5, 18–24, and *St. Lawrence Waterway: Message from the President ...*, 169. The expanded Joint Board of Engineers recommended the cheaper north shore canal and power dams in the St. Lawrence; see Senate of Canada, *Proceedings of the Special Committee Appointed to Inquire into the Development and Improvement of the St. Lawrence River*, Ottawa, 1928, ix–xv, xxv–xxxii, which compares the 1922 and 1926 reports; the *Final Report of the Joint Board of Engineers, April 9, 1932*, really an updated version of the 1926 report of the Canadian engineers, appears in AO, F1055, *Frederick A. Gaby Papers* under Papers re: The St. Lawrence Deep Waterways Report, 1932. H. Blair Neatby, *William Lyon Mackenzie King: The Lonely Heights, 1924–1932*, Vol. 2 (Toronto, Buffalo, and London, 1963; reprinted 1970), 369–83; Mabee, *op. cit.*, 76–77. For an example of the efforts of Craig's experts, see note 19.

27. Quoted in "Calvin Coolidge," part of *American President: An Online Reference Resource*, at the Miller Center of Public Affairs, University of Virginia, accessed at *millercenter.org/academic/americanpresident*, January 23, 2009.

28. *Ibid.*, "Herbert Hoover," *New York Times*, March 12, 1926; the engineering report appears as House of Representatives, *House Document 288*, 69th Congress, 1st Session; The Great Lakes–Tidewater Association reprinted the report, with negative comments on the Hudson route added by the Chief of Engineers, United States Army, suggesting that the St. Lawrence would cost far less to deepen; see reprint of a letter from the Chief of Engineers, Washington, December 6, 1926, in AO, F1198, Frederick Innes Ker Fonds, Box 4, Folder 4.6. The composition of the American national advisory commission, the St. Lawrence Commission, is found in Senate of Canada, *Proceedings of the Special Committee Appointed to Inquire into the Development and Improvement of the St. Lawrence River*, Ottawa, 1928, xi.

29. Mabee, *op. cit.*, 78–79; Willoughby, *op. cit.*, 107.

30. Willoughby, *op. cit.*, 113–15, 119, 121, 124–25.

31. LAC, *Mackenzie King Diaries*, November 21, 1927; AO, *Ferguson Papers*, Hamilton Chamber of Commerce to Ferguson, May 30, 1930.

32. Quoted, Larry A. Glassford, *Reaction and Reform: The Politics of the Conservative Party Under R.B. Bennett, 1927–1938* (Toronto, Buffalo, and London, 1992), 78; King's ambivalence on the issue of federal control of power generation in riverbeds is discussed in Neatby, *op. cit.*, Vol. 2, 226–27.

33. The resolution of the 1927 convention is quoted in Oliver, *op. cit.*, 292; AO, *Ferguson Papers*, clipping, February [13?], 1929.

34. AO, *Ferguson Papers*, telegrams King to Ferguson, February 25, 1930, and Ferguson to King, February 27, 1930; Oliver, *op. cit.*, 366; *Canadian Annual Review of Public Affairs, 1929–30* (Toronto, 1930), 105–06.

35. Ernest Watkins, *R.B. Bennett* (Toronto, 1963), 193; Willoughby, *op. cit.*, 139–41; Parliament of Canada, *White Paper, Agreement Made the 11th Day of July A.D. 1932, Between the Dominion of Canada and the Province of Ontario, Concerning the Development of Power in the International Rapids Section of the St. Lawrence River, 1932*.

36. Quoted in Watkins, *op. cit.*, 193.

37. Canada, Parliament, *House of Commons Debates*, February 8, 1932.

38. Kenneth H. Davis, *FDR: The New York Years, 1928–1933* (New York, 1979), 41–42, 93–100; Mabee, *op. cit.*, 88–95; Willoughby, *op. cit.*, 107–08.

39. Davis, *FDR: The New York Years*, 100; Mabee, *op. cit.*, 100.

40. Piper, *op. cit.*, 90–91 and appendix H; Philip P. Jessup, "The Great Lakes–St. Lawrence Deep Waterway Treaty," in *The American Journal of International Law*, Vol. 26, No. 4 (October 1932), 814–19; for the issue of protecting the level of Lake Ontario, see *Final Report of the Joint Board of Engineers*, April 9, 1932, in AO, F 1055, *Frederick A. Gaby Papers*, re: The St. Lawrence Deep Waterways Report, 1932; Willoughby, *op. cit.*, 104, 145–46.

41. Telegram, Governor Franklin D. Roosevelt of New York to President Hoover, July 9, 1932, appears under President Hoover, telegram to Governor Franklin D. Roosevelt of New York about the Great Lakes–St. Lawrence deep waterway, July 10, 1932, in John T.

Woolley and Gerhard Peters, *The American Presidency Project*, University of California, Santa Barbara, accessed at *www.presidency.ucsb.edu/ws/?pid=23154*, March 5, 2009.

42. *Massena Observer*, Massena, July 28, 1932; AO, F8, *Howard Ferguson Papers*, Resolution passed unanimously at a meeting of the County of Dundas Conservative Association, September 19, 1927; Gary Pennanen, "Battle of the Titans: Mitchell Hepburn, Mackenzie King, Franklin Roosevelt and the St. Lawrence Seaway," page 4 and note 7, page 18, in Ontario Historical Society, *Ontario History*, Vol. 89, No. 1, March 1997, 1–21. The same concern about the effects of flooding was expressed when the 1941 agreement was signed; see AO, RG3, *Mitchell Hepburn Correspondence*, letter, J. McDonald, Warden and A. MacMillan, Clerk, Council of the United Counties of Stormont, Dundas, and Glengarry to Hepburn, February 15, 1941, on behalf of same and the United Counties of Leeds and Grenville.

43. Power Authority of the State of New York, *Annual Report*, 1933, 30–32; *Congressional Record*, 73rd Congress, 1st Session, 2,348–65, 2,412–14, 4,477–4,509, 4,584–89, 4,971–74, 5,403–04; Mabee, *op. cit.*, 106.

44. Mabee, *op. cit.*, 107–08; Willoughby, *op. cit.*, 152; One of two interviews with the press is reproduced in Frank Freidel, *Franklin D. Roosevelt: Launching the New Deal* (Boston and Toronto, 1973), 440–41; SLU, Collection 40, *The St. Lawrence Seaway Collection*, Mabee Series, Box 52, Item 3, Interviews with E.B. Crosby, Massena, September 18, 1958, and January 22, 1959, and with Philip Falter, Massena Banking and Trust, Massena, November 6, 1959.

45. For comments on the opposition of coal interests, see Ireland, *op. cit.*, 138–39; SLU, Collection 40, Mabee Series, Box 52, Item 3, Interview with Philip Falter, Massena Banking and Trust, Massena, September 12, 1959 (Falter identified the main New York State opponents as the railroads, New York City, which had a large share of the population of the state, as well as Rochester, Syracuse, and the Niagara Mohawk Corporation, with Alcoa opposed, but not actively. He identified the chief congressional opponents as Robert Wagner and S. Copeland of New York, who spoke for the port of New York, J.H. Lewis of Illinois, who was attorney for the power interests, and Huey Long of Louisiana); Interviews, E.B. Crosby, September 18, 1958 (Crosby said that opposition was so strong that, after holding a few meetings at St. Lawrence University and Syracuse University during the Depression, the pro-seaway forces were told that they were no longer welcome), and January 22, 1959; Interviews, Harry C. Brockel, Municipal Port Director, Milwaukee, November 6 and 12, 1959 (Brockel identified the chief railway opponents as the New York Central and the Pennsylvania, which dominated the American Association of Railroads, and the Baltimore and Ohio. In testimony before a subcommittee of the Senate Committee on Foreign Relations examining the St. Lawrence Seaway project in 1947, Julius Barnes said the same thing — see Hearings, 80th Congress, 1st Session, 1947); Interview, John C. Beukema, Muskegon, MI, October 5, 1959.

46. SLU, Collection 40, Mabee Series, Box 52, Item 3, Interviews with Edward B. Crosby, Massena, October 18, 1956, September 18, 1958, January 22, 1959; Interview with Harry C. Brockel, Milwaukee, November 6, 1959.

47. "Message to the Senate Requesting Ratification of the St. Lawrence Treaty with Canada," January 10, 1934, in *The American Presidency Project*, accessed at *www.*

*presidency.ucsb.edu/ws/?pid=23154*, March 5, 2009.

48. Roosevelt Press Conference, March 14, 1934, *The American Presidency Project*, accessed at *www.presidency.ucsb.edu/ws/?pid=23154*, March 10, 2009. Seaway supporters met with Roosevelt and he said that he was three votes short. They could not understand why he did not use his considerable influence on Congress; see SLU, Collection 40, Mabee Series, Box 52, Item 3, Interview with Philip Falter, September 12, 1958.

49. Roosevelt Press Conference, March 14, 1934, *The American Presidency Project*, accessed at *www.presidency.ucsb.edu/ws/?pid=23154*, March 10, 2009.

50. SLU, Collection 40, Mabee Series, Box 52, Item 3, Interviews with Harry C. Brockel, Milwaukee, November 6, 1959 and with E.B. Crosby, Massena, September 18, 1958.

51. SLU, Collection 40, Mabee Series, Box 52, Item 3, Interviews with Harry C. Brockel, Milwaukee, November 6, 1959, and with E.B. Crosby, Massena, September 18, 1958, and January 22, 1959, and with John C. Beukema, Muskegon, MI, October 1959.

52. Neil McKenty, *Mitch Hepburn* (Toronto and Montreal, 1967), 24, 30–38, 54–57, 65–67, 94, 159; Pennanen, *op. cit.*, 5–6 and notes 10 and 11, 18.

53. H. Blair Neatby, *William Lyon Mackenzie King, Vol. 3, 1932–1939: The Prism of Unity* (Toronto and Buffalo, 1976), 242–44.

54. The treaty is reproduced in Baxter, ed. *op. cit.*, 11–17; A discussion of the terms and a comparison with the terms of the 1932 agreement is found in AO, RG3-10, item B307951, *Great Lakes-St. Lawrence Agreement Report*; Pennanen, *op. cit.*, 6–13; McKenty, *op. cit.*, 145–49, 152–56, 199–200; Neatby, *op. cit.*, Vol. 3, 117, 201–02, 239–42, 269–70; *Massena Observer*, October 18, November 8, 1940; Mabee, *op. cit.*, 129–30.

55. Mabee, *op. cit.*, 132–33; Noble was never involved with the pro-seaway organizations, but supported the project independently for some years; see SLU, Collection 40, Mabee Series, Box 52, Item 3, Interview with E.B. Crosby, January 22, 1959.

56. Message to the Great Lakes Seaway and Power Conference, December 5, 1940, *The American Presidency Project*, accessed at *www.presidency.ucsb.edu/ws/?pid=23154*, March 10, 2009. For opposition, see *New York Times*, January 10, March 25, 1941, *Wall Street Journal*, New York, March 21, 1941.

57. AO, RG3, *Mitchell Hepburn Correspondence*, G.D. Conant to Hon. T.B. McQuesten, Hon. Peter Heenan, Hon. H.J. Kinby, and Hon. Farquar Oliver, February 19, 1941; Same, letter J. McDonald, Warden, and A. MacMillan, Clerk of the Council of the United Counties of Stormont, Dundas and Glengarry, February 15, 1941, to Hepburn, on behalf of same and United Council of Leeds and Grenville; Hon. Lionel Chevrier M.P., *The St. Lawrence Seaway* (Toronto, 1959), 40; Mabee, *op. cit.*, 133–35.

58. Willoughby, *op. cit.*, 188, 202; House of Representatives, *House Report 1431*, 77th Congress, 1st Session, Section 2, 105–11; Dave Kenney, *Minnesota Goes To War: The Home Front During World War II* (Saint Paul, MN, 2005), 116–21; New York Division of Military and Naval Affairs, "Military History, Forts, Sampson Naval Training Base," accessed at *www.dmna.state.ny.us/forts/fortsQ_S/sampsonNavalTrainingBase.htm*, March 17, 2009.

59. Mabee, *op. cit.*, 130, 135–39.

60. Ingham, *op. cit.*, "Julius Howland Barnes"; *Time* magazine, May 5, June 9, 1930 (Barnes was featured on the cover on June 9. He wound up his business as a grain broker at about that time, having suffered losses in the crash of 1929, and his

shipbuilding business in Duluth was not competitive after wartime construction in the Second World War, but he added other businesses, including insurance and investment companies to his holdings); SLU, Collection 40, Mabee Series, Box 52, Item 3, quotation on Barnes from Interview with Emery Henshell, Duluth Industrial Bureau Director, Duluth, October 29, 1959; also Interviews with Harry A. Bullard, former president of the Northern Federation of Chambers of Commerce, Potsdam, NY, January 18, June 29, 1959; Biographical material on N.R. Danielian appears in the outline of an oral interview conducted by John Luter for the *Columbia University Oral History Project* in 1972, accessed at *www.eisenhower.archives.gov/Research/ Oral_Histories/oral_history_finding_aids/ohfa177.pdf*, March 12, 2009, and in obituary in the *New York Times*, May 14, 1974.

61. Willoughby, *op. cit.*, 193, 195.
62. *Ibid.*, 201–09; Chevrier, *op. cit.*, 33.
63. Chevier, *op. cit.*, 33; Willoughby, *op. cit.*, 212–15; Mabee, *op. cit.*, 145–47.
64. Willoughby, *op. cit.*, 214; Mabee, *op. cit.*, 140.
65. "Harry S. Truman," in *American President: An Online Reference Resource*.
66. "Annual Message to the Congress on the State of the Union," January 4, 1950, and "Special Message to the Senate Transmitting Treaty with Canada Concerning Uses of the Waters of the Niagara River," May 2, 1950, *The American Presidency Project*; Willoughby, *op. cit.*, 225–26.
67. Mabee, *op. cit.*, 148–49; new extraction techniques actually made it possible to prolong the life of the Mesabi field, employing low-grade ore, but these had not been discovered in the late 1940s and early 1950s.
68. Mabee, *op. cit.*, 149.
69. *Ibid.*, 151–53; SLU, Collection 40, Mabee Series, Box 52, Item 3, Interview with Harry Brockel, Milwaukee, November 12, 1959; Foreign Affairs and International Trade Canada, *Documents on Canadian External Relations*, Vol. 18, No. 786, July 25, 1952; No. 789, August 27, 1952, accessed at *www.international.gc.ca/department/ history-histoire/dcer/menu-en.asp*, April 5, 2009.
70. SLU, Collection 40, Mabee Series, Box 52, Item 3, Interview with Harry A. Bullard, former president of the Northern Federation of Chambers of Commerce, Potsdam, NY, June 18, 1959: Willoughby, *op. cit.*, 216, 220–23.
71. Annual Message to the Congress: The President's Economic Report, January 12, 1951, and Annual Budget Message to the Congress, fiscal year 1952, January 15, 1951, *The American Presidency Project*.
72. Willoughby, *op. cit.*, 226–31; SLU, Collection 40, Mabee Series, Interview with Harry S. Truman, Independence, MO, November 25, 1959.
73. Dale C. Thomson, *Louis St. Laurent: Canadian* (Toronto, 1967), 115–16, 265.
74. *Ibid.*, 258–59, 289–90; Willoughby, *op. cit.*, 224.
75. Chevrier, *op. cit.*, 43–46; Thomson, *op. cit.*, 307, 319–20; another Chevrier speech was reported in the *Toronto Daily Star*, February 13, 1951, and one by Defence Minister Claxton, given in New York, appears in the *Globe and Mail*, Toronto, March 21, 1951; the *Saturday Evening Post* commented on the suggestion that Canada would go it alone, saying in an editorial "that we must see, if strictly from amazement." See AO, RG3-24, Hydro-Electric Power Commission, Seaway Bill, undated article

commenting on *Post* editorial; the *Toronto Daily Star*, April 1951, quotes the head of the anti-seaway lobby in Washington as saying that Canada was bluffing. When Robert H. Saunders, head of the Hydro-Electric Commission of Ontario was told this, he replied bluntly, "I know our Canadian government never bluffs."

76. Chevrier, *op. cit.*, 46–47.

77. Annual Message to the Congress: The President's Economic Report, January 16, 1952, Annual Budget Message to the Congress: fiscal year 1953, January 21, 1952, Special Message to the Congress Urging Action on the St. Lawrence Seaway, January 28, 1952, *The American Presidency Project*.

78. Willoughby, *op. cit.*, 238–40; Mabee, *op. cit.*, 160; Foreign Affairs and International Trade Canada, *Documents on Canadian External Relations*, Vol. 18, No. 788, August 1, 1952; No. 789, August 27, 1952. Danielian later urged Canada not to state that it had started the Seaway without the United States, out of concern that this might help opponents of American participation. See Vol. 18, No. 804, December 12, 1952.

79. Curiously, given how much energy Truman put into getting Congress to adopt the 1941 agreement, his memoirs make only the vaguest of reference to the seaway issue; see Harry S. Truman, *Memoirs: Years of Trial and Hope, 1946–1952* (Garden City, NY, 1956). Standard biographies of Truman also give little attention to the subject.

80. Thomson, *op. cit.*, 346, 348; Willoughby, *op. cit.*, 243–45; *Documents on Canadian External Relations*, Vol. 18, No. 783, July 8, 1952, No. 794, October 3, 1952, No. 795, October 31, 1952.

81. Willoughby, *op. cit.*, 245, 248; Mabee, *op. cit.*, 161; "Annual Budget Message to the Congress: Fiscal Year 1954," *The American Presidency Project*.

82. Willoughby, *op. cit.*, 246; Editorial, "How Long Must Canada Wait?" *The Telegram*, Toronto, April 26, 1951, and article on the need for power, dated Ottawa, November 30, 1951, in AO, F12, Gordon D. Conant Papers, Package 4. The American cabinet recognized the extreme patience of the Canadian government; see *Documents on Canadian External Relations*, Vol. 18, No. 774, April 14, 1952.

83. Robert Donovan, *Eisenhower: The Inside Story* (New York, 1956), 76–78; Sherman Adams, *Firsthand Report: The Story of the Eisenhower Administration* (1961; reprinted Westport, CT, 1974), 4–5; Departmental Opinions on the St. Lawrence Seaway Project, March 11, 1953, quoted in Robert L. Branyan and Lawrence H. Larsen, *The Eisenhower Administration, 1953–1961: A Documentary History* (New York, 1971), 258–59; and in a memo from Assistant Budget Director Roger Jones to President Eisenhower, May 11, 1954, *Ibid.*, 271–73; Presidential Press Conference of April 23, 1953, *The American Presidency Project*; Agenda for the Permanent Joint Board on Defense, April 2, 1953, quoted in Branyan and Larsen, *op. cit.*, 259–63; President Eisenhower to Senator Alexander Wiley, April 23, 1953, quoted in *Ibid.*, 263.

84. Mabee, *op. cit.*, 163–64; the ministers' speeches are summarized in Willoughby, *op. cit.*, 250; Chevrier, *op. cit.*, 62–63.

85. Mabee, *op. cit.*, 165; Homer Gruenther to the Special Assistant to the President Sherman Adams, January 14, 1954; same to Special Counsel to the President Bernard Shanley, January 26, 1954; same to Special Assistant Wilton Persons, February 23, 1954; and Special Counsel to the President Bernard Shanley to Homer Gruenther, January 28, 1954; quoted in Branyan and Larsen, *op. cit.*, 265–67; Admiral Arthur

Radford to Senator Homer Ferguson, January 18, 1954, quoted in Branyan and Larsen, *op. cit.*, 267–70; "Remarks of John F. Kennedy on the Saint Lawrence Seaway Before the Senate, Washington, January 14, 1954," John F. Kennedy Presidential Library and Museum, accessed at *www.jfklibrary.org/search.htm*, January 19, 2009.

86. President Eisenhower to Guy Brown, February 16, 1954, quoted in Branyan and Larsen, *op. cit.*, 270–71; Mabee, *op. cit.*, 153; SLU, Mabee Series, Interviews with E.B. Crosby, September 1 and 18, 1958, and Harry C. Brockel, November 6, 1959; *Congressional Record*, 83rd Congress, 2nd Session, 6,050–52.

87. *New York Times*, May 16, 1954; Mabee, *op. cit.*, 166–67.

88. SLU, Collection 40, Mabee Series, Box 52, Item 3, Interview with Emery Henshell, Duluth Industrial Bureau Director, Duluth, MN, October 29, 1959.

89. Willougby, *op. cit.*, 253–54.

90. Chevrier makes a very personal interpretation of these negotiations; see Chevrier, *op. cit.*, 61–62; the actual points agreed to are contained in an exchange of notes between the two governments, found in 83rd Congress, 2nd Session, Senate Document 165 (Washington, 1954), 171–73.

**Chapter 4: Building a Dream: Seaway Construction**

1. These figures appear in various sources, including government publications. The quantities of earth and concrete vary slightly and an exact count of the number of people moved was not kept; see Chevrier, *op. cit.*, 39. He deals only with earth and cement related to the power facilities, as does AO, F12, Gordon D. Conant Papers, undated article, *circa* 1960, "St. Lawrence Power Project."

2. Lionel Chevrier discusses the problems of working with so many entities; see Chevrier, *op. cit.*, 53–54, 58–63.

3. Chevrier, *op. cit.*, 52–53; Thomson, *op. cit.*, 373–74, says that Chevrier asked to be given the position, but this is not inconsistent with the idea that he hesitated for some time before deciding that this was the right move for him.

4. Mabee, *op. cit.*, 191–92, SLU, Collection 40, Mabee Series, Box 52, Interview with Harry A. Bullard, former president of the Northern Federation of Chambers of Commerce, Potsdam, NY, June 29, 1959.

5. H. Becker, *From the Atlantic to the Great Lakes: A History of the U.S. Army Corps of Engineers and the St. Lawrence Seaway* (Washington, D.C., 1984?), vii, 23, 28–31, 33.

6. *Ibid.*, 8–16, 20–22, 25, 35–36.

7. *Ibid.*, 26, 52; Mabee, *op. cit.*, 205; SLU, Collection 40, Mabee Series, Item 3, Interview with A.W. Lamport, Project Property Office, Ontario Hydro, Cornwall, August 5, 1958.

8. *Toronto Telegram*, January 17, 1955; Saunders speeches to the Empire Club, Toronto, January 27, 1949, and October 11, 1951, accessed at *speeches.empireclub.org/details. asp?r=vs&ID=60242&number=1* and *60296&number=3*, November 9, 2009.

9. *Globe and Mail*, Toronto, September 24, 1953.

10. Quoted Chevrier, *op. cit.*, 30.

11. *The Atlantic Monthly*, February 1939; Obituary, *New York Times*, July 30, 1981; Willoughby, *op. cit.*, 269. Moses's reputation with Americans was further damaged

by the Pulitzer Prize-winning biography, *The Power Broker*, by Robert A. Caro, published in 1974, which praised Moses for is early work, but attacked his support of expressways and urban renewal, and suggested that Moses took steps to ensure that the poor and racial minorities be excluded from his parks.

12. Chevrier, *op. cit.*, 30–31; Becker, *op. cit.*, vi–vii, 1, 16.

13. Chevrier, *op. cit.*, 54–55; the Canadian government originally told the United States in June of 1952 that it planned to build its own system of canals in the International Section after arrangements for the completion of the power dam had been made. It became more specific when it informed the United States in August of 1954 that it would build a lock at Iroquois and would build its own canal around the Barnhart Island power dam "when it considers that parallel facilities are required to accommodate existing or potential traffic …" The United States government indicated in 1955 that it was under some pressure from various quarters, but agreed with the Canadian position. It needed a joint statement to put matters to rest. Because of disagreements about dredging the North Channel, the possibility of continuing the 14-foot navigation, and lock sizes, it took about a month and a half to come up with a letter seemingly agreeable to both (see *Documents on Canadian External Relations*, Vol. 21, No. 413, January 5, 1955, to No. 431, February 21, 1955; Baxter, *op. cit.*, 54–57); At that point, a disagreement arose over the Canadian insistence on providing for 27-foot navigation by dredging the North Channel. This disagreement dragged on until November 21, 1956, when the United States, in a sharply worded note, acknowledged that it recognized, de facto, what Canada was doing, but reserved the right to protect its interests; see *Documents on Canadian External Relations*, Vol. 21, No. 434, July 7, 1955, and Vol. 23, No. 173, February 21, 1956, to No. 192, November 21, 1956.

14. Becker, *op. cit.*, 96–97; Chevrier, *op. cit.*, 62–63. Duplessis indicated that he would not oppose the Seaway, but insisted on being consulted on any aspect which involved Quebec; see *Documents on Canadian External Relations*, Vol. 18, No. 790, August 27, 1952. Canadian insistence on being able to dredge the North Channel to 27 feet, both to allow for a later Canadian canal and to keep the flow in the two channels at the same rate as before can be seen in Vol. 21, No. 419, February 3, 1955, No. 424, February 8, 1955, No. 425, February 8, 1955, No. 434, July 7, 1955, and in the series from Vol. 23, No. 173, February 21, 1956, to No. 192, November 21, 1956.

15. Chevrier, *op. cit.*, 58–61.

16. Becker, *op. cit.*, 62, 64–65; Chevrier, *op. cit.*, 63, 111; SLU, Collection 40, Mabee Series, Box 52, Item 3, Lieutenant Colonel James E. Hammer, Corps of Engineers, U.S. Army, addressing the Society of Military Engineers at Clarkson College of Technology, Potsdam, NY, March 30, 1955.

17. SLU, Collection 40, Mabee Series, Box 52, Item 3, Interview with Stanley Frost, M.E.I.C., P. Eng., Engineering Consultant, *circa* August 1955; Same, Reverend A.E. Wilfong, United Church Moulinette Pastoral Charge, July 6, 1957; Interview with George Beavers, Reeve, December 6, 1955; Discussion of the early history of the villages and the lack of progress after a seaway was proposed early in the twentieth century, together with extensive photographs, can be found at the Lost Villages Historical Society website, *lostvillages.ca*, accessed May 4, 2009.

18. Mabee, *op. cit.*, 204–07; AO, RG37-6-7, Expropriation Hearings; SLU, Collection 40, Mabee Series, Box 52, Item 3, Interview with A.W. Lamport, Project Property Officer, Ontario Hydro, Cornwall, August 5, 1958, and Interview with Garnet De Rosie, former president of the Mille Roches-Moulinette Chamber of Commerce, and store owner, Mille Roches, April 1957; AO, RG19-27, Intergovernmental Correspondence, 1942–58, Box V8, b354418, File 19.11, M.R. Sloan, Director, municipal assessment, September 11, 1956.

19. Mabee, *op. cit.*, 211–12, SLU, Collection 40, Mabee Series, Box 52, Item 3, Interview with A.W. Lamport, August 5, 1958; Roger Graham, *Old Man Ontario: Leslie M. Frost* (Toronto, Buffalo, London, 1990), 212–17. There was to be only one new town to encompass all of the communities east of Morrisburg under the Hydro plan, but since the existing communities were in two different townships, neither wished to lose the tax revenue, so each township received one of the new communities.

20. SLU, Collection 40, Mabee Series, Box 52, Item 3, Interviews with Mr. and Mrs. Mert Simser, near the Massena canal, August 1956, Walter F. Wilson, Louisville, August 27, 1956, Daniel Conglas (?), head of the landowners association, Louisville, March 21, 1957, Thomas Fay, Postmaster, Massena, September 15, 1958.

21. Becker, *op. cit.*, 51; Moses on land speculators, quoted in Mabee, *op. cit.*, 210.

22. Mabee, *op. cit.*, 179–80, 184, gives examples of individuals who found work on the project. He obtained a job as a photographer, his first experience as such, in order to do research for his book on the Seaway.

23. *Ibid.*, 239–43.

24. Carleton Mabee based his account of the trip by "The Gentleman" on a talk given by Ellis Armstrong in Massena on May 14, 1957, but there are obvious inaccuracies, not the least of which is that a report in *Excavating Engineer* for August 1955, "Draglines Float to Seaway," dealing with the early portion of the trip, not only mentions that there were two draglines, but provides photographs. A second report of the latter part of the trip, Daniel J. McConville, "Seaway To Nowhere," in *Invention and Technology* magazine, Fall 1995, Vol. 11, Issue 2, accessed at *www.americanheritage.com/articles/magazine/it/1995/2/1995_2_34.shtml*, June 7, 2009, provides an alternative, more logical version of the latter portion of the trip to that given by Mabee, based on the reminiscences of the pilot on the tug that accompanied the barge through the rapids; see Mabee, *op. cit.*, 177–78 and 289, note 5, for his version. The second, smaller dragline may have been "The Madam," which also worked on the Seaway.

25. *Ibid.*, 178–79; Becker, *op. cit.*, 101–03.

26. Chevrier, *op. cit.*, 65–71, 85–91.

27. Gerald A. Alfred, *Heeding the Voices of Our Ancestors* (Toronto, New York, Oxford, 1995), 52, 63–64; Laurence M. Hauptman, *The Iroquois Struggle for Survival: World War II to Red Power* (Syracuse, 1986), 136–37; Mabee, *op. cit.*, 208.

28. Chevrier, *op. cit.*, 105–06; Mabee, *op. cit.*, 208; Hauptman, *op. cit.*, 137; SLU, Collection 40, Mabee Series, Box 52, Item 3, Interview, no date, with George A. Laframbose, Administration Officer, Cote St. Catherine Division, and Donald H. Stevens, Administration Office of Construction, St. Lawrence Seaway Authority.

29. Chevrier, *op. cit.*, 92–93; Mabee, *op. cit.*, 184.

30. Becker, *op. cit.*, 50–51.

31. *Toronto Telegram*, January 17, 1955.

32. Becker, *op. cit.*, 31–33; SLU, Collection 40, Mabee Series, Item 3, Interviews with Harry C. Brockel, November 6, 1959, and John C. Beukema, October 5, 1959. The American government also expressed annoyance at the pressure Danielian was applying to do things the way his organization wanted; see *Documents on Canadian External Relations*, Vol. 21, No. 431, February 21, 1955.

33. Willoughby, *op. cit.*, 267; Becker, *op. cit.*, 67. Castle originally suggested larger locks to the Canadians, but then withdrew the request, agreeing that the locks on the American side would be of Welland dimensions; see *Documents on Canadian External Relations*, Vol. 21, No. 418, January 28, 1955, No. 419, February 3, 1955, No. 423, February 5, 1955, and No. 428, February 10, 1955.

34. Mabee, *op. cit.*, 179. It should be remembered that Carleton Mabee worked on the International Section of the Seaway and either had first-hand information about construction, or access to those who did; the Mabee references to the construction phase reflect his experience; Willoughby, *op. cit.*, 268; Chevrier, *op. cit.*, 83–84. The exemptions covered work on "international" portions of the work, but not portions occurring entirely within each country; see *Documents on Canadian External Relations*, Vol. 21, No. 426, February 8, 1955, and No. 433, May 4, 1955. Another example of the exemptions from normal customs and immigration policies can be found in an exchange of notes between the two countries in November and December of 1956; see Baxter, *op. cit.*, 60.

35. Chevrier, *op. cit.*, 111–12; Mabee, *op. cit.*, 180–81. While Chevrier only acknowledges pressure from Lake Ontario residents, there was also pressure from the American section of the IJC, probably because of complaints by American residents along Lake Ontario; see *Documents on Canadian External Relations*, Vol. 18, No. 790, August 27, 1952.

36. Mabee, 181–83; Chevrier, *op. cit.*, 94–95.

37. Mabee, *op. cit.*, 182–83, 198–201; photographs of the dry riverbed and the cannon balls appeared in newspapers such as the *Toronto Telegram*.

38. *Ibid.*, 176, 180–81, 186–87; Chevrier, *op. cit.*, 82.

39. McConville, *op. cit.*

40. *Ibid.*; Mabee, *op. cit.*, 186. The naming of the lock after Senator Bertrand Snell was controversial among seaway supporters. He had always claimed that he had authored the first bill in the United States Congress to propose the building of power and navigation facilities, but this was not true. Also, while he spoke in support of the seaway when in his home district in Upstate New York, he did not do much to further the cause when in Congress, because, critics said, he was tied closely to private power interests. Seaway supporters did acknowledge, however, that his pressure on New York senators had greatly assisted in creating PASNY. See SLU, Collection 40, Mabee series, Box 52, Item 3, Interviews with E.B. Crosby, Massena, September 18, 1958, Thomas Fay, Postmaster, Massena, September 15, 1958, and George S. Reed, Trustee of PASNY 1934–50, Lowville, NY, July 18, 1959; Mabee, *op. cit.*, note 3, 289.

41. McConville, *op. cit.*

42. SLU, Collection 40, Mabee Series, Box 52, Item 3, Interview with Gordon Mitchell, Project Director, Ontario Hydro, July 9, 1958; Chevrier, *op. cit.*, 83; Becker, *op. cit.*, 73.

43. Mabee, *op. cit.*, 186, 188–89.

44. Becker, *op. cit.*, 101–03.

45. *Ibid.*, 72, 73, 76–77.

46. Chevrier, *op. cit.*, 84–85; Hauptman, *op. cit.*, 145; Mabee, *op. cit.*, 181, 182, note 42, 290.

47. *Documents on Canadian External Relations*, Vol. 23, No. 173, February 21, 1956, No. 177, May 10, 1956, to No. 182, May 31, 1956, and No. 188, October 2, 1956; Chevrier, *op. cit.*, 74–75; Mabee, *op. cit.*, 190–91, Becker, *op. cit.*, 67–68, 97–98; Moses quoted in Willoughby, *op. cit.*, 268.

48. *Ibid.*, SLU, Collection 40, Mabee Series, Box 52, Item 3, Interview with Lewis Castle, September 18, 1958; Becker, *op. cit.*, 55–58; Moses quoted in Mabee, *op. cit.*, 194; discussions of the low level versus high level bridges by the Canadian cabinet and officials can be found in *Documents on Canadian External Relations*, Vol. 21, No. 436, September 20, 1955, and Vol. 23, No. 183, July 9, 1956.

49. Chevrier had the idea of dredging the North Channel early in the process, but did not push it with the Americans until they suggested that, because the South Channel was being deepened, a large hole should be dug in the North Channel to keep the flow rate in the two channels the same as it had been previously; see Chevrier, *op. cit.*, 75–76; Mabee, *op. cit.*, 191, 193, 194–95. The American government expressed its displeasure at the Canadian idea of dredging the North Channel, insisting that it was not in keeping with American legislation and with subsequent agreements with Canada, but it indicated that it did not want to hinder construction. Canada countered that the matter had been raised several times, starting in August of 1954, and that dredging would accomplish the intention of the Boundary Waters Treaty to keep the flow of water in the two channels the same as it was before the project started; see Baxter, *op. cit.*, 58–60 and note 13 of this chapter. The desire for an all-Canadian canal through the International Section (and on through the Welland) never went away. The Toronto *Globe and Mail*, for instance, had endorsed the idea when put forward by premier Leslie Frost in 1951, but was still advocating a Canadian seaway after the Seaway opened; see May 4 and May 10, 1951, and July 4, 1958.

50. Mabee, *op. cit.*, 191–93; NEMHC, Lewis G. Castle Papers, S2425b1f2, unidentified newspaper clippings, "Seaway Squabble Flairs," dated Milwaukee, April 27, 1957, and "Charge Seaway Bungling May Cause Canada to Quit," dated Washington, April 27 [1957].

51. NEMHC, Lewis G. Castle Papers, S2425b1f2, unidentified newspaper clippings, "Seaway Squabble Flairs," dated Milwaukee, April 27, 1957; "Charge Seaway Bungling May Cause Canada to Quit," dated Washington, April 27 [1957]; "Castle Raps Seaway Toll Testimony," *Duluth News-Tribune*, April 15, 1957; "Danielian's Pessimism Assailed by Port Director," *Massena Observer*, April 29, 1957; "Kilburn Hits Tolls Issue, Democrats," *Watertown Daily Times* article dated January 8 [1957]; "Bacon Given Seaway Job," *Milwaukee Journal*, May 9, 1957; Castle's handwritten notes marked "NRD"; Interview with N.R. Danielian by John Luter, 1972, "Columbia University Oral History Project"; *New York Times*, May 14, 1974. See also note 32 of this chapter.

52. Becker, *op. cit.*, 111–20.

53. *Standard Freeholder*, Cornwall, April 27, 1957.

54. Becker, *op. cit.*, 52–53; Hauptman, *op. cit.*, 144–47.

55. Becker, *op. cit.*, 104; Mabee, *op. cit.*, 102; Chevrier, *op. cit.*, 98; *Documents on Canadian External Relations*, Vol. 21, No. 435, July 19, 1955.

56. Willoughby, *op. cit.*, 270–72.

57. *Ibid.*, 272–75; Becker, *op. cit.*, 109–13; Chevrier, *op. cit.*, 118–24.

58. Mabee, *op. cit.*, 213–14, 217, 219; SLU, Collection 40, Mabee Series, Box 52, Item 3, Interviews with Mr. Stanley Frost, M.E.I.C., P. Eng., Engineering Consultant, December, 1955; Eunice Armstrong, Iroquois, April 4, 1956; A.W. Lamport, Project Property Officer, Ontario Hydro, Cornwall, August 5, 1958; and a Sheek Island cottager, tearing down his cottage, April 8, 1957. The original proposals for the parks and new communities, which were largely followed by HEPCO, except that it did not provide all new housing, were developed in 1943; see Norman D. Wilson, *Factors in the Rehabilitation of the St. Lawrence Communities*, a report done for the federal government; Chevrier, *op. cit.*, 40, makes reference to this report and its influence.

59. SLU, Collection 40, Mabee Series, Box 52, Item 3, Interviews with A.W. Lamport, Project Property Officer, Ontario Hydro, Cornwall, August 5, 1958, and Reverend A.E. Wilfong, United Church Moulinette Pastoral Charge, July 6, 1957.

60. See The Lost Villages Historical Society website, accessed at *lostvillages.ca*.

61. The experiments are detailed in the documentary, *Setting Fires for Science*, Donald Brittain, writer and director, National Film Board, Montreal, 1958.

62. Mabee, *op. cit.*, 220–21; some of this information comes from The Lost Villages Historical Society website, and from aerial photographs of the town sites after the buildings and other man-made objects had been removed.

63. HEPCO's plans for the communities were published in Hydro-Electric Power Commission of Ontario, *Proposals for the Rehabilitation of Communities Affected by St. Lawrence Power Project* (Toronto, August 1954); Mabee, *op. cit.*, 214–18; The Lost Villages Historical Society website.

64. SLU, Collection 40, Mabee Series, Box 52, Item 3, Interview with Reverend A.E. Wilfong, United Church Moulinette Pastoral Charge, July 1957; Mabee, *op. cit.*, 217–18; over the years, newspapers, both local and provincial, have featured stories about residents and their comments about returning to see the place where they used to live. The Lost Villages Historical Society website also features some of this material.

65. The schedule of when the generators were brought on line can be found at *www.opg.com/power/hydro/ottawa_st_lawrence/rh_saunders.asp*, accessed April 24, 2009.

66. Mabee discusses power rates and their effects at some length. Mabee, *op. cit.*, 223–38.

67. SLU, Collection 40, Mabee Series, Box 52, Item 3, Interviews with Miss ___ Linden, Secretary to Lewis Castle, September 18, 1958, and with Emery Henshell, Director, Duluth Industrial Bureau, Duluth, October 29, 1959; David Helberg, former Duluth Port Director; "When the Ocean Met the Lake," *Lake Superior Journal* (online portion of *Lake Superior Magazine*), accessed at *www.lakesuperior.com/online/311/311jrnl.html*, posted June 21, 2009.

68. *New York Times*, June 26 and 27, 1959.

## Chapter 5: Reassessing the Dream: The Seaway in Operation

1. *Newsweek*, New York, late fall, 1955.
2. *Toronto Telegram*, Toronto, August 14, 1958.
3. *Minneapolis Star*, Minneapolis, June 6 and 24, 1955.
4. *Newsweek,* August 15, 1955. The magazine ran a series of stories in 1955 on several cities in the United States and some in Canada that would benefit from the Seaway.
5. *The Chicago American*, Chicago, June 7, 1957.
6. *Newsweek*, August 15, 1955; Syracuse *Post-Standard*, August 21, 1955.
7. Mabee, *op. cit.*, 253–54.
8. *Ibid.*, 254–55; Willoughby, *op. cit.*, 275–777.
9. Mabee, *op. cit.*, 255; Willoughby, *op. cit.*, 276.
10. Willoughby, *op. cit.*, 276, 278.
11. The two agencies now record all tonnage in metric tons, or tonnes; Great Lakes–St. Lawrence Seaway, *Traffic Results 1959–1992*, and *Traffic Results 1982–2001*, accessed at *www.greatlakes-seaway.com/en/pdf/traffic_report_hist.pdf*, June 25, 2009; see also Great Lakes–St. Lawrence Seaway, *Monthly Traffic Results* and tonnage information, covering years since 1998, accessed at *www.greatlakes-seaway.com/en/pdf/seaway/facts/traffic/index.html*, June 25, 2009; Transport Canada provides similar information for the years 1993–2007, accessed at *www.tc.gc.ca/policy/Report/anre2007/add/table-m20.htm*, June 25, 2009. The two Seaway agencies list totals of both upbound and downbound cargoes, and subtract from this half the cargoes of vessels which have been counted twice, once going through the Montreal–Lake Ontario section, and once going through the Welland. Some authors use total numbers, double counting certain vessels, thus inflating figures; see, for example, Legget, *The Seaway*, 77–78. Some authors have tended to use lower figures, the origin of which is not clear; see, for example, *Gale Encyclopedia of U.S. Economic History* (2000), accessed at *www.accessmylibray.com/coms2/summary_0193-1344_-ITM*, June 26, 2009; the figures from the Seaway Authority and the Seaway Corporation are a good general reflection of traffic volume, but need to be used with some caution, as transiting as little as one lock in the system results in the cargo being included in tonnage figures for the system. The two agencies made it even more difficult to interpret data when, in 1999, they changed from recording a tug and barge combination (the barge having a specially constructed indentation in the stern to hold the tug) as one vessel, to recording it as two, thereby increasing the number of vessels listed as using the system.
12. Gennifer Sussman, *The St. Lawrence Seaway: History and Analysis of a Joint Water Highway* (Montreal and Washington, 1978), 30–31, 40, 43–44, 58–60. Sussman's work highlighted some of the issues that had emerged or were emerging by 1978; Robert J. McCalla, *Water Transportation in Canada* (Halifax, 1994), 178–79; Becker, *op. cit.*, 126; Canadian National, *Initial Submission to the Canada Transportation Act Review Panel: Perspectives on Competitive Rail Access Issues*, October 6, 2000, accessed at *www.reviewcta-examenltc.gc.ca/Submissions-Soumissions/Txt/Canadian%20Nationa%20(1)%20English.txt*, June 30, 2009; Presentation to the Canada Grains Council by William Rowat, President and CEO, Railway Association of Canada, April 7, 2004, Winnipeg, accessed at *www.railcan.ca/documents/*

*presentations/2004_04_08_CanadaGrainsCouncil_en.ppt*, June 30, 2009; Norman Bonsor, "Competition, Regulation, and Efficiency in the Canadian Railways and Highway Industries" (The Fraser Institute, October 20, 1999), accessed at *oldfraser. lexi.net/publications/books/essays/chapter2.html*, June 30, 2009.

13. At least one ship owner was still ordering 14-footers from England (where they were cheaper to build) as late as 1956, claiming that he could more than make the money back in the three years before the Seaway opened, though he acknowledged that they would not be used on the Seaway; see SLU, Collection 40, Mabee Series, Box 52, Interview with Captain A.E. Brown, in port at Ogdensburg unloading pulpwood, July 24, 1956.

14. Becker, *op. cit.*, 130–34.

15. Becker, *op. cit.*, 134–35; Sussman, *op. cit.*, 36.

16. Sussman, *op. cit.*, 30–33, 36–37; Becker, *op. cit.*, 124.

17. Becker, *op. cit.*, 135; CBC report, *The End of the St. Lawrence Seaway?* November 6, 1994.

18. McCalla, *op. cit.*, 178–79; Becker, *op. cit.*, 135; "St. Lawrence Seaway to Get Makeover," *Toledo Free Press*, June 4, 2009, accessed at *www.toledofreepress.com/2009/06/04/st-lawrence-seaway-to-get-makeover*, June 25, 2009.

19. Becker, *op. cit.*, 135–40.

20. *Ibid.*, 140–41.

21. "Seaway Strives to Stay Afloat," Milwaukee *Journal Sentinel*, November 30, 2007, accessed at *www.jsonline.com/story/index.aspx?id=691994*, February 1, 2008.

22. CBC report, *The End of the St. Lawrence Seaway?* November 6, 1994; *Exchange of Notes Between the Government of Canada and the Government of the United States of America: Amending the Agreement Concerning the Application of Tolls on the St. Lawrence Seaway, Signed at Ottawa, March 9, 1959, as Amended (with Memorandum of Agreement)*, Washington, June 10, 1994, *Canada Gazette*, Vol. 132, No. 17, April 25, 1998; Transport Canada news release, No. H095/98, October 2, 1998, accessed at *www.tc.gc.ca/mediaroom/releases/nat/1998/98_h095e.htm*, June 25, 2009.

23. "St. Lawrence Seaway Wins New Cargo as Marketing Drive Takes Hold," *Port Engineering Management*, November/December 2005, accessed at *www.toledoseaport.org/documents/Lawrence.pdf*, June 25, 2009; Hamilton Chamber of Commerce, *St. Lawrence Seaway* (2007), accessed at *www.hamiltonchamber. on.ca/policies/Provincial/St%20Lawrence%20/Seaway%20/2007.pdf*, June 25, 2009.

24. "St. Lawrence Seaway to Get Makeover," *Toledo Free Press*, June 4, 2009.

25. Great Lakes–St. Lawrence Seaway, *Seaway Monthly Traffic Results, 2007, 2008*.

26. Courtney Tower, "St. Lawrence Seaway Traffic Plunges," *Breakbulk*, June 3, 2009, accessed at *www.breakbulk.com/content/?=711*, June 25, 2009.

27. Hamilton Chamber of Commerce, *St. Lawrence Seaway* (2007).

28. Environment Canada, *The State of Canada's Environment, 1996*, accessed at *www. ec.gc.ca/soer-ree/English/soer/1996Report/Doc/1-6-6-5-5-3-1.cfm*, January 29, 2009.

29. *Great Lakes St. Lawrence Seaway Study*, Final Report (Washington and Ottawa, Fall 2007), 57. In August 2007 the Ontario government announced that it was committing more than $1.5 million in a joint Canada–Ontario program toward the further cleaning up of the Cornwall Area of Concern. News release, August 21, 2007, accessed at *www.ene.gov.on.ca/en/news/2007/082101.php*, February 7, 2008.

30. For examples of attacks on the power dam and on Seaway navigation, see American Rivers, and Save the River, Upper St. Lawrence Riverkeeper, "St. Lawrence River on Most Endangered River List," April 17, 2008, accessed at *www.great-lakes.net/lists/ glin-announce/2008-04/msg00037.html*, June 3, 2009, and Barbara A. Gray, Mohawk National Council of Chiefs, "Socio-Cultural Impacts of Icebreaking Activities and Winter Navigation," presented October 28, 2004, accessed at *www.mohawknation. org/pages/MNCCicebreakingOnCulture.htm*, June 26, 2009; the website of the Save the River, Upper St. Lawrence Riverkeeper organization discusses criticisms of the Seaway; see *www.savetheriver.org*; Becker, *op. cit.*, 137; the successful campaign by the people of Akwesasne to have a say in the opening date of the Seaway and to have a study done of the effects of icebreaking is detailed in a press release from the United States Department of Transportation, dated June 29, 2006, accessed at *www. dot.gov/affairs slsdc0306.htm*, June 25, 2009.
31. *Great Lakes St. Lawrence Seaway Study*, 3–4, 11, 54–71.
32. Response to the Great Lakes St. Lawrence Study, January 18, 2008, accessed at *www. cela.ca/files/uploads/596_GLSLS.pdf*, June 26, 2009.
33. *Great Lakes St. Lawrence Seaway Study*, 8–10, 96–106, 109–11.
34. See, for example, Martin Associates, *Economic Impact Study of the Great Lakes St. Lawrence Seaway System*, August 1, 2001, accessed at *www.greatlakes-seaway.com/ en/pdf/impact_study_en.pdf*, June 26, 2009.
35. "St. Lawrence Seaway to Get Makeover," *Toledo Free Press*, June 4, 2009; "Chicago's Port Awash in Criticism: Longshoremen Say District Does Little to Keep or Entice Shipping Companies to Illinois Waterfront," *Chicago Tribune*, January 23, 2005, accessed at *www.geoffdougherty.com/port.html*, July 3, 2009; "St. Lawrence Seaway at 50: A Bypass for Buffalo's Port," *The Buffalo News*, June 25, 2009; CBC report, *The End of the St. Lawrence Seaway?* November 6, 1994.

# BIBLIOGRAPHY

Comments about sources will also be found in the preface. Individual files and items from the archival collections are listed when only one file was used. Negotiations and agreements between Canada and the United States were sometimes published in one country but not in the other. Thus an American or Canadian government document may contain information relative to both countries. In some cases, assignment of a printed source is somewhat arbitrary. For instance, Carleton Mabee's book on the Seaway is primarily a secondary source, but a portion of it comprises his own observations and information collected from others while he worked on the Seaway. Noble E. Whitford's history of the New York Barge Canal, while a secondary account, is based on direct observation and on government records.

## PRIMARY SOURCES

### Abbreviations

AO        Archives of Ontario
EL        Dwight D. Eisenhower Presidential Library and Museum
JFKL      John F. Kennedy Presidential Library and Museum
LAC       Library and Archives Canada
NLA       National Library of Australia
NEMHC  Northeast Minnesota Historical Center, University of Minnesota–Duluth
SLU       St. Lawrence University, Owen D. Young Library, Special Collections and Vance University Archives

AO, F8, Howard Ferguson Papers.
AO, F1055, Frederick A. Gaby Papers.
AO, RG3, Mitchell Hepburn Correspondence.
AO, F1198, Frederick Innes Ker Fonds.
AO, F5-1, Correspondence of James Whitney.
AO, RG3-10, Item B307951, Great Lakes–St. Lawrence Agreement, Report.
AO, RG19-27, Intergovernmental Correspondence, 1942–58, Box V8, b354418, File 19.11.
AO, RG37-6-7, Expropriation Hearings.

EL, interview with N.R. Danielian, 1972, by John Luter for the Columbia Oral History Project, accessed at *www.eisenhower.archives.gov/Research/Oral_Histories/oral_ history_finding_aids/ohfa177.pdf*, March 12, 2009.

Remarks of John F. Kennedy on the Saint Lawrence Seaway before the Senate, Washington, January 14, 1954, John F. Kennedy Presidential Library and Museum, accessed at *www.jfklibrary.org/search.htm*, January 14, 2009.

LAC, MG26 J13, Mackenzie King Diaries, accessed at *www.collectionscanada.gc.ca/ databases/king/index-e.html*, November 9, 2009.

LAC, R5500-0-6-E, Andrew Audubon Merilee Fonds.

LAC, R5500-7-9-E, Views of Canada and the United States, *circa* 1858–1934.

LAC, R9726-0-4-E, John Boyd Fonds.

NLA, MS51, Papers of Sir Edmund Barton, Series 1, Correspondence 1827–1921, Correspondence 1903, Item 1071a-6a, accessed at *nla.gov.au/nla.ms-ms51-1-1071a*, December 5, 2008.

NEMHC, Lewis G. Castle Papers, S2425b1f2.

SLU, Collection 40, St. Lawrence Seaway Collection, Mabee Series, Sillcox Series.

**PRINTED PRIMARY SOURCES**

**Government Documents**

**United States**

*Congressional Record*

*Exchange of Notes Between the Government of Canada and the Government of the United States of America Concerning the Application of Tolls on the St. Lawrence Seaway, Signed at Ottawa, March 9, 1959, As Amended (with Memorandum of Agreement )*, Washington, June 10, 1994.

House of Representatives, *Preliminary Examination and Survey of Deeper Waterway from Great Lakes to Hudson River*, House Document 288, 69th Congress, 1st Session.

International Joint Commission, *St. Lawrence Waterway: Message from the President of the United States Transmitting a Letter from the Secretary of State Submitting the Report of the International Joint Commission Concerning the Improvement of the St. Lawrence River Between Montreal and Lake Ontario for Navigation and Power*, printed as Senate Document 114, 67th Congress, 2nd Session.

Power Commission of the State of New York, *Annual Report*, 1933.

*St. Lawrence Waterway Report of the United States and Canadian Government Engineers on the Improvement of the St. Lawrence River from Montreal to Lake Ontario Made to the International Joint Commission*. Printed as supplementary to Senate Document No. 114, 67th Congress (Washington, 1922).

### Canada

Canada, *Annual Report of the Department of Railways and Canals*, 1891–92 (Ottawa, 1893), 1898–99 (Ottawa, 1900), 1902–03 (Ottawa, 1904).

*Canada Gazette.*

Canada, House of Commons Debates (Hansard).

Canada, *Sessional Papers*, 1893.

Canada, *White Paper, Agreement Made the 11th Day of July A D. 1932, Between the Dominion of Canada and the Province of Ontario, Concerning the Development of Power in the International Rapids Section of the St. Lawrence River, 1932.*

Canal Commission, *Letter to the Hon. The Secretary of State from the Canal Commissioners Respecting the Improvement of Inland Navigation of the Dominion of Canada* (Ottawa, February 24, 1871).

Foreign Affairs and International Trade Canada, Documents on Canadian External Relations, accessed at *www.international.gc.ca/department/history-histoire/dcer/menu-en.asp*, April 5, July 16, July 28, 2009.

*Final Report of the Joint Board of Engineers*, April 9, 1932 (*see* AO, *Gaby Papers*).

Hydro-Electric Commission of Ontario, *Proposals for the Rehabilitation of Communities Affected by St. Lawrence Power Project* (Toronto, August 1954).

Senate of Canada, *Proceedings of the Special Committee Appointed to Inquire into the Development and Improvement of the St. Lawrence River* (Ottawa, 1928).

Transport Canada, tonnage figures, 1993–2007, accessed at *www.tc.gc.ca/policy/Report/anre2007/add/table-m20.htm*, June 25, 2009.

Upper Canada, Journals of the House of Assembly of Upper Canada, 1836–37.

Additional government material regarding treaties can be found in:

Baxter, R.R., *Documents on the St. Lawrence Seaway* (London and New York, 1960).

Piper, Don Courtney, *The International Law of the Great Lakes: A Study of Canadian–United States Co-operation* (Durham, North Carolina, 1967).

Public statements and public documents of the presidents can be found in:

Woolley, John T. and Gerhard Peters, *The American Presidency Project*, University of California, Santa Barbara, accessed at *www.presidency.ucsb.edu*, March 5, 10, 12, 17, 20, 30, April 8, 2009.

### OTHER PRINTED PRIMARY SOURCES

Adams, Sherman, *Firsthand Report: The Story of the Eisenhower Administration* (1961; reprinted Westport, CT: Greenwood Press, 1974).

Branyan, Robert L., and Lawrence H. Larsen, *The Eisenhower Administration 1953–1961 A Documentary History* (New York: Random House, 1971).

Catermole, William, *Emigration* (London, 1831, reprint, Carlisle, MA: Applewood Books, 2006).

Chevrier, Honourable Lionel, M.P., *The St. Lawrence Seaway* (Toronto: Macmillan, 1959).

Donovan, Robert J., *Eisenhower: The Inside Story* (New York: Harper & Brothers, 1956).

Duncan, John M., *Travels Through Part of the United States and Canada in 1818 and 1819* (Glasgow: University Press, 1823).

Dunlop, William, *Recollections of the American War*, in *The Literary Garland*, Montreal, June to November 1847 (reprinted Toronto: McClelland and Stewart, 1967).

Great Lakes St. Lawrence Seaway System, tonnage information, accessed at *www.greatlakes-seaway.com/en/seaway/facts/traffic/index.html*, June 25, 2009.

Great Lakes St. Lawrence Seaway System, traffic results, accessed at *www.greatlakes-seaway.com/en/seaway/facts/traffic/index.html*, September 23, 2009.

Heriot, George, *Travels Through the Canadas, Containing a Description of the Picturesque Scenery on Some of the Rivers and Lakes, With an Account of the Productions, Commerce, and Inhabitants of Those Provinces* (London, UK: R. Phillips, 1807).

Saunders, Robert S., Speeches to the Empire Club, Toronto, January 27, 1949 and October 11, 1951, accessed at *speeches.empireclub.org/details.asp?r=vs&ID=60242&number=1* and *speeches.empireclub.org/details.asp?r=vs&ID=60296&number=3*, September 23, 2009.

Smith, M., *A Geographical View of the Province of Upper Canada, and Promiscuous Remarks Upon the Government* (Hartford, 1813), quoted in Gerald Craig, *Early Travellers in the Canadas* (Toronto, 1955).

Styran, Roberta M. and Robert R. Taylor, *The "Great Swivel Link": Canada's Welland Canal* (Toronto: The Champlain Society, 2001).

Transport Canada, U.S. Army Corps of Engineers, U.S. Department of Transportation, The St. Lawrence Seaway Management Corporation, Saint Lawrence Seaway Development Corporation, Environment Canada, U.S, Fish and Wildlife Service, *Great Lakes St. Lawrence Seaway Study, Final Report* (Washington and Ottawa, Fall 2007).

Truman, Harry S., *Memoirs: Years of Hope, 1946–1952* (Garden City, NY: Doubleday, 1956).

**SECONDARY SOURCES**

**Books**

Aitken, Hugh G.J., *The Welland Canal A Study in Canadian Enterprise* (Cambridge, MA: Harvard University Press, 1954).

Alfred, Gerald A., *Heeding the Voices of Our Ancestors: Kahnawake Mohawk Politics and the Rise of Native Nationalism* (Toronto, New York, Oxford: Oxford University Press, 1995).

Annin, Peter, *The Great Lakes Water Wars* (Washington, DC: Island Press, 2006).

Becker, H., *From the Atlantic to the Great Lakes: A History of the U.S. Army Corps of Engineers and the St. Lawrence Seaway* (Washington, DC: 1984?).

Brown, Robert Craig, *Robert Laird Borden: A Biography* (Toronto: Macmillan, 1975).

*Canadian Annual Review of Public Affairs 1929–30* (Toronto: The Canadian Review Company, 1931).

Careless, J.M.S., *The Union of the Canadas: The Growth of Canadian Institutions, 1841–1857* (Toronto: McClelland and Stewart, 1967).

Craig, Gerald (ed.), *Lord Durham's Report* (Toronto: McClelland and Stewart, 1963).

Craig, G.M. *Upper Canada: The Formative Years, 1784-1841* (London and New York: McClelland and Stewart, 1963).

Creighton, Donald, *John A. Macdonald: The Old Chieftain* (Toronto: Macmillan, 1955).

Creighton, Donald, *The Road to Confederation: The Emergence of Canada, 1863-1867* (Toronto: Macmillan, 1964).

Davis, Kenneth H., *FDR: The New York Years, 1928-1933* (New York: Random House, 1985).

Dent, J.C., *The Last Forty Years: Canada Since the Union of 1841* (Toronto: George Virtue, 1881; abridged edition, Donald Swainson, ed., Toronto: McClelland and Stewart, 1972).

Eccles, W.J., *Canada Under Louis XIV, 1663-1701* (Toronto: McClelland and Stewart, 1964).

Forbes, Ernest R., *The Maritime Rights Movement, 1919-1927: A Study in Canadian Regionalism* (Kingston and Montreal: McGill-Queen's University Press, 1979).

Freidel, Frank, *Franklin D. Roosevelt: Launching the New Deal* (Boston and Toronto: Little Brown & Co., 1973).

Glassford, Larry A., *Reaction and Reform: The Politics of the Conservative Party Under R.B. Bennett, 1927-1938* (Toronto, Buffalo, and London: University of Toronto Press, 1992).

Glazebrook, G.P. de T., *A History of Transportation in Canada* (Toronto: McClelland and Stewart, 1964).

Gould, Lewis L., *The Presidency of Theodore Roosevelt* (Lawrence, KS: University Press of Kansas, 1991).

Graham, Roger, *Old Man Ontario: Leslie M. Frost* (Toronto, Buffalo, London: University of Toronto Press, 1990).

Greenwald, Michelle, Alan Levitt and Elaine Peebles, *The Welland Canals; Historical Resource Analysis and Preservation Alternatives* (Published by the Historical Research Branch, Government of Ontario, 1979).

Hauptman, Laurence M., *The Iroquois Struggle for Survival: World War II to Red Power* (Syracuse, NY: Syracuse University Press, 1986).

Heisler, John P., *The Canals of Canada* (Ottawa: National Historic Sites Service, 1973).

Hill, Libby, *The Chicago River: A Natural and Unnatural History* (Chicago: Lake Claremont Press, 2000).

Hitsman, J. Mackay, *The Incredible War of 1812* (Toronto: University of Toronto Press, 1965).

Innis, Mary Quayle, *An Economic History of Canada*, revised edition (Toronto: Ryerson Press, 1954).

Ireland, Tom, *Great Lakes–St. Lawrence Deep Waterway to the Sea* (New York: Putnam, 1934).

Kenney, Dave, *Minnesota Goes To War: The Home Front During World War II* (St. Paul, MN: Minnesota Historical Society Press, 2005).

Legget, Robert, *Ottawa River Canals and the Defence of British North America* (Toronto, Buffalo, and London: University of Toronto Press, 1988).

Legget, Robert, *Rideau Waterway* (Toronto: University of Toronto Press, 1955; revised 1972).

Legget, Robert F., *The Seaway* (Toronto and Vancouver: Clarke Irwin, 1979).

Lower, Arthur M., *Great Britain's Woodyard: British America and the Timber Trade 1763–1867* (Montreal and London: McGill-Queen's University Press, 1973).

Mabee, Carleton, *The Seaway Story* (New York: Macmillan, 1961).

Mansfield, J.B. (ed.), *History of the Great Lakes* (Chicago: J.H. Beers & Co., 1899) Vol. 1, transcribed by Walter Lewis and Brendon Baillod, accessed at *www. maritimehistoryofthegreatlakes.ca/Documents/HGL/default.asp?ID=c006*, January 23, 2009.

Marks, Frederick W., *Velvet on Iron: The Diplomacy of Theodore Roosevelt* (Lincoln, NE: University of Nebraska Press, 1979).

McCalla, Robert J., *Water Transportation in Canada* (Halifax: Formac Publishing, 1994).

McKenty, Neil, *Mitch Hepburn* (Toronto and Montreal: McClelland and Stewart, 1967).

Neatby, H. Blair, *William Lyon Mackenzie King, Vol. 2: The Lonely Heights* (Toronto, Buffalo and London: University of Toronto Press, 1963; reprinted 1970).

Neatby, H. Blair, *William Lyon Mackenzie King, Vol. 3: The Prism of Unity* (Toronto and Buffalo: University of Toronto Press, 1976).

Nute, Grace Lee, *Lake Superior* (Indianapolis and New York: University of Minnesota Press, 1944).

Oliver, Peter, *G. Howard Ferguson: Ontario Tory* (Toronto and Buffalo: University of Toronto Press, 1977).

Passfield, Robert W., *Building the Rideau Canal: A Pictorial History* (Don Mills, ON: Fitzhenry & Whiteside, 1982).

Senior, Elinor Kyte, *From Royal Township to Industrial City: Cornwall, 1784–1984* (Belleville, ON: Mika Publishing, 1983).

Shaw, Ronald E., *Erie Water West: A History of the Erie Canal, 1792–1854* (Lexington, KY: University of Kentucky Press, *circa* 1966; reprinted American Council of Learned Societies, 1990 as an e-book).

Stacey, C.P., *Canada and the Age of Conflict A History of Canadian External Relations, Vol. 1: 1867–1921* (Toronto, Buffalo, and London: University of Toronto Press, 1977).

Stacey, C.P., *Canada and the Age of Conflict, Vol. 2: 1921–1948: The Mackenzie King Era* (Toronto, Buffalo, London: University of Toronto Press, 1981).

Stanley, George F.G., *The War of 1812 Land Operations* (Ottawa: Macmillan, 1983).

Sussman, Gennifer, *The St. Lawrence Seaway: History and Analysis of a Joint Water Highway* (Montreal and Washington: National Planning Association, 1978).

Thomson, Dale C., *Louis St. Laurent: Canadian* (Toronto: Macmillan, 1967).

Trudel, Marcel, *The Beginnings of New France, 1524–1663* (Toronto: McClelland and Stewart, 1973).

Tucker, Gilbert N., *The Canadian Commercial Revolution, 1845–51* (New Haven, CT, 1936; republished Toronto: McClelland and Stewart, 1964).

Uttley, William Velores, *A History of Kitchener, Ontario* (1937; reprinted Waterloo: Wilfrid Laurier University Press, 1975).

Vigod, Bernard L., *Quebec Before Duplessis: The Political Career of Louis-Alexandre Taschereau* (Kingston and Montreal: McGill-Queen's University Press, 1986).

Waite, P.B., *The Life and Times of Confederation, 1864–1867* (Toronto: University of Toronto Press, 1962).

Watkins, Ernest, *R.B. Bennett* (Toronto: Kingswood House, 1963).

Welles, Frederick Dunbar, and George S. May, *Michigan: A History of the Wolverine State* (third revised edition, Grand Rapids, MI: Wm. B. Eerdmans Publishing, 1995).

Whitford, Noble E., *History of the Barge Canal of New York State: Supplement to the Annual Report of the State Engineer and Surveyor for the Year Ended June 30, 1921* (Albany: J.B. Lyon Company, 1922) Transcription 1999, accessed at *www.history. rochester.edu/canal/bib/whitford/1921/contents.html*, November 15, 2008.

Willoughby, William R., *The St. Lawrence Waterway: A Study in Politics and Diplomacy* (Madison, WI: University of Wisconsin Press, 1961).

## Articles

Aitken, Hugh, G.J., "The Family Compact and the Welland Canal Company," *Canadian Journal of Economics and Political Science*, Vol. 18 (1952).

Benidickson, Jamie, "Francis Henry Keefer," *Dictionary of Canadian Biography*, Vol. 15 (University of Toronto Press: Toronto, Buffalo, London, 2000).

Cooke, O.A., "Frederick Charles Denison," in *Dictionary of Canadian Biography*, Vol. 15 (University of Toronto Press: Toronto, Buffalo, London, 2000).

Craig, Charles P., "From the Great Lakes to the Atlantic," *Saturday Evening Post*, January 20, 1920.

"Draglines Float to Seaway," *Excavating Engineer*, August 1955.

Gardner, H.C., "The Great Lakes–St. Lawrence Tidewater Project," *The Ohio State Engineer*, March 1921, accessed at *kb.osu.edu/dspace/handle/1811/34082/1/os_ENG_v04_i03_009.pdf*, February 3, 2009.

Gilmore, James, "The St. Lawrence River Canals Vessel," Society of Naval Architects and Marine Engineers, Transactions 1957, reproduced in sections at *www.hhpl.on.ca/ GreatLakes/Documents/Gilmore/default.asp*; accessed July 13, 2008.

Goodrich, Hon. James P., "Lakes–St. Lawrence Seaway: From the Viewpoint of National Welfare," address to the Ohio Bankers Association, Toledo, OH, June 22, 1923, accessed at *www.archive.org/stream/lakesstlawrences00gooduoft/lakestlawrences00gooduoft_ djvu.txt*, February 3, 2009.

Helberg, David, "When the Ocean Met the Lake," *Lake Superior Journal* (online portion of *Lake Superior Magazine*), at *www.lakesuperior.com/online/311/311jrnl.html*, posted June 21, 2009; accessed June 21, 2009.

Jessup, Philip P., "The Great Lakes–St. Lawrence Deep Waterway Treaty," in *The American Journal of International Law*, Vol. 26, No. 4 (October 1932).

"Julius Howland Barnes," in John H. Ingham, *Biographical Dictionary of American Business Leaders: A–G* (Westport, CT, and London, England: Greenwood Press, 1983).

Manitoba Historical Society, "James Fisher," accessed at *www.mhs.mb.ca/docs/people/ fisher_j.shtml*, January 11, 2008.

McConville, Daniel J., "Seaway to Nowhere," *Invention and Technology Magazine*, Fall 1995, Vol. 11, Issue 2, accessed at *www.americanheritage.com/articles/magazine/ it/1995/2/1995_2_34.shtml*, June 7, 2009

Michigan Family History Network, "James S. Dunham," accessed at *www.mfhn.com/ forum/topic.asp?TOPIC_ID=16*, January 11, 2009.

Nelles, H.V., "Sir Adam Beck," in *Dictionary of Canadian Biography*, Vol. 15 (University of Toronto Press: Toronto, Buffalo, London, 2000).

Pennanen, Gary, "Battle of the Titans: Mitchell Hepburn, Mackenzie King, Franklin

Roosevelt and the St. Lawrence Seaway," Ontario Historical Society, *Ontario History*, Vol. 89, No. 1, March 1997.

Talman, J.J., "William Hamilton Merritt," in *Dictionary of Canadian Biography* , Vol. 12 (University of Toronto Press: Toronto, Buffalo, London, 1990).

Andrew Thomson, "Elias Weber Bingeman Snider," *Dictionary of Canadian Biography*, Vol. 15 (University of Toronto Press: Toronto, Buffalo, London, 2000).

"Charles Elroy Townsend (1856–1924)" in *Biographical Directory of the United States Congress 1774–Present,* accessed at *bioguide.congress.gov/scripts/biodisplay. pl?index=T000330*, December 10, 2008.

**Newspapers and Magazines**

With a few exceptions, some noted above, individual articles are not singled out. They will be found in the endnotes. Specialized publications are treated differently.

*The Atlantic Monthly*
*Breakbulk*, June 3, 2009; Courtney Tower, "St. Lawrence Seaway Traffic Plunges," accessed at *www.breakbulk.com/content/?=711*, June 25, 2009.
*The Buffalo News*
*Canadian Agriculturalist,* Toronto
*The Chicago American*
*Chicago Tribune*
*Duluth News-Tribune*
*Gazette*, Montreal
*Globe and Mail*, Toronto
*Journal Sentinel*, Milwaukee
*Massena Observer*, Massena, New York
*Milwaukee Journal*
*Minneapolis Star*
*Newsweek*
*New York Times*
*Port Engineering Management*, November/December 2005, "St. Lawrence Seaway Wins New Cargo as Marketing Drive Takes Hold," accessed at *www.toledoseaport.org/ documents/Lawrence.pdf*, June 25, 2009.
*Post-Standard*, Syracuse
*Saturday Evening Post*
*Standard-Freeholder*, Cornwall
*Time*
*Toledo Free Press*
*Toronto Daily Star*
*Toronto Telegram*
*Wall Street Journal*
*Watertown Daily Times,* Watertown, New York

## Online Sources

Some materials were designed for the Internet, or are more easily located there, as they are highly specialized. All websites were current in the summer of 2009, but some may later be updated or closed.

American President: An Online Reference Resource, at the Miller Centre of Public Affairs, University of Virginia, accessed at *millercenter.org/academic/americanpresident*, March 5, 10, 15, 16, 19, 2009.

American Rivers, and Save the River, Upper St. Lawrence Riverkeeper, "St. Lawrence River on Most Endangered River List," April 17, 2008, accessed at *www.great-lakes. net/lists/glin-announce/2008-04/msg00037.html*, June 3, 2009.

Bonsor, Norman, "Competition, Regulation, and Efficiency in the Canadian Railways and Highway Industries," (The Fraser Institute, October 20, 1999), accessed at *oldfraser. lexi.net/publications/books/essays/chapter2.htm*, June 30, 2009.

Canadian National, *Initial Submission to the Canada Transportation Act Review Panel, Perspectives on Competitive Rail access Issues*, October 6, 2000, accessed at *www.reviewcta-examenltc.gc.ca/Submissions-Soumissions/Txt/Canadian%20 National%29(1)%20English.txt*, June 30, 2009.

Environment Canada, *The State of Canada's Environment-1996*, accessed at *www.ec.gc.ca/ soer-ree/English/soer/1996Report/Doc/1-6-6-5-5-3-1.cfm*, March 5, 2009.

"Erie Canal Chronology," accessed at *www.history.rochester.edu/canal/chron.htm*, March 7, 2008.

"The Erie Canal and De Witt Clinton," accessed at *xroads.virginia.edu/~HYPER/DETOC/ transport/erie.htm*, July 30, 2008.

Gale Encyclopedia of U.S. Economic History (2000), accessed at *www.accessmylibray. com/coms2/summary_0193-13448-ITM*, June 26, 2009.

Gray, Barbara A., Mohawk National Council of Chiefs, "Socio-Cultural Impacts of Icebreaking Activities and Winter Navigation," presented October 28, 2004, accessed at *www.mohawknation.org/pages/MNCCicebreakingOnCulture.htm*, June 26, 2009.

Hamilton Chamber of Commerce, *St. Lawrence Seaway* (2007), accessed at *www. hamiltonchamber.on.ca/policies/Provincial/St%20Lawrence%20Seaway%20/2007. pdf*, June 25, 2009.

"The History of the Soo Locks," accessed at *huron.lre.usace.army.mil/SOO/lockhist.html*, September 16, 2008.

Illinois State Museum, *Harvesting the River*, accessed at *www.museum.state.il.us/ RiverWeb/harvesting/transportation/boats/timeline.html*, October 19, 2008.

Lost Villages Historical Society website: *lostvillages.ca*, accessed January 24 and 29, 2008.

Martin Associates, *Economic Impact Study of the Great Lakes St. Lawrence Seaway System*, Prepared for the U.S. St. Lawrence Seaway Development Corporation, August 1, 2001, accessed at *www.greatlakes-seaway.com/en/pdf/impact_study_ en.pdf*, June 27, 2009.

New York Division of Military and Naval Affairs, "Military History, Forts, Sampson Naval Training Base," accessed at *www.dmna.state.ny.us/forts/fortsQ_S/ sampsonNavalTrainingBase.htm*, March 17, 2009.

Ontario Power Generation, R.H. Saunders Dam, accessed at *www.opg.com/power/hydro/ ottawa_st_lawrence/rh_saunders.asp*, April 24, 2009.

Parks Canada, Coteau-du-Lac National Historic Site of Canada, accessed at *www.pc.gc. ca/lhn-nhs/qc/coteaudulac/natcul/natcul1d_e.asp*, July 13, 2008.

Presentation to: the Canada Grains Council by William Rowat, president and CEO, Railway Association of Canada, April 7, 2004, Winnipeg, accessed at *www.railcan.ca/ documents/presentations/2004_04_08_CanadaGrainsCouncil_en.ppt*, June 30, 2009.

Press release from the United States Department of Transportation, dated June 29, 2006, accessed at *www.dot.gov/affairs slsdc0306.htm*, June 25, 2009

Response to the Great Lakes–St. Lawrence Study, January 18, 2008, accessed at *www.cela. ca/files/uploads/596_GLSLS.pdf*, June 26, 2009.

Save the River, Upper St. Lawrence Riverkeeper: *www.savethe river.org.*

"The Soo Locks," accessed at *www.geo.msu.edu/geo333/SooLock.html*, September 16, 2008.

Transport Canada, news release, No. H095/98, October 2, 1998, accessed at *www.tc.gc.ca/ mediaroom/releases/nat/1998/98-h095e.htm*, June 25, 2009.

**Other Media**

CBC Television report, "The End of the St. Lawrence Seaway?" broadcast November 6, 1994, accessed at *archives.cbc.ca/science_technology/transportation/clips/3523*, December 18, 2009.

National Film Board of Canada, *Setting Fires for Science*, Donald Brittain, writer and director, Montreal, 1958.

# INDEX

# Of Related Interest

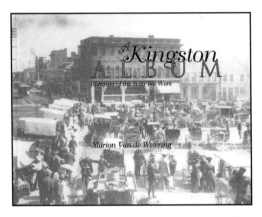

**A KINGSTON ALBUM:**
**GLIMPSES OF THE**
**WAY WE WERE**
Marion Van de Wetering
978-0-88882-200-0  $19.99

This album follows the history of Kingston from the founding of Fort Frontenac and the accompanying French settlement of Cataraqui in 1673 to its present-day incarnation as a popular tourist and travel destination. In addition to its fine military tradition, Kingston has also been the centre of commerce, shipping, industry, education, and government in the region.

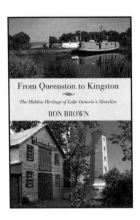

**FROM QUEENSTON TO KINGSTON:**
**THE HIDDEN HERITAGE OF LAKE**
**ONTARIO'S SHORELINE**
Ron Brown
978-1-55488-716-3  $26.99

Author, geographer, and travel writer Ron Brown has long had a love affair with the landscapes of Canada. Travel with him as he probes the shoreline of the Canadian side of Lake Ontario and discover its hidden heritage.

 **DUNDURN PRESS**
www.dundurn.com

Available at your favourite bookseller